This Distracted Globe

This Distracted Globe

Worldmaking in Early Modern Literature

Marcie Frank, Jonathan Goldberg,
and Karen Newman
Editors

FORDHAM UNIVERSITY PRESS
New York 2016

Fordham University Press also publishes its books in a variety of electronic formats. Some content that appears in print may not be available in electronic books.

Visit us online at www.fordhampress.com.

Library of Congress Cataloging-in-Publication Data

Names: Frank, Marcie, editor.
Goldberg, Jonathan, editor.
Newman, Karen, 1949– editor.
Title: This distracted globe : worldmaking in early modern literature / edited by Marcie Frank, Jonathan Goldberg, Karen Newman.
Description: New York : Fordham University Press, 2016.
Includes bibliographical references and index.
Identifiers: LCCN 2015036362
ISBN 9780823270286 (hardback)
ISBN 9780823270293 (paper)
Subjects: LCSH: English literature—Early modern, 1500–1700—History and criticism.
Material culture in literature.
Literature and society—England—History—16th century.
Literature and society—England—History—17th century.
BISAC: LITERARY CRITICISM / Renaissance.
Classification: LCC PR428.M38 D57 2016
DDC 820.9/003—dc23 LC record available at http://lccn.loc.gov/2015036362

Printed in the United States of America
18 17 16 5 4 3 2 1
First edition

CONTENTS

PREFACE

The essays in this volume were prompted by "Writing Sex and Other Matters with Jonathan Goldberg," a conference held at Brown University on September 21–22, 2012. Papers presented at the conference lie behind about half of the essays found in the pages that follow. These essays, we found, spoke to essays offered subsequently by other contributors, often in surprising, unplanned ways, across markedly different scholarly styles. This confluence furthered the prospect of a collection, of which this book is the result. The various contributions take up questions of materiality—of bodies, of writing—that project and encompass the multiple worlds we inhabit and from which we imagine our world differently, a distracted relationality, to recall Hamlet's phrase about the globe that has come to title this collection of essays. Hamlet's "globe" is a figure for the world, for his head, and for the stage on which he performs and speaks the words provided for him in a script he is at that moment claiming to attempt to remember and inscribe within. These concerns about multiple materialities reflect an abiding interest for Goldberg as a literary theorist and prime mover of queer theory, but it is especially gratifying that a conference in his honor helped to produce scholarship with a freestanding life of its own, for dynamic generativity is at the heart of his scholarly and pedagogical ethos.

In their different ways, these essays reflect the worldmaking power of Renaissance literature. As the entry in the recent *Dictionary of Untranslatables* reminds us, *world* is not a term with singular meaning. It includes cosmological, ontological, theological, chronological, sociological, anthropological, and existential senses.[1] As Roland Greene observes in the "World" section of his recent *Five Words*, an exploration of five generative concepts in early modernity, the questions that move through *world* in the period were provoked by the scientific and philosophic theories of multiple worlds as well as by colonialist ventures into the so-called New World that threw the relations between subject formation and worldmaking into question. "World" is about relations between the whole and the partial, the singular and the multiple, the corporeal and the abstract, the natural and the constructed, the human and the divine, the subjective and the corporate, questions central for early modernity. These are not questions simply confined to the word *world*.[2] So, although that word is not sounded in every essay in this collection (the introduction addresses a Spenserian etymology for *world*), the questions raised in these essays resonate with the multiple meanings of *world*. Ranging across the canonical writers of the period, the essays collected here treat the world as cosmos, globe, earth, universe, social sphere, and mundanity in order to explore these meanings. Although most of the essays focus on early modern English literature, these forays into worldmaking extend beyond the boundaries of a single literary tradition. This is most palpably evident in the wide range of theoretical concerns engaged in the volume, as well as in their rich contextualization that ranges from Pauline doctrines to the throne of Saint Peter, from classical sources to the creation of Urdu.

Reflecting on the range of meanings of *world*, the essays are grouped into three categories: Materiality, Sociality, and Universality—rubrics meant to suggest some of the ways essays on disparate authors, genres, and topics, and displaying differences in methodology and outlook, nonetheless speak to one another as well as to concerns that may engage readers with interests in these topics more broadly. The first group—with essays by Brent Dawson on Edmund Spenser, David Glimp on Elizabeth Cary, and Aaron Kunin on Christopher Marlowe—explores the stuff of which the world is made and the objects it fails to contain. The second group—featuring Robert Matz on Shakespeare's sonnets, James Kuzner on friendship in *Hamlet*, Lara Bovilsky on the extremity of male-male relations in *The Merchant of Venice*, and Meredith Evans on pirates and global relations of belonging—deals with the social relations the world enables or disables. The third group—with essays by Daniel Juan Gil on religious bodies in Henry Vaughan, Lynn Maxwell on microcosm/macrocosm tropes in John Donne and Shakespeare, and Madhavi Menon on Chouboli's *Dastan*—contemplates the applicability of the norms of one world to another, whether that transfer happens between this world and the hereafter, within the gendered spheres of male and female, or in relations between the "first" and "third" worlds. Equally invested in exposing the worldmaking and world-destroying energies of the texts they analyze, these essays' shared interest in the instability of their texts' worlds means that they also overlap across the rubrics in which we have grouped them. The introduction to the volume offers further discussion of *world* and *worldmaking* by way of ruminations on the multiple ways these essays speak to one another; it also offers a theoretical framework for reflecting on worldmaking in early modern literature through readings of Spenser as well as Sir Thomas Browne, John Milton, and Andrew Marvell (the last three not addressed at length elsewhere in this collection). It ends by considering how this volume furthers the work of queering the Renaissance.

NOTES

1. Barbara Cassin, ed., *Dictionary of Untranslatables: A Philosophical Lexicon*, trans. Steven Rendall, Christian Hubert, Jeffrey Mehlman, Nathanael Stein, and Michael Syrotinski; trans. ed. Emily Apter, Jacques Lezra, and Michael Wood (Princeton, NJ: Princeton University Press, 2014), 1265. Originally published as *Vocabulaire européen des philosophies: Dictionnaire des intraduisibles* (Paris: Éditions de Seuil, 2004). An entry for "Welt" can be found on 1217–34 and an entry on "planetary" on 1223.

2. Roland Greene, *Five Words* (Chicago: University of Chicago Press, 2013), 143–72.

This Distracted Globe

Introduction: World Enough and Time

Jonathan Goldberg (with Karen Newman and Marcie Frank)

Prince Arthur first appears in book 4 of *The Faerie Queene* in canto 8. His squire, Timias, has just been described as "mindlesse of his owne deare Lord" (4.8.18.4), and, in typical Spenserian fashion, the distracted mindlessness of one character seems to be the catalyst for the other forgotten character's textual manifestation.[1] Arthur appears in the vicinity of the Cave of Lust that had housed Aemylia and Amoret and from which they were rescued by Belphoebe and Timias. The prince, in fact, is seeking the squire who has forgotten him when he chances on the two women. Like Timias before him, Arthur is attracted to Amoret's plight; he ministers to her wounds—the wounds she received when Timias saved her. (Those wounds had led Belphoebe to abandon the squire, for she read them as signs of his desire for Amoret.) Arthur hears from Aemylia and Amoret their story of capture and rescue and sees the figure of Lust dead before him (as Belphoebe had earlier after she killed him). He wants to know more about what all this means, but cannot, and is left in a situation readers of the poem can easily acknowledge as their own as they parse this narrative in which identification, substitution, difference, and sameness all seem uncannily in play: "he wondred much, when all those signes he found" (4.8.21.9).

Arthur's inability to decipher a world of signs describes a familiar situation in Spenser. As is usually the case, Spenserian opacity has to do with the tangled nature of desire. Is Arthur rescuing these women or about to replicate their experience in the Cave of Lust? His actions with Amoret match those of his squire: just as Belphoebe had read rescue as seduction, Arthur is apprehended similarly by an old woman who sees him with the two young women. She may resemble the woman in the cave who fulfilled Lust's desire, sparing Aemylia and Amoret thereby, and vilified for doing so. This woman who reviles Arthur is called a "queane" (4.8.28.8); her vilification resembles Belphoebe's rage at Timias. This queen is named Sclaunder. Spenser's narrator worries that the filth she spews may match what the reader thinks about the threesome. He worries, that is, about the very misreading that seems to be the only possible kind of reading on offer in *The Faerie Queene*, the "misregard" of a "misled" reader who will "misdeem" the "conversing" of Spenser's characters (4.8.29.1–3).

Worrying that his "rimes" may "be red" wrongly (4.8.29.1), the poet intervenes to suggest how not to misread his poem. He insists that it is set in a time when things were different, an innocent "antique age" (4.8.30.1) inapprehensible now: "But when the world woxe old, it woxe warre old, / (Whereof it hight)," he explains (4.8.31.6–7). This explanation depends upon a difference between now and then that the explanation in fact baffles.[2] It posits a "world" before, one that only seems to become and be named "world" in the present. The word *world* used to refer to past time is a present formation that depends precisely on coming after, on aging, on not being that previous world. Nonetheless, it is supposed to name a before unlike the present. Such naming seems to be no different from the misnaming that the poet worries and tries to dispel by adducing a "world" before our "world." Stunningly, too, the temporality of aftering is attached to a signifier, *world*, that might be assumed to be spatial, not temporal.

In her recent edition of books 3 and 4 of *The Faerie Queene*, Dorothy Stephens labels Spenser's a "false etymology for 'world' suggested by the Old English 'worold.'"[3] The *Oxford English Dictionary*, however, countenances this etymology. Perhaps what makes Spenser's etymology false is what he does to the Germanic root *wer*, meaning "man," that lies behind the Old English word *worold* that gives it the literal meaning "the age or life span of man." *Wer* becomes *warre*, a past tense that defines waxing as its usual opposite, waning. Either it does that or perhaps *warre* functions as an adjective; if so, the effect is similar, waxing becomes a process of worsening or wearing out.

The Old English *worold* makes *world* mean something like the sum of subjective experience, the meaning of a life. It suggests that the world arises from and is one's sphere of making meaning: making intelligibility constitutes the world or, as we sometimes say, the world is what one makes of it. Spenser's etymology glimpses a process that occurs in time without any such human agency; it takes place in a temporality that does not move forward in the supposed orderly procession of a lifetime that could culminate in a backward glance making sense of what came before. Spenser's temporality is not in a time that has the coherence that would produce a worldview, a totality that sums up a life; it is, rather, a temporality that utterly confuses before and after, just as the etymology of *world* confuses time and space. Attempting to explain a relationship in the poem and to the poem (the possible mirroring of the reader of the text by the baffled reader in the text), the account we are given seems entirely impersonal; it is generated in an order of words that produces the world as, at once, other than itself at the very moment of its coming-to-be. In a word, it offers a distracted, drawn apart totality.

The "world" that Spenser proffers in this opaque moment of paradoxical elucidation speaks to the salience of "world" as an overarching rubric for this collection of essays, their manifest concern with very different ways in which worldmaking figures in early modernity: world as earth and world as matter; world as social configuration, including gendered and sexual configurations; world in the colonial and imperial contexts of early modern territorial expansion; world as a version of the global, the universal; and world in relation to the spiritual. Spenser's foray into the etymology of *world* resonates with Brent Dawson's opening essay on Spenserian worldmaking in its relationship to a matter bent on unmaking and dissolution. Does Spenser give us a world or take it away at the moment he ventures his etymology? Spenser's "world" might also anticipate the question Quentin Meillassoux asks in *After Finitude*: "How are we to grasp the *meaning* of scientific statements bearing explicitly upon a manifestation of the world that is posited as anterior to the emergence of thought and even of life—*posited, that is, as anterior to every form of human relation to the world*?"[4] Spenser's poem engages such philosophical questions about the world and, in its own way, muses on the questions raised in the entries on "world" and "Welt" in the recent *Dictionary of Untranslatables*.[5] Dawson's essay, and those that follow his, raise these kinds of theoretical questions in their readings of literary texts that imagine the conditions and possibilities of worldmaking, often in highly self-reflexive ways, as when, to take a phrase from Meredith Evans, "the intermissive discontinuities we are" lead to the notion of communities without definition as a "topos of worldmaking."

For however literary their focus, philosophical implication and political questions arise in these essays as they reflect upon both "a cosmological sense [of world] corresponding to the universe and a cosmo-political, anthropological, or existential sense referring to a way of relating to both the universe and the community of human beings," to quote again from the *Dictionary of Untranslatables*.[6] Madhavi Menon's closing essay, the one piece not located entirely in early modern English literature, finds Shakespearean resonance in the multilinguistic, palimpsestic textuality of an Indian performance tradition of "stories from everywhere and nowhere at once" that might as easily be thought to displace a Shakespearean universal in offering a literariness without bounds. Similarly, Dawson's essay moves from materiality to the presumed settled relation of body and empire in book 2 of *The Faerie Queene* and then on to questions of language and representation, poetry-making as worldmaking. Dawson raises questions about literature, temporality, and sovereignty when Spenser's "world" becomes the object of his reflection, as he contemplates an order of words that has everything to do with the kind of poem he writes and the world he inhabits. The spatiotemporal coordinates of this world, moreover, might not line up the way we expect, with "before" situated behind and "after" ahead. Not in Shakespeare either. Referring to the future, Macbeth says, "The greatest is behind," while to Marvell in "To His Coy Mistress" the future also comes from behind: "at my back I alwaies hear/Times winged Charriot hurrying near."[7] Questions about the coincidence of spatial and temporal conceptions of world(s), about language and writing, about life and temporality, about the cosmos and the polis, are intertwined for Spenser with questions of desire and sociality ("conversation"). So, too, in this volume, in which Shakespeare's world can reappear in contemporary India in Menon's essay, for example, or, in Evans's discovery that Hamlet's movement across water can involve the suspension of a law presumed to be universally applicable, an exception that nonetheless, Carl Schmitt avers, points to a "new global order of land and sea."[8]

What, then, does *world* mean? The question of worlds was raised for early modernists as early as Harry Berger Jr.'s seminal "The Renaissance Imagination: Second World and Green World," published fifty years ago.[9] There Berger considered the philosophical ramifications of literature as worldmaking, often in literary works that themselves encompass made-up worlds. Recently, Eric Hayot has offered a taxonomy of the worldmaking properties of modern literature as a system transcending national literatures and narrow periodization.[10] Hayot's work derives from Heidegger's sense of worldview as worldmaking that in turn can be related to the philosophical explorations of Jean-Luc Nancy at least since his 1993 book, *Le sens du monde* (*The Sense of the World*).[11] (Nancy, along with Simon Palfrey in *Shakespeare's Possible Worlds*, owes a debt to Leibniz and his speculations on possible worlds.)[12] Lauren Berlant's work, often alluded to in this collection, contemplates possibilities for worldmaking under the conditions of constraint marked by gender, race, and sexuality—issues that she and Lee Edelman discuss as "worlding" in their recent *Sex, or the Unbearable*.[13] These questions arise, in different ways, in all the essays collected here, as when Lynn Maxwell parses the ways in which familiar gender binarisms both constrain and overstep their limits when placed in the analogical sphere of the world, or when Menon notes the way in which texts can simultaneously maintain and ignore differences whose recognitions can be mobilized as forms of categorical constraint: it is particularly in the mapping of gender and sexuality, of identity and desire, as drawn apart, distracted, that she opens worlds of possibility.

So, what *world* means is never to be answered in the singular. We speak, after all, of a "social world," as Robert Matz does, as a place of complicated belonging; and we recall Hamlet's "distracted globe" as Maxwell does, a world of the mind that in being imagined as a globe also must recall the name of the theater in which Hamlet speaks. The coincidence of multiple globes in that single word also marks a distance between them already indicated by Hamlet's distracted and abstracted mind. Where Hamlet is located, in what world, is a question Evans raises in contemplating his encounter with pirates on the way to England. Is all the world a stage? Although he is writing about Marlowe, Aaron Kunin glimpses something akin to Hamlet's antics when he remarks on the distance between the stage and the utterances that take place on it as "a world distinct from the scene in which they are spoken." The worldmaking of a text may not coincide with a representational aim of reproducing a known world. Such distinctions are in question when James Kuzner considers Hamlet contemplating the fate of Alexander, in death returned to the matter from which he was made, as if such contemplation could stand apart from what one is a part. Can sullied solid flesh melt into thought? These questions of apartness are, as Dawson remarks on the opening page of his essay, a question of synecdoche housed in the Greek for world—*kosmos*, a word for world that names both a totality and an ornamental part. This relationship of part and whole is pursued in Maxwell's contribution on the relationship of microcosm to macrocosm. If man is "a little world made cunningly," as Donne famously claims opening one of his holy sonnets, is woman, asks Maxwell? Is woman part of the world that is reflected in "man" or apart from it? Menon likewise pursues related questions arising from the equation of woman and world. Is woman a reflection of a reflection, a part of the whole ("He for God only, she for God in him," as Milton would have it); or does the chain stop and in woman do we glimpse something else, some other world, the sex that is not one, as Luce Irigaray would put it, or something between, as Menon avers?[14] Is the world one or are there many? Kunin allows himself to wonder, when two popes appear at once, whether Marlowe's rival Pope Bruno might take his name from Giordano Bruno, the contemporary materialist philosopher who imagined and theorized multiple worlds.[15]

Does *world*, modernizing Spenser's *worold*, translate *kosmos* or *mundus*? Or is *world* what the French would call "*le monde*," naming thereby the social stratum that counts? Or is *world* closer to the French *peuple*, mundane, debased, proletarian? Do we live in one world or more than one? A universe or a university? In which world—the first world, the second, or the third? The New World? Moving across worlds, as Evans and Menon do, raises questions about the many worlds that are in the world. Is the world something we make or simply where we find ourselves—are we located in nature (in the flesh) or in what we make, in art (when dust becomes a bottle stop)? Or when nature turns unnatural (a bung stop)? Is our body our world? Is our world our flesh? Our mind? Our soul? Is our life worldly or otherworldly in its impetus and direction? Or somewhere in between? When/where do we truly live? Is Hamlet's distraction antisocial and unworldly or is it aimed at some other mode of being in this very world? Is it, perhaps, a debased worldliness?

"Thus is Man that great and true *Amphibium*," Sir Thomas Browne writes in *Religio Medici*, in a trope worth pausing over and to which Evans turns briefly, "whose nature is disposed to live, not onely like other creatures in divers elements, but in divided and distinguished worlds."[16] At the same time that Browne likens humans to animals that live on both land and sea, he refuses this likeness by distinguishing and dividing humans from their animal confreres. The disposition of human nature to live a double life seems as much a human inclination (an expression of choice and desire) as simply a situation in which people find themselves. This life is in "divided and distinguished worlds," Browne continues, "for though there be but one to sense, there are two to reason, the one visible, the other invisible." Browne's separations of mind and body, of thought and sensation, of visible and invisible, of physical and metaphysical, are immediately belied. First, by the multiple meanings of *sense* that cross from body to mind, but even more so by the fact that this very doubleness and division is simultaneously singularly available in the very sentence he writes.[17] Elsewhere Browne professes his admiration for paradox, for two truths that exist at the same time. David Glimp's foray into geopolitical crisis leads him to note how paradox functions in Niklas Luhmann's systems theory, enabling, Glimp writes, a "second-order perspective from which it is possible to see the larger unity that organizes the conflict and to access the 'unsaid' that is excluded when a set of distinctions are introduced to make sense of the world." To see not just what divides and distinguishes, that is, to see further than (often binary) categories allow, perhaps offers a glimpse of totality, an alternative as yet unvoiced and unthought. It is to these terrains that Maxwell and Menon guide us as well beyond and within the categorical differences of gender.

Daniel Juan Gil pursues another such parallel in reading Henry Vaughan's resurrection beliefs in relation to humoral theory. Like Browne, Vaughan writes some version of a *religio medici*. He believes in the resurrection of the body at the end of time. Like Milton (Donne, too, in his holy sonnet on man as microcosm), he is a mortalist: there is a great gap in time—the gap, in fact, is all of time—between this life and the next life, this world and the next world. Nonetheless, following Saint Paul, Vaughan avers that there is a seed planted and growing here and now, in the human soil and soul, that enables a reading of worldly existence from the perspective of an otherworldliness that inhabits and grows in us.[18] As Gil argues, this double view opens a kind of sociological perspective (Gil conjures Pierre Bourdieu into his analysis) enabling one to see this life and this world from an elsewhere even in a *habitus* that, nonetheless, is here and now. Vaughan's immanent and monist resurrection theory produces "a change in the basic way a person is habituated in the world." It enables a recognition of and a distantiation from social habitation to discover a vitality in the body now that will be that of the resurrected body at the end of time. This figuration of this seed also coincides with the language Lucretius uses for the atomic matter of which we are all made, the invisible atoms that constitute us and make us indistinguishable from the material world. Browne's *invisibilia* may intend spirit; similarly, Lucretian matter also resists visibility not just because atoms are too small to be seen, but because they also intimate that they are the very matter of thought. The precarity of material existence (of life that coincides with matter) runs through many of these essays. In Browne's words, "Though I feel his pulse, I dare not say he lives."[19] For Gil, following Vaughan, we experience futurity now.

Between a world nullified by Saint Paul as merely worldly and a world promised but entirely otherworldly, between a world destroyed and a world remade, these essays seek to understand the work of both division and distinction, even as they also seek to undo the full force of such division in order to glimpse something sustaining in life, the "flourishing" of "a poetic of immanent worldmaking," to quote Lauren Berlant, to grasp the seed in us to quote Saint Paul against himself.[20] Over and again, that is, these essays demarcate anti-dualist positions. Gil studies resurrection theory precisely because it belies the body/soul division upon which it seems to rely to adumbrate the social. Glimp looks at a moment of emergency in Cary's *Tragedy of Mariam*, exploring the possibilities opened by the death of Herod and its promise of a world remade that are shattered when the tyrant lives to exercise his state of exception; Mariam, the heroine of Cary's play, suspended between life and death, is herself put to death. Precisely in, and despite the maintenance of, the absoluteness of division and distinction, of life and death, something else seems at least momentarily possible, Glimp avers. So, too, Kunin plays with Marlovian fantasies of world domination that reduce others to seemingly inanimate objects—footstools—only to observe how these differences—the human, the movable object—refuse to be stable. The ruler seeks the power of the inanimate, unchanging being symbolized by a throne. Perhaps paradoxically the sovereign wishes for the king's body that never dies but in his very wishing signals his own lack. The desire to reduce others to earth that can be trampled on houses the contradictory desire that those abased should nevertheless testify to their abasement. If a footstool speaks, it is animate and has a life that exceeds the ambition to turn it into a thing, but it is thus also subject to death. Such Marlovian scenes intimate a world of vibrant matter, as Jane Bennett might put it, or Giordano Bruno, a world vitalized beyond any easy distinction between animate and inanimate. In Menon's text, a necklace speaks.

Questions about distinction and difference also haunt the social world, the world of friend and enemy upon which Carl Schmitt (invoked in several of these essays) founds the concept of the political (or on land and ocean upon which definitions of political sovereignty teeter, as Evans argues). The distinction of friend and enemy founders on the classical requirement that friends die for each other, as James Kuzner explores in the relationship of Hamlet and Horatio, and Lara Bovilsky in the relationship between Antonio and Shylock. Hamlet insists that Horatio not die, but live on to tell his tale. Horatio thus finds himself in an impossible position, as Kuzner notes: How much of the truth, what truth, must he tell? His promise to speak of "unnatural acts;/ . . . accidental judgments, casual slaughters" sounds more like an Aristotelian parsing of a tragedy—a rather old-fashioned one like that mimed in the play-within-the-play—than a "factual" account of the truth. Kuzner shows how Horatio glances obliquely at some of the ways Hamlet falls short, neither exemplary hero nor ideal friend. In Kuzner's account, Hamlet occupies the impossible position imposed by sociality, the inhabitation of a vulnerability that, following Judith Butler, Kuzner affirms as what it means to live in the world. To uphold the dictates of friendship (a world where two truths are told at once) is to create a world that affirms our openness to others. "The play's world," Kuzner writes, "is a wound that will always be open." Bovilsky also reads friendship differently. Antonio's masochistic drive in *The Merchant of Venice*, his refusal of self-care, she argues, undermines normative economic, sexual, political, and social institutions. Instead of seeking to normalize Antonio and Bassanio's queer friendship, as some recent readings have sought to do, she seeks to identify an "affective and queer idiosyncrasy" in Antonio akin to Marlowe's fully negativized sodomitical affirmations.

Responding to impossibility and difficulty rather than insisting on closure and boundary, worldmaking is always precarious. As Matz suggests, that precarity teeters toward a dissolution that can seem utopic in its imagined freedom from the constraints of boundedness and identity, but that can also be dystopic, for the loss of markers of individual identity makes escape from definition also dangerous and raises the possibility of being seized. This is the condition of the utterly confused category of sodomy in early modernity, as Foucault claimed.[21] But it might also be our fate, Matz argues, in the corporate university whose globalizing interests seek to monopolize who is speaking and to close down difference. As Glimp suggests, the friend/enemy difference is not easily sustained, for it is one more version of the old question of difference and sameness. Perhaps, in fact, as Evans reflects, difference is not a matter of identity at all; Menon raises a similar question when she explores how maintaining normative distinctions of sex and gender identity are suspended in a play world that refuses to name as difference a difference that repeatedly recurs. Are two women married to each other, one of them cross-dressed, lesbian, or are gender and sexuality indeterminate? Not answering this question suspends categorical differences that can at the same time be desired and assumed—a possibility that exists in fictional worlds, in any case, whatever their relations to "our" "real" world might be taken to be.

Contemplating ambiguity, contradiction, ambivalence, these essays suggest that the possibilities of theory have not been exhausted. The list of theorists whose work is marshaled here would be a long one: to those already named (Berlant, Bourdieu, Butler, Foucault, Irigaray, Luhmann, Schmitt) must be added Giorgio Agamben, Hannah Arendt, Étienne Balibar, Roland Barthes, Georges Bataille, Walter Benjamin, Leo Bersani, Maurice Blanchot, Elias Canetti, Paul de Man, Jacques Derrida, Jean-Luc Nancy, Derek Parfit, Eve Kosofsky Sedgwick. Nothing like a singular theoretical perspective or "school" obtains in these essays, nor are they instrumentalizing exercises in applied theory. Rather, the collection limns the ways in which the possibility of leaving behind the categorical and addressing what it takes to make a world requires the thinking exemplified by "theory." It animates, for example, Meillassoux's questions about what exists before and beyond our own existence, or Nancy's reflections on the difference between "freedoms" and the rights' claims such freedoms are said to underwrite, and freedom. We "do not grasp the stakes of 'freedom,'" he argues, "for [freedoms] delimit necessary conditions of contemporary human life, without considering existence as such."[22] The task of thinking is to think the unthinkable, as Agamben avers, following the lead provided by Aby Warburg and his formulation of *Pathosformeln*, connections of thought and emotion that might persist across space and time through figuration and representation. For Warburg, that persistence was exemplified in the art and writing of early modernity.[23] No wonder, then, that these essays are intensely theoretical, motivated as they are by thinking beyond impasses and at the sites of impossible divisions. No wonder, too, that they are intent upon literature as a place to pursue such questions. Kunin, in fact, quotes Allen Grossman's speculation that the function of literature may be to try to manifest, against our vanishing, a making that cannot be destroyed or, at the very least, that might last longer than individual life, or that of any given empire, and thereby might transform worldly muck and precarious matter into something worth poetic worldmaking. "Almost anything that appears in a poem looks more or less like a king," Kunin writes. Ozymandias?

> As one who in his journey bates at noon,
> Though bent on speed, so here the archangel paused
> Betwixt the world destroyed and world restored,
> If Adam aught perhaps might interpose;
> Then with transition sweet new speech resumes. (*Paradise Lost*, 12.1–5)

These lines (very likely the last Milton wrote, added to *Paradise Lost* in 1674 when the 1667 book 10 was divided into books 11 and 12) slow as they approach an apex to which they also rush; this apex also is a midpoint that marks at once a high point and the beginning of decline. Milton writes in the wake of Spenserian worlding. His simile may summon a life approaching its end (Milton died in 1674), a poem coming to its conclusion, a day hastening to rise to its inevitable fall: the story of paradise lost. It is also a circle that recurs daily, although in this context, a circulation within the brackets of a time before and a time after that is no time at all. This is the world without thought and life that Meillassoux contemplates. Nevertheless, between an ending that seems the absolute end of "the world destroyed," and a "world restored," there is a relation: one follows from the other. Both moments in time are called "the world." These lines take place in a pause, a caesura, a between that is neither of these seeming opposites. Between the angel and the human there is the possibility of something interposed, an "aught" that seems contentless, non-referential, a letter away from "naught" and yet something that might exceed the division between destruction and restoration. "New speech" resumes in the empty place of Adam's silence; its potential opens perhaps the position that Meillassoux marks out—the space of/for saying the unsaid, the space/time of the inoperable, the emergent. Our analysis of Milton here echoes Evans, Kuzner, Glimp, and Menon, a place of theoretical utterance that articulates our relationship to what is necessarily other and unrelated to us, and yet what we are nevertheless part of, the life before and after that goes on without us. "New speech" resumes as if it were that future restoration (as if the Last Judgment and the afterlife and the other world were to be had now, as they are for Vaughan); it resumes too as if Adam's interposition had taken place in the pause. Literally, Adam has not spoken; yet he has insofar as the voice of the angel is a human voice. Milton wrote these lines and has inserted this pause in the narrative just as he supplied the words the angel speaks. The silent partner in this moment of human/angelic exchange is the voice speaking anew past or just before the midpoint marked as located between worlds. Characteristic of what Gordon Teskey calls Milton's delirium, this speech, offered as angelic, dissimulates Milton's writing as the "new speech" of the sweet transition between the world destroyed and the world restored.[24] The place of literature, the impossible locale in which we can see all the world at once, is what Evans characterizes as Milton's view. Characteristically, these lines opening the final book of *Paradise Lost* imagine a scene between men; yet there is another silent partner: Eve sleeping, dreaming, as she will report when she awakens, to know everything there is to know. Hers also is Milton's own nightly visitation that delivers the poem to him.[25]

The space in Milton's lines of the thought and the unthought, the said and the unsaid, constitutes a literary world seeking a way past binding dualisms comparable to the many early modern instances discussed in other essays in this volume; in this context William Empson's reading of a moment in Marvell's "The Garden" in *Some Versions of Pastoral* comes to mind.[26] Empson begins his discussion with a "crucial double meaning" that he finds in the notes to the Oxford edition of Marvell's poem, a gloss on the lines that are the pivot of his chapter: "Annihilating all that's made / To a green Thought in a green shade."[27] Does "To" mean, "in comparison to" or does it mean "transformed into"? These lines are about the activity of mind. The mind is said to have withdrawn from "pleasure less" into itself:

> The Mind, that Ocean where each kind
> Does streight its own resemblance find;
> Yet it creates, transcending these,
> Far other Worlds, and other Seas;
> Annihilating all that's made
> To a green Thought in a green Shade. (41–48)

The mind is first described as a site of reflection, but it immediately exceeds resemblance to create other worlds—worlds in the sea that is the mind. In the course of his analysis of this moment, Empson recalls the watery world of Donne's lovers in "A Valediction: Of Weeping," a poem Maxwell explores, also following Empson's critical lead, but in *Seven Types of Ambiguity*.[28] The world made between the lovers, she argues, exceeds the straitening/straightening plots of gender difference. In his reading of Marvell, Empson is interested in gendered questions too, framing them in terms of activity and passivity, wondering about the desire expressed in withdrawal, destruction, and creation. This ocean that exceeds resemblance finds its echo in Evans pausing with Hamlet in his sea journey to inquire about possibilities of agency and self-resemblance, or in Antipholus of Syracuse in *The Comedy of Errors*, who reflects, "I to the world am like a drop of water / That in the ocean seeks another drop, / Who, falling there to find his fellow forth / Unseen, inquisitive, confounds himself" (1.2.34–40).[29] The green thought in a green shade of "The Garden" is self-reflexively "The Garden." Mentation here may be that of a distracted/abstracted globe or an exercise of what Sir Philip Sidney names as the "zodiac" of the poet's own creative "wit," bent on making golden worlds.[30]

As Empson insists, the knotty double meaning in this moment of annihilation and creation of worlds may mean a passive withdrawal of the mind into itself, or it might mean an active resistance to merely mundane pleasure and thus a transcendence of itself. The mind into which the poet withdraws and from which he makes something may be a withdrawal into a nothingness in which mind and thinking is lost as itself, or it could be a conscious grasping of everything that exceeds itself. Green thought into green shade splits the same word, *green*, into alternative and yet simultaneous possibilities. "Shade" carries menace and pleasure at once: death and something beyond that nonetheless is located in what is or in what can be made of what is. Empson links Marvell's poem to Buddhist thought only to suggest that the poem raises a kind of universal philosophical question (he offers a quick sketch of western thought and western literature in his chapter, which ranges from Homer to Shakespeare, Donne, and beyond). Empson is offering a version of pastoral by way of Marvell's poem to ask about the relations of mind and nature, of body and spirit, in which this poem operates. He is asking, in essence, in what world we divided and distinguished beings exist and the degree to which poetry, through its difficult language, offers a way of arresting contradiction by its restatements, its sweet resumings in the pause of stultifying abyssal thought.

Although Empson appears in these essays only in citation by Maxwell, he has a place in the most significant literary engagement in this volume, we would suggest, with the poet who inevitably signifies early modern literature, Shakespeare. There is considerable Shakespeare here, perhaps because, as Palfrey has recently observed, "his work is symptomatic of an age in which worlds and perspectives were multiplying;" yet the Shakespeare on offer here resists simply instantiating a period as well as his incorporation into his canonical position of transcendence.[31] Matz's essay examines how Shakespeare's own bids to such a position reek of convention; those bids, moreover, are made in the sonnets, poems whose sexuality has always made them suspect to conventional humanist canonizers of Shakespeare, as Matz notes. Until late in the eighteenth century, Shakespeare's sonnets and his plays were never bound within the same book, and then only with resistance, as Menon observes.[32] Gertrude Stein, as late as her *Four in America* (1947), still keeps the poems separate from the plays as kinds of writing, though since it is Stein, what starts as strict division becomes indistinction, *individual* in the early modern sense.[33] Matz notices how, anticipating Foucault, Shakespeare's sonnets deconstruct the very claims to authorship that they make; but, he insists, Shakespeare is not easily mistaken for someone else and thereby finds value in Shakespeare's idiosyncrasy, his utterly contingent historical formation, against a dissolution into non-self-identity, which Matz sees as dangerously close to a kind of corporatizing identity, a commodified cultural object with readymade meaning.

Shakespeare in this volume is no such item. Marlowe serves as a significant counter to Shakespeare here—in the Marlovian Cary of Glimp's essay and in Kunin's reading of human-object relations in Marlowe. And the essays that do read Shakespeare posit a Shakespeare on the verge of extremities that Marlowe espouses more openly: Kuzner's, with its focus on the impossibility of friendship and a Hamlet who is scarcely exemplary, or Bovilsky's attention to the extremity of Antonio, or Evans's, which locates Hamlet in a hiatus of sovereignty. Empson could well be behind the extreme Marlowe adduced in this volume, especially his brief essay "Two Proper Crimes," where Marlowe's atheism and his support for sodomy are taken as key to his poetic achievement: "The unmentionable sin for which the punishment was death was *the proper thing to do*. . . . It seems to me that this is the primary fact about his work, and that a critic who muffles it up, from whatever kindly intentions, cannot be saying anything important about him."[34] Those "kindly intentions" might well include the desire to make Marlowe seem an anticipation of Shakespeare, especially the Shakespeare hailed as the inventor of the human. Repeatedly in these essays Shakespeare is measured against the Marlovian critical demand that Empson voices. This is explicit in Bovilsky's reading of *The Merchant of Venice* and in her refusal to allow Antonio to be understood either as some exemplary, if extreme, version of everyone's plight as a subject or as some simple exception as a proto-homosexual. Antonio's desire for annihilation, which can be placed beside the inoperable friendship that Kuzner explores between Hamlet and Horatio, glimpses Marlowe's fundamental negation of the world as a way of reframing the proper, refusing limitation, embracing an extremity from which something can yet be made. That making, Empson seems to suggest, is coincident with being in a world indifferent to human exceptionality. It is the space of being part of what one is necessarily also separate from; participation in the world is participation in a vitality and a life that exceeds mortal limits, a life that is here and elsewhere at once, insofar as the other world is in this world. The other world racks to the uttermost the complacencies of canonical Shakespeare: a world of what we might term, with Dawson, "queer sovereignty," or with Menon, "queer universalism," the latter attached to a Shakespeare affirmed/negated as an "empty signifier."

Twenty years ago, *Queering the Renaissance* gathered a group of writers, many, as here, at early stages of their careers. Although this volume is not offered under the rubric "queer," and only Bovilsky's essay situates itself explicitly as a contribution to sexuality studies, "queer" is sounded in the opening and closing essays as a frame that highlights the participation of these essays in practices that follow from the work that *Queering the Renais-*

sance initiated and sought to foster. Arguably, one need no longer queer the Renaissance; it is queered. But, as the concluding section of Matz's essay suggests, such efforts do not safeguard early modern studies or literary studies more broadly; in the corporate university, the canonical humanist Shakespeare is apt to be the only value for which we are valued, our "value added." Against such institutional and political antagonism, queer work is needed perhaps as never before, whether explicitly under that label or not; the multitude of theoretical approaches in this volume figures these possibilities. No monolithic agenda attaches itself to "queer"; its transformations are the risks of participation in the very categorical thinking it deconstructs.[35] As Glimp suggests, moments of emergency are those in which the direction of a discourse, the intentions of those in positions of power, are especially precarious. To queer the sovereign is to show the value of precarity, as Matz or Dawson or Evans argues in quite different ways. Another shared impulse in this collection is its non-reductive sense of the historical; this runs quite counter to much in our current disciplinary climate, in the historicist practices prevailing in literary studies today, which all too often reduce literature to little more than an empirical, even positivist, history assumed reducible to the factual and the singular.

Queer work is needed, as Bovilsky's work attests, at least indirectly, to complicate what too easily is seen as the triumph of gay/lesbian politics, today so frequently reduced to the gay marriage movement. *Queering the Renaissance* was framed by essays contemplating the damage done by the 1986 U.S. Supreme Court *Bowers v. Hardwick* decision; this volume comes after the 2013 overthrow of the Defense of Marriage Act, itself presaged by the 2003 Supreme Court decision in *Lawrence v. Texas* and now fulfilled in *Obergefell v. Hodges* in 2015. In "Gay Rights versus Queer Theory: What Is Left of Sodomy after *Lawrence v. Texas*," Teemu Ruskola argues against the normalizing of gay intimacy and shows the dangers of modeling same-sex relations on heterosexual coupledom. Recognizing that gay people are capable of intimacy, Ruskola notes, is welcome after the disavowals of *Bowers v. Hardwick* but erasing the specificity and differences of gay people is not.[36] Ruskola invokes sodomy as the term for an antisocial dissidence denied by the marriage model. Sodomy is sexuality, as Dawson avers. LGBT politics stands behind queer work even as queer work seeks to complicate the identitarian, minoritizing, rights-driven ambitions of movement politics. As Eve Kosofsky Sedgwick argues in "Making Gay Meanings," it is one of the paradoxes of gay politics to insist that difference should be no bar to inclusion.[37] The desire to be included by those who would exclude has a price: conformism and, thereby, ironically, participation in such exclusions; conformism and, thereby, ironically, the very denial of the difference upon which identity politics battens as it makes its case for the right to inclusion. In "Thinking Sex," Gayle Rubin noted as long ago as 1984 how LGBT politics marginalized those thought to taint the image of proper gays; today, not marrying and having children poses a similar potential for marginalization.[38] The gay defense of marriage forgets the critiques of marriage inequalities once fundamental to feminist critique. It hands movement politics over to the state, to the courts, perhaps even the church, with worrisome political costs, as Wendy Brown and Janet Halley would remind us.[39]

Bovilsky's essay seeks to make Antonio's resistance to socialization palpable. So doing, it speaks to these current issues as much as it does to those Shakespeareans whose bard teaches the timeless truths of a not-so-liberal society. Her essay continues the unfinished work Empson's reading practice enacts, arguably deconstructive avant la lettre. Bovilsky's reading of Shakespeare's "*nearly* Marlovian" merchant is like Kunin's reading of a Marlowe whose absolutism pushes so hard on difference as to make indifferent the human/object relationship ("A man acting as a footstool declares his submission to a chair acting as man"). Absolute difference is impossible. The rebellion that Empson located in Marlowe is the rebellion of a double agent not in fact likely to be martyred, as Empson supposed would have been his fate had he not been murdered, but not likely either to be comfortably included; this is the position finally occupied by Shylock. In their different ways, Dawson's and Menon's framing essays articulate a queerness that inhabits the norm because it is not one. This volume need not appear under the rubric "queer" for it to further the ambitions of work done under that name: to practice literary analysis otherwise and to inflect those practices in the direction of social and political critique. These ambitions are captured in the work of Lauren Berlant, especially in her advocacy of worldmaking. *Sex, or the Unbearable*, as we have noted, offers a dialogue in worldmaking, world-annihilating, that shares many of the aims of this volume. Or with the scene at whose sexuality Kunin glances ("sit on me," "stand on me," "tell me you like it," "tell me you don't") that needs no further naming since it is a "basic, universal, unspoken desire."

NOTES

1. All citations to book, canto, stanza, and line from *The Faerie Queene* are from Edmund Spenser, *Poetical Works*, ed. J. C. Smith and E. De Selincourt (London: Oxford University Press, 1970).

2. The analysis here depends upon Jonathan Goldberg, *Endlesse Worke: Spenser and the Structures of Discourse* (Baltimore, MD: Johns Hopkins University Press, 1981), 69–70.

3. Edmund Spenser, *The Faerie Queene: Books Three and Four*, ed. Dorothy Stephens (Indianapolis: Hackett, 2006), 375n8.

4. Quentin Meillassoux, *After Finitude: An Essay on the Necessity of Contingency*, trans. Ray Brassier (London: Bloomsbury, 2008), 9–10.

5. Pascal David, "Welt," in *Dictionary of Untranslatables: A Philosophical Lexicon*, ed. Barbara Cassin, trans. Steven Rendall, Christian Hubert, Jeffrey Mehlman, Nathanael Stein, and Michael Syrotinski, trans. ed. Emily Apter, Jacques Lezra, and Michael Wood (Princeton, NJ: Princeton University Press, 2014), 1217–24. Originally published as *Vocabulaire européen des philosophies: Dictionnaire des intraduisibles* (Paris: Éditions de Seuil, 2004).

6. David, "Welt," *Dictionary of Untranslatables*, 1217.

7. William Shakespeare, *Macbeth*, in *The Riverside Shakespeare* (Boston: Houghton Mifflin, 1974), 1.3.116; Andrew Marvell, "To His Coy Mistress," in *The Poems and Letters of Andrew Marvell*, 2nd ed., ed. H. M. Margoliouth, 26–27 (Oxford: Clarendon, 1951).

8. Carl Schmitt, *Hamlet or Hecuba: The Intrusion of the Time into the Play*, trans. David Pan and Jennifer Rust (New York: Telos, 2009), 64.

9. Harry Berger Jr., "The Renaissance Imagination: Second World and Green World," *Centennial Review* 9 (1965): 36–78.

10. Eric Hayot, *On Literary Worlds* (Oxford: Oxford University Press, 2012).

11. Jean-Luc Nancy, *Le sens du monde* (Paris: Galilée, 1993), translated by Jeffrey Librett as *The Sense of the World* (Minneapolis: University of Minnesota Press, 1997); see also his *The Creation of the World or Globalization*, trans. François Raffoul and David Pettigrew (Albany: State University of New York Press, 2007), which argues against a homogenizing globalization and for multiple worldmaking.

12. Simon Palfrey, *Shakespeare's Possible Worlds* (Cambridge: Cambridge University Press, 2014).

13. Lauren Berlant and Lee Edelman, *Sex, or the Unbearable* (Durham, NC: Duke University Press, 2014). Gayatri Chakravorty Spivak raises similar questions about worlds in *An Aesthetic Education in the Era of Globalization* (Cambridge, MA: Harvard University Press, 2012) in such essays as "The Imperative to Re-imagine the Planet" (335–50) or, in terms of transnational literary practice (also a concern of Hayot's), in "Teaching for the Time" (137–57).

14. Luce Irigaray, *This Sex Which Is Not One*, trans. Catherine Porter (Ithaca, NY: Cornell University Press, 1985). *Paradise Lost*, 4.299. Milton

citations are from *John Milton: The Major Works*, ed. Stephen Orgel and Jonathan Goldberg (Oxford: Oxford University Press, 1991).

15. On Bruno and worldmaking, see May Baine Campbell, *Wonder and Science: Imagining Worlds in Early Modern Europe* (Ithaca, NY: Cornell University Press, 1999).

16. Sir Thomas Browne, *Religio Medici and Other Writings* (New York: Dutton, 1951), 39.

17. On the meanings of *sense*, see William Empson, *The Structure of Complex Words* (Ann Arbor: University of Michigan Press, 1967), 250–310.

18. For a cognate exploration see Giorgio Agamben, "The Glorious Body," in *Nudities*, trans. David Kishik and Stefan Pedatella (Stanford, CA: Stanford University Press, 2011), 91–103.

19. Browne, *Religio Medici*, 36.

20. Lauren Berlant, *Cruel Optimism* (Durham, NC: Duke University Press, 2011), 8; David Glimp alludes to this moment in Berlant.

21. See Michel Foucault, *The History of Sexuality: An Introduction*, trans. Robert Hurley (New York: Pantheon, 1978), 101.

22. Jean-Luc Nancy, *The Experience of Freedom*, trans. Bridget McDonald (Palo Alto, CA: Stanford University Press, 1993), 2.

23. See Giorgio Agamben, "Nymphs," in *Releasing the Image: From Literature to New Media*, ed. Jacques Khalip and Robert Mitchell, 60–80 (Stanford, CA: Stanford University Press, 2011).

24. See Gordon Teskey, *Delirious Milton: The Fate of the Poet in Modernity* (Cambridge, MA: Harvard University Press, 2006).

25. This connection was made by Brent Dawson in conversation with Jonathan Goldberg.

26. William Empson, "Marvell's Garden," in *Some Versions of Pastoral* (New York: New Directions, 1974), 119–48.

27. Ibid., 119.

28. William Empson, *Seven Types of Ambiguity* (New York: New Directions Press, 1947), 139–45.

29. William Shakespeare, *The Comedy of Errors in The Riverside Shakespeare* (Boston: Houghton Mifflin, 1974), 83–105.

30. Sir Philip Sidney, *A Defence of Poetry*, ed. J. A. Van Dorsten (Oxford: Oxford University Press, 1966), 24.

31. Palfrey, *Shakespeare's Possible Worlds*, 6.

32. The definitive study of Edmond Malone's joining the poet and the playwright in his 1790 edition of Shakespeare is Margreta de Grazia, *Shakespeare Verbatim: The Reproduction of Authenticity and the 1790 Apparatus* (Oxford, UK: Clarendon, 1991).

33. For further discussion, see Jonathan Goldberg, "Exclusive of," *Renaissance Drama* 40 (2012): 9–17, esp. 14–15.

34. William Empson, "Two Proper Crimes," is a book review that appeared in the *Nation* of October 10, 1946. I cite its reprinting in *The Strengths of Shakespeare's Shrew*, ed. John Haffenden, 86–88 (Sheffield, UK: Sheffield Academic Press, 1996), 87.

35. In the concluding page of her 2008 new preface to *Epistemology of the Closet* (Berkeley: University of California Press, 1990, 2008, xiii-xviii), Eve Kosofsky Sedgwick talks about finding herself located "in the yet unlabeled realm of queer theory" that her book was creating. By *Tendencies* (Durham, NC: Duke University Press, 1993), "queer" had arrived and Sedgwick was already imagining its volatization well beyond concerns with sexuality and identity that had first mobilized it; see Sedgwick, "Queer and Now," in *Tendencies*, 1–20, esp. 8–9.

36. Teemu Ruskola, "Gay Rights versus Queer Theory: What Is Left of Sodomy after *Lawrence v. Texas*," *Social Text* 84–85 (Fall-Winter 2005): 235–49.

37. Eve Kosofsky Sedgwick, "Making Gay Meanings," in *The Weather in Proust*, ed. Jonathan Goldberg, 183–89 (Durham, NC: Duke University Press, 2011).

38. For a reprinting of "Thinking Sex," along with 1993 further thoughts and 2010 reflections, see Gayle Rubin, *Deviations* (Durham, NC: Duke University Press, 2011), 137–223.

39. See Wendy Brown and Janet Halley, ed., *Left Legalism/Left Critique* (Durham, NC: Duke University Press, 2002).

PART I

Materiality

CHAPTER I

Worldly Muck: Translating Matter in Book 2 of *The Faerie Queene*

Brent Dawson

Spenser's famous set-piece, the House of Alma, begins with a comparison of the human body and the world, the tangible physicality of what we all have and a vast expanse that stretches beyond its reach:

> Of all Gods workes, which do this world adorne,
> There is no one more faire and excellent,
> Then is mans body both for powre and forme,
> Whiles it is kept in sober gouernment.
>
> (Spenser, *The Faerie Queene*, 2.9.1.1–4)[1]

Playing on the Latin sense of *mundus* as both "cosmos" and "ornament," the passage suggests the body is a microcosm, that crowning jewel of the world most like the world's own pristine beauty. The rest of the canto develops the synecdoche, expanding the human body into a well-run castle, the House of Alma, whose chambers and fortifications map precisely onto the different human organs. The integrity of the human body, its ability to regulate what it incorporates and expels of the outside world, is made the model of well-run government. As here, the body and its matter are tightly interlinked throughout book 2 of *The Faerie Queene* with ideals of politics and empire: the temperate body is a colonial fortress; the pursuit of gold is appetite in the Cave of Mammon; maritime adventure verges on self-pleasure at the Idle Lake; acceding to sexual desire is going native in the Bower of Bliss. These organic metaphors serve ideological ends, naturalizing capitalism and imperialism as forms of civilizational health and rendering savages and other cultures as disorders to be contained or overcome.

But can these analogies among body, state, and world move in directions less comforting for imperial ideology? How might flesh, with all its traditional attributes of mutability and impurity, open different ways of thinking politics in Spenser? Jonathan Goldberg raises the possibility of such a reading of the house in *The Seeds of Things*, arguing that while the practices of bodily discipline explored in the canto "easily correlate with colonialism," given that colonialism claims to bring order to civilization's unruly outsides, if one follows the affirmative possibilities Foucault's later work finds in these regimes, "such linkages do not exhaust the work of these labors on oneself."[2] The possibility Goldberg raises, that Spenserian flesh might cut across the boundaries raised by colonial ideology, is supported by Spenser's longest description of the matter of the body in the Alma canto, which compares human flesh to the cosmopolitan Tower of Babel:

> Not built of bricke, ne yet of stone and lime,
> But of thing like to that *AEgyptian* slime,
> Whereof king *Nine* whilome built *Babell* towre;
> But ô great pitty, that no lenger time
> So goodly workemanship should not endure:
> Soone it must turne to earth; no earthly thing is sure. (2.9.21.4–9)

Where the canto as a whole dwells on the body as a beautiful and exemplary structure, these lines shift focus toward the viscous matter of which that structure is formed. While the shape of the organism might be beautiful, the matter within it is given to rotting, never permanent or "sure." The passage raises a number of perplexing questions: Why, in a celebration of organic form, this sickly lingering on the body's rotten flesh? What is the relation between the two opposed functions of flesh in the passage, composition and decomposition? Finally, what links together the fatal weakness of the body with which the stanza ends and the dream of a united humanity suggested by the reference to Babel in its middle? Does the lowest form of ecstasy, the body's dissipation into dirt, and the highest, humanity's tran-

calling up connotations of "the mud of the Nile, from which crocodiles and hippopotami were alleged to be spontaneously generated after the yearly floods."[22] However, the spontaneous generation associated with the Nile, in its ontological leap from nonliving matter to living organisms, has little to do with traditional hetero notions of reproduction, insofar as reproduction is imagined as reproduction of the same, the continuation of the father in the son. Classical accounts of the Nile's life-creation suggest a hypergenerativity that bears no resemblance to the formation of discrete individuals. Virgil's *Georgics*, for example, describes how in the Nile's banks "miraculous creatures. . . . / swarm together . . . / until, like rain pouring from the clouds of summer, / they burst forth."[23] The droves of creatures emerging from the Nile resemble less the regulated life of Alma's house than the hordes of troops assaulting the house. Indeed, Spenser compares these beings to "a swarme of Gnats" rising "Out of the fennes of Allan" in Ireland (2.9.16.1, 2). Virgil's bees are described as "miraculous" [*mirus*], that is, unexpected and incredible. Spenser similarly gives slime something of the miraculous in the birth of the Christ-child "in fleshly slime / Enwombed" (2.10.50.2–3). If the body's slime ties the body to Adam and his crime, then it also gives the body something in common with Christ and his miraculous entrance into the world. Reproduction in these descriptions is not the stable perpetuation of organic life; rather, reproduction here marks the discontinuity of the organism, its monstrous division.

What is most interesting about Egyptian slime is that, according to Spenser, it can change places with Babylonian asphalt. The substitution has long baffled editors; why the misleading name "Egyptian slime" is used, the eighteenth-century editor John Jortin remarks, "I can't conceive," while A. E. Sawtelle finds Spenser's phrase "somewhat careless[]." John Upton, defending Spenser, argues that it is a meaningless change and, in any case, "even historians confound neighboring nations," using the proper names of different places "promiscuously."[24] But it is just this sort of promiscuous and confounding use that Spenser finds generative. Whether or not the substitution is a mistake, it is certainly not insignificant; nor is it singular, for the description of the house's walls are not the only time Spenser will make this error. Indeed, in book 1, the creature named Error vomits another toxic substance that initially looks like bitumen: "Therewith she spewd out of her filthy maw / A floud of poyson horrible and blacke / Full of great lumpes of flesh and gobbets raw" (1.1.20.1–2). But Spenser transforms the poison to Egyptian mud: "As when old father *Nilus* gins to swell / With timely pride aboue the *Aegyptian* vale, / His fattie waues do fertile slime outwell," just so does Error's bile spawn swarms of "loathly frogs and toades" (21.1–3, 20.7). The conflation suggests that in Spenser the generativity of Egyptian mud cannot be separated from the toxicity of Babylonian bitumen. Life thrives in Spenser on this seething, fatal stuff. Spenserian slime suggests, as does Pauline flesh, that the stuff of the body is alien to the organism. If matter makes the body strange to itself, it also makes the body's negotiation with that alterity into its life, its worldly existence.

One name for the crossings between life and death, the body and the world, culture and its outsides, might be given by a place that is conspicuously absent from Spenser's account. As Teskey notes, there were "three points along the Fertile Crescent where asphalt boiled up": Babylon, Egypt, and, between the two, Sodom.[25] Foucault calls sodomy "that utterly confused category," and Sodom here would mark the non-place between the unstable life-giving origin of Egypt and the deadly remainder of Babylon, between life that exceeds itself and death that lays the foundation of life.[26] Sodom too would mark the necessary point of indistinction between the categories of sexuality that hang around the divisions of matter in *The Faerie Queene*: the fruitfully reproductive slime of the tower and the sterile, perverse gold of the cave. Bataille notes at the outset of *Erotism* that human erotic activity, "unlike simple sexual activity, is a psychological quest independent of the natural goal . . . [of] reproduction and the desire for children." Insofar as reproduction might be understood as a simple desire for the perpetuation of life, for life to continue, erotic activity breaks from the reproductive understanding of life, for "although erotic activity is in the first place an exuberance of life, the object of this psychological quest . . . is not alien to death."[27] In that case, the idea that there might be any healthy or natural erotic pleasure, to which sodomy could be contrasted as sterile or perverse, is no more than a ruse of power. Sexuality just is sodomy and, conversely, reproduction has nothing to do with sex outside some accidents of biology. In Spenser, similarly, the erased, though still legible, place of Sodom in this passage suggests that slime suspends any meaningful final distinctions between healthy and unhealthy desire.

To return to Alma's house, the intertextual allusions around slime suggest how the material of the body in Spenser is not entirely the purified, healthy stuff Schoenfeldt finds nor Landreth's nourishing *prima materia*. In making the walls, or structure, of the body out of slime, Spenser suggests that the body is not an organism. For even as the walls of the body keep out the dangerous assaults of Maleger and his horde, the walls also endanger the body through breaking down, since "no earthly thing is sure." That ambivalence toward matter continues within Alma's house as well.

Schoenfeldt points out that the nourishment of the body as described in the house "continually produc[es] 'superfluous excrements' from the very matter which nourishes it," that is, that matter in its basic form is both healthy and toxic.[28] While Schoenfeldt focuses on the body's ability to separate waste from nutrients, other moments suggest that the purgation of contaminants from nutritive stuff is never full or final. Though there are cooks who "remoue the scum" that rises during digestive processes, there are others who take these dregs "to vse according to his kind" (2.9.31.7, 31.9). Furthermore, the heart is depicted as a "mighty furnace," that burns up the fuel placed in its cauldron to generate the body's energy (29.6). That energy, or "heat," while it keeps the body running, also risks "break[ing] out, and set[ting] the whole on fire" (30.1, 30.2). In the house, the body is set running by what consumes it. And that heat can only be "delay[ed]" by the cooling air of the lungs, not entirely stabilized, for total stability is the same as death (30.1). While the narrator in the opening lines of the canto asserts that Alma's house is a moral *exemplum* of a well-governed body, the description of the house itself suggests that bodies in Spenser cannot be orderly. For the material processes of life that keep them in order, functioning smoothly, and alive are always doing more or less than what they should: breaking down, catching fire, bursting forth in unexpected growths. The life of the self is fueled in Spenser by a relation to its death and destruction, and the self can only partially delay these forces.

And if even Alma's house, the most ideally organized body in the poem, is monstrous, it ought to call attention to just how normal monstrous bodies are in *The Faerie Queene*, whose inhabitance is made up of knights never seen but in their metallic exoskeletons, shape-shifting wizards and temptresses, Ovidian metamorphoses of humans into plants and animals, pairs who seem in terms of allegory and plot to be disjointed pieces of the same being (Guyon and the Palmer, Furor and Occasion, Acrasia and her knight). Indeed, the cast of Spenserian characters could well be described as "a monstrous rablement / Of . . . misshapen wights" like the hordes outside Alma's house (2.11.8.1–2). Spenser's seeming division between human and monstrous life, a division that recurs in the distinction of civil from savage and Christian from heathen, is undercut by the fact that all life exceeds form in the poem. It is certainly true that the self is embodied in Spenser, not dualistically separated into an ideal realm; it is also true that, in Spenser, embodiment is essentially monstrous. That essence is commented on at the end of book 2, when Grille, one among the men whom Guyon and the Palmer free from Acrasia's spell, complains bitterly about having been returned to human form.[29] The Palmer describes Grille as being of "the donghill kind" that "delights in filth and foule incontinence" (2.12.87.6, 87.7). The shit the Palmer recognizes in Grille, though, is a matter common to all life in the book, recalling the "slime" that composes the human form in Alma's house. Grille's doubled state, both or neither human nor beast, is the basic, irreducible stratum of life, the same doubled state that the first stanza of the Alma canto invites the reader to "behold" in the human body, "both one and other," fairest of God's works and unruly monster (2.9.1.9). The base materiality of slime is foundational to life. This matter exists in excess to life conceived as an organism, as productive being; its vitality is bound up with its own waste, decay, and death. Whatever boundaries Spenser's ontology draws between high and low, civil and savage, or human and animal life, this common materiality cuts through them. That is not to say that differences between beings and kinds of life do not exist in Spenser, or that those differences are more or less meaningless in the face of this overarching material sameness. Rather, slime is what prescribes that there be difference, that life never be identical to itself within a kind or individual.

Politics

If the House of Alma figures the ideal state through the metaphor of the body, then how might the slimy materiality of the body translate into politics? One answer might be in what Giorgio Agamben has called "bare life," a zero degree of life detached from the particular shapes and forms given through membership in a body politic. Such life might be glimpsed in the figure of Grille, the residual being who refuses Guyon's civilizing mission. In Agamben's account, the sovereign, who founds the law and order of the state and yet is outside it, leaves, as a sort of residue of that foundation, this bare life, humans whose lives do not count as lives.[30] In Bataille as well, both sovereign and lower orders are part of the "heterogeneous world," that life that cannot be assimilated within the "homogeneous society" of equivalent individuals, society essentially conceived on the order of the commodity.[31] Like the body in its relation to slime, politics in these accounts is a relation toward a residue that resists assimilation to the political order. There is a personage in the slime passage who figures, in Spenser, this materiality of the body politic. This figure is conspicuous through her absence from Spenser's description of the foundation of Babel. She haunts the ambiguously named "king *Nine*" who constructs the tower (2.9.21.6). "*Nine*" most likely refers to Ninus, in Greek history the founder of Nineveh, who is traditionally conflated with the biblical "Nimrod," the king of Babel. Spenser at times fuses Ninus with Nimrod, although in book 1 he shows he knows the two are distinct by making Nimrod Ninus's father (1.5.48.1–3). "*Nine*" could also refer to Ninyas, Nimrod's son, to whom I will return in a moment. The ambiguity of Spenser's "*Nine*" invites a reader to investigate who is or is not being named in this passage. For whoever "*Nine*" may be, he curiously seems to have taken the place of a woman, Semiramis, whom the two major classical sources on Babylon, Diodorus and Justin, credit with the foundation of the city. Making her absence more glaring in the passage, Semiramis is acknowledged by both Diodorus and Justin as responsible for the idea to use bitumen for Babylon's walls.[32] Ovid likewise comments, "Within the towne . . . of whose huge walles so monstrous high and thicke,/The fame is given Semyramis for making them of bricke."[33] Spenser himself seems aware of this association, as one of the two references to Semiramis in the poem plays on the architectural trope by transforming her into a "famous moniment of womens prayse" (2.10.56.1). Semiramis, through a sort of metonymic contagion, is attached to the materiality of her state, the walls of Babylon. As the other associations around her suggest, Semiramis stands in, on the level of politics, for the strange and paradoxical materiality Spenser traces through slime.

Like slime in Spenser, a fundamental contradiction surrounds the historical narratives about Semiramis. As Spenser's base materiality is both toxic and yet the source of life, so too Semiramis is at once the ideal ruler, founder of a glorious empire, and a loathsome example of tyrannical disregard for the law. Semiramis figures all the characteristics that sovereignty, in traditional accounts, is not: female, transgressive of sexual and gender norms, criminal, deceptive. One way to read Semiramis, then, is as a queer sovereign who holds a place within social order for the queer life that society normally excludes. Another way, which will be my focus here, is that she brings out a queerness, or monstrosity, within the idea of sovereignty. Accounts of Semiramis register, I argue, the paradox of sovereignty that both Bataille and Agamben note, that the sovereign, while founder of law and order, is herself outside that order and, thus, in a way closer to those seen as excluded from that order: criminals, women, slaves, the sexually transgressive, and so on.

Semiramis, in some of the legends about her and in one of the two mentions of her in *The Faerie Queene*, is an exemplary emperor, not far from how Spenser imagines Elizabeth. She beautifies her city, expands its territory, and fortifies its walls. Her association with materiality casts her as productive, forging not only a vast but powerful and free state. Diodorus's account is largely celebratory, and Christine de Pizan makes Semiramis the first stone in *The Book of the City of Ladies*.[34] Her erasure from Spenser's description of Babylon, however, likely has to do with the traditions that accrue around her of uncontrollable sexuality and its effects on political rule. The only other reference to Semiramis in *The Faerie Queene*, drawing on such traditions, locates her in the dungeon of the House of Pride, where among the "Proud wemen, vaine, forgetfull of their yoke" is "The bold *Semiramis*, whose sides transfixt / With sonnes owne blade, her fowle reproches spoke" (1.5.50.2, 50.3–4). Justin, whose account is the source of the story to which Spenser here refers, claims that, in order to assume power, Semiramis dressed in the garb of a man and claimed to be her husband's son, Ninyas. This gendered disguise is possible only because the two already closely resemble one another, their faces, heights, and voices being similar. Semiramis is so successful as emperor that eventually she decides it is safe to announce she is a woman, a confession that, according to Justin, only increases her subjects' admiration for her. Her return to her true form is complicated by the love she then conceives for Ninyas. Whether Ninyas reciprocates her love is unknown, but Justin relates that later he kills her, assuming the throne she had originally occupied as him.[35]

While Justin remains somewhat neutral toward Semiramis's turn as (drag?) king and subsequent imperial love, his account fed many narratives that equated her allegedly uncontrollable lust with tyrannical rule. The medieval historian Orosius describes her as "burning with lust and thirsting for blood, in the midst of unceasing adulteries and homicides." Orosius, drawing on the same conflation of Babylon and Babel as Spenser, blames her "swollen ferment of vainglory" for the building of the Tower of Babel. For Dante, to whom Spenser may allude in placing Semiramis in a kind of Hell, Semiramis's "vicious tastes" connect her to the orientalist "Sultan" who in Dante's day rules her former land, another figure in which sinful pleasure and tyrannical rule are perniciously conflated.[36] These misogynist accounts equate bad political rulership with the transgression of gender and sexuality, such that Semiramis's inability to control her bodily desires is equated with her failure to control the state. At the same time, these accusations against Semiramis point up, despite their intent, a queerness to the normative ideal of the sovereign. For Semiramis is attacked for being above the law, for transgressing the laws of incest and gender in the name of pursuing her passions. Her desires, at first to be Ninyas and then to have sex with him, are essentially the same: she wishes to screw the law, the law constraining who or what the sovereign can do. This criminal passion connects Semiramis with those who try to escape the law from below, Bataille's motley rabble of criminals and outcasts. But her desire is also the desire common to sovereignty insofar as it is sovereignty: to be above the law, to have the power to found or suspend rule and order. Moreover, Semiramis's negativity is not purely destructive, for her ability to conceal her gender is initially tied to her ability to rule well, and what her detractors frame as her excessive desire seems akin to her expansive aims to grow her kingdom. The doubled, contradictory accounts of Semiramis reveal a monstrous, queer element within sovereignty, a lawless passion internal to the foundation of law and order.

If Semiramis haunts sovereignty in later accounts, that haunting is itself part of Semiramis's story, where after her death, her son/lover Ninyas seems possessed by her, losing interest in being king "as if," Justin writes, "he had exchanged sex with his mother."[37] Spenser, in substituting Ninus for Semiramis as builder of Babylon, likely aims to arrest an unfortunate chain of associations that would connect Semiramis to Alma to Elizabeth as figures of feminine rule and would make less easy the separation between well-ordered empire and its allegedly monstrous lower orders. But Spenser can only do so by extending a chain of reversals within Semiramis's history: Semiramis becomes Ninyas who becomes Semiramis. Semiramis's haunting of later figures of sovereignty suggests that all the doubled figures of female rule in the poem are reflections of this original, base, and basic principle of sovereignty: Una and Duessa, Belphoebe and Acrasia, Alma and Philotime. Who better mirrors Semiramis in *The Faerie Queene* than Elizabeth herself, shadowed in both Belphoebe and Gloriana?

How does the House of Alma look different once the erased figure of Semiramis is taken into consideration? For all that the description makes the house appear a functionalist state in which every member has a precise role, there are several odd moments where the house reveals its monstrous order. Take, as a matter of comparison, the hordes outside the house's gates making war upon it. The enemies of Alma's state are not another state, equal to her own, but, as I have quoted previously, "a monstrous rablement/Of fowle misshapen wights," a savage multitude incapable of order (2.11.8.1–2). On the most surface and ideological level of the poem's politics, war and colonization are justified because the enemies of the state are not civilized but half-animal creatures over whom rational control must be exerted. But that ideological analogy breaks down since the hordes of Maleger are not quite foreign to the state. When the narrator commands the reader to view the body as "both one and other" at the beginning of the canto, the obvious sense is that the hordes as well as the house are part of the body (2.9.1.9). The hordes allegorically stand for sensations, and sensations are not external to the body but occur liminally between the body and the world. Maleger, the leader of the assailants, symbolizes death and decay, a condition that belongs to the body itself, as its slimy walls indicate.

These unruly hordes are mirrored within the house by the aristocratic lovers that stand in for the passions. Unlike the industrious servants in the heart and stomach, these nobles do not work, nor do they, like the higher officers in the house's tower, assist rule. Instead, they "idly s[i]t at ease," singing, laughing, and courting (2.9.35.3). This loose, wanton group lacks discipline, much like those bunched outside the house's walls. The variety and incongruity of the horde's monstrous members are paralleled in the upper class's mixture of feelings: "This fround, that faund, the third for shame did blush" (35.6). This state of indolence seems to lead them back into some pre-civilized form of savagery, as one "did gnaw a rush" (35.8). Spenser's precise anatomization of the state, in which each member serves a specific function, runs into trouble in depicting the literary and amorous aristocracy, who seem to do nothing at all of value. The canto brings out in the aristocracy something that is generally true for Spenser's political society. Society is not order in Spenser; all collective life shares a monstrous element and a desire for de-individuation, for freeing itself from the bounds of social role and the norms that shape selfhood. The erased figure of Semiramis suggests that such "monstrous" desire is not outside social life; indeed, it is the drive that makes any kind of social relation possible.

World

When Spenser compares the body to "*Babell* towre," he suggests a relation between the base materiality of the body and the dream of a common human culture (2.9.21.6). The lowest of the low in human existence, the refuse of the body, is connected to the greatest harmony, the reunion of all the world's peoples. This section traces the complex relation between the base materiality of slime and cosmopolitan universality. The same tension between organization and heterogeneity seen in the slimy body plays out in Spenser on the level of international relations. In the last stop on Alma's tour of the house, the library of Eumnestes, or memory, the book of *Briton moniments* tells a sordid tale of the impure beginnings of the British nation. The British were not, as it turns out, native to their own land, which was originally occupied by a race of "hideous Giants" born, in a manner akin to Virgil's bees, from England's "natiue slime" (2.10.7.2, 9.5). The autochthonous giants mark, then, an impurity tainting the origin of the British nation, their alien relation to their own land. The language surrounding the giants is marked by the same vacillation between decay and miraculous power found in the description of slime: on the one hand, the giants' "filthinesse/polluted" the "gentle soyle"; on the other, their "stature huge" and "courage bold" makes them seem more manly than the "sonnes of men" who encounter them (9.1–2, 7.8, 7.9).[38] The conquest of the giants by Brutus, the legendary Roman founder of Britain, is, on its most overt level, a historical precedent for imperial colonization in that Brutus "frees" the land of its filthy monstrous inhabitants. However, on closer inspection, this conquest marks a lingering impurity to the British nation that will return throughout the history Spenser tells. That ancestral taint is figured in the narrative through the marks the giants leave on the land, particularly the slimy "gore" of a slain giant that "besprincle[s]" Plymouth Hoe (10.7). That gore, sign of impure lineage as well as violent division, recurs in the way in which even the noblest of British kings beget monstrously treacherous children, what Harry Berger notes in this canto as "the apparently haphazard operations of nature in the matter of supplying heirs."[39] Indeed, decay, as Berger suggests, is one of the overarching themes of Spenser's national history lesson, seen in the "sad decay" of Roman rule overrun by Anglo-Saxon invaders (62.5) and even in the sacred spread of Christianity in the land, which "greatly did decay" from its initial seeding by Joseph of Arimathea (53.9). It would not be hard to show how rottenness is associated with other forms of international relations in *The Faerie Queene*, from the gold described as "worldly mucke" in the Cave of Mammon to the hyper-fertile putrescence of the exotic Bower of Bliss (2.7.10.5). Worldhood has two contradictory yet joined senses in Spenser: on the one hand, the unifying spread of the nation, of order, civility, and holy truth throughout the world, and on the other hand, the rotten decay of that homogeneous nationhood in its expansion through intermixture, migration, and unsure succession. These two, just like the slime of the earth and the heaven-reaching Tower of Babel, cannot be separated from one another, for the decomposing muck, figured as giant's blood, is also what founds the English nation. This monstrous origin story should not be mistaken as peculiar to England; given that the giants arise from the Earth, they can be taken as the general figure for the lost connection to the harmonious and universal world out of which culture in general arises and which remains "within" culture only as the guarantor of its impurity.

The contamination of the nation seen in the giants' story could also be told through the reference to the Tower of Babel in the slime passage. That retelling would be a translation from international relations to translation itself, as Babel is the story of the division of human languages. The lines describing slime are, as I have shown, riddled with errors and conflations.

Babel and Babylon are merged; "Nine" fuses Ninas and Nimrod while displacing Semiramis; "slime" may mean flesh, tar, or mud. These ambiguities might appear to be the result of hasty writing on Spenser's part; but in describing the Tower of Babel, is it really an accident that Spenser's language is confusing? If it is not possible to fully determine the referent of Spenser's "slime," then it goes to show that matter, at least insofar as humans have access to it, is not outside language and linguistic play. Indeed, Spenser's "slime" may not refer so much as it enacts, within language, the unstable yet generative overflowing of individual languages and traditions that base materiality accomplishes on the level of the organism.

In the Genesis account of Babel, too, the connection is made between the building of bricks into a tower and the unity of culture and language:

> And the whole earth was of one language, and of one speech. And it came to pass, as they journeyed from the east, that they found a plain in the land of Shinar; and they dwelt there. And they said one to another, Go to, let us make brick, and burn them thoroughly. And they had brick for stone, and slime had they for morter. And they said, Go to, let us build us a city and a tower, whose top may reach unto heaven; and let us make us a name, lest we be scattered abroad upon the face of the whole earth. And the LORD came down to see the city and the tower, which the children of men builded. And the LORD said, Behold, the people is one, and they have all one language; and this they begin to do: and now nothing will be restrained from them, which they have imagined to do. Go to, let us go down, and there confound their language, that they may not understand one another's speech. So the LORD scattered them abroad from thence upon the face of all the earth: and they left off to build the city. Therefore is the name of it called Babel; because the LORD did there confound the language of all the earth: and from thence did the LORD scatter them abroad upon the face of all the earth. (Gen. 11:1–9)

The passage sketches a compact trajectory shared by matter and humanity, from amorphous mass to joined structure to ruins. Jacques Derrida, reading this passage, comments that the transmutation of slime into brick "already resembles a translation, a translation of translation."[40] The biblical scene suggests that the base materiality I have located in slime bears a trace of human universality, a scattered ruin of the Tower of Babel. The paradoxical relation between contamination and organization found in slime also inheres in relations between cultures.

Walter Benjamin's essay "The Task of the Translator," like the passage from Spenser I dwell on, compares the lost universality of languages to broken material. In Benjamin, this comparison is made through the metaphor of a shattered vessel: "a translation, instead of resembling the meaning of the original, must lovingly and in detail incorporate the original's mode of signification, thus making both the original and the translation recognizable as fragments of a greater language, just as fragments are part of a vessel."[41] When one uses a word in one's native language, one might think there is a direct correlation between word and thing. But in translation one gets a sense of what is sometimes called the *materiality* of language, the uniqueness of *brot* as the word for bread in German, as Benjamin suggests, that comes from its homonyms, rhymes, and anagrams.[42] What appears fleetingly in the process of translation is the desire for a universal language and the fact that such a language is, in human life, impossible. There can only be, translation makes clear, fragments and ruins, but fragments and ruins *of* a universal tongue.[43] It's no accident if, in describing the relation between languages, Benjamin employs at times a vocabulary of interpersonal and international relations. All languages partake, he suggests, in a "suprahistorical kinship," a kinship that has nothing to do with connections of blood or nationality. Paul de Man, reading Benjamin's essay, also draws on such a language, arguing that translations reveal in their originals "a wandering, an *errance*, a kind of permanent exile if you wish, but it is not really an exile, for there is no homeland, nothing from which one has been exiled."[44] The materiality of language, that which in a language cannot be translated (and translation would here have to be something that occurs within a single language as well), is itself translated by Benjamin and de Man into the register of international relations. The suprahistorical kinship among nations, imagined mythologically in the Tower of Babel story, cannot ever be realized; it can only be glimpsed in the state of exile that one bears in relation to the culture that is allegedly one's own.

Benjamin's shattered vessel translates on the level of language a similar pattern found in Bataille's base materialism. Materiality, now the materiality of language, is connected to the shattering of the whole and the organic. Benjamin's emphasis on what is lost, on the rupture *of* the universal, invites speculation on the relation between materiality and universality, of the common conditions of speaking in a language that is partial and incomplete just as of living in a body that is by nature decomposing. These common conditions are not the grounds for any kind of utopian cosmopolitanism of mutual understanding or accord—in fact, they proscribe such final harmony. But they do offer what might be called a negative universality, the bare fact that one is not an organism or a member of a state. Life grows out of its social bounds and toward a universal state that is nowhere. Both Benjamin and Bataille proclaim not a universality of the material, which would risk subsuming all the violent heterogeneity of life into an overarching and neutralizing sameness, but a materiality of the universal, a universality that is dispersed and divided, glimpsed in the rupture of the familiar and organized. To translate these terms back into Spenser, the fatal slime of human life is the residue of Babel's tower.

Writing at the beginning of the era in which vernacular language first becomes a prominent symbol of national identity, Spenser also meditates on this strange materiality of language that, in not belonging to any one language, marks all as fragmentary. In the late sixteenth century, as England is trying to establish itself as a nation comparable to Rome or the continental nations, poetry establishes the purity and worthiness of the English language. From *The Shepheardes Calender* onward, Spenser writes in a style of conscious anachronism and opaque allusion. In the epistle that prefaces the *Calender*, E.K. (often identified with Spenser) comments on the strangeness of Spenser's language and his use of archaic words. Spenser's language comes close but is not quite, for E.K., a "disorderly and ruinous" old building.[45] (An English Babel?) However, E.K. believes Spenser's language to be restoring the English language to the "rightfull heritage" from which it has been "almost cleare disherited"; his archaism, in fact, a restoration of an allegedly pure English nation (79, 81). The fault belongs to other writers who, thinking the English language incapable of poetry, have "patched vp the holes with peces and rags of other languages" (85–86). The degraded stuff of foreign tongues is pulled from its proper home and inserted into a ragtag English. The result is that English has become "a gallimaufray or hodgepodge of al other speeches" (90–91). A gallimaufry is a French term for a stew of heterogeneous elements, and E.K.'s example is one of the earliest citations in the *Oxford English Dictionary*; the word has not yet at this point been well-digested into the English language. One must suspect that E.K.'s accusations toward these false poets describe no one's writing so well as Spenser's, whose language is constantly creating new words and images out of mixtures of the old and foreign. As in Benjamin, that foreign materiality of language is connected to an alienation toward one's "own" country, for E.K. argues that these false poets ought to be ashamed that they are "in their own mother tonge straungers to be counted and alienes" (96–97). This imagery of stew and rags anticipates *The Faerie Queene*'s slime, a stuff that resists incorporation into the body. It should thus not be surprising that the bitumenic substance Error vomits out in book 1 is transformed not only into monstrous shapes but also into "bookes and papers" (1.1.20.6). Slime, then, is a figure for Spenser's own writing. Just as slime is a foreign substance within the body, so too Spenser writes in a foreign language within English.

The House of Alma canto begins with analogies between the body, state, and world as instances of beautiful form. That analogic outlook offers a way of understanding universal connection that is deeply connected to hierarchy and order: the body is well-governed by its head just as the state is by its sovereign and the world is by divine providence, a providence executed by God's chosen nation. Slime offers a different mode of universal relation, one in which what all living beings share is the fact that they emerge out of a heterogeneous muck to which they also return, for "no earthly thing is sure." Bataille imagines that "our random and ephemeral individuality," the precipitation of a specific life out of that basic sludge, produces, alongside the "tormenting desire that this evanescent thing should last," a "yearn[ing] for our lost continuity," a nostalgia for the union with other material beings that comes closest to achievement in death.[46] That de-individuating desire, an ecstatic movement toward an impossible universality, is what I locate in Spenserian materiality where it seems most useless and even destructive. Spenserian slime cuts across the hierarchical lines separating higher from lower life, including the relation between civilized and savage, sovereign and rabble, human and animal. This slimy matter bears a nonarbitrary relation to those monstrous beings in Spenser associated with uncontrolled desire and improper organization, beings like Grille, the hordes assaulting the house, and England's native giants. Yet in Spenser such creatures are marked, again and again, as figures for the common life from which so-called civilization only superficially and imperfectly departs. Slime offers a place to begin thinking in Spenser the longing for de-individuation and de-hierarchization as a common condition of life across lines of society, culture, and species.

NOTES

1. All text citations to *The Faerie Queene* refer to Edmund Spenser, *The Faerie Queene*, ed. Thomas P. Roche (London: Penguin Books, 1978).

2. Jonathan Goldberg, *The Seeds of Things: Theorizing Sexuality and Materiality in Renaissance Representations* (New York: Fordham University Press, 2009), 89–90.

3. Stephen Greenblatt, *Renaissance Self-Fashioning: From More to Shakespeare* (Chicago: University of Chicago Press, 1980), 157–92.

4. Michael C. Schoenfeldt, *Bodies and Selves in Early Modern England: Physiology and Inwardness in Spenser, Shakespeare, Herbert, and Milton* (Cambridge: Cambridge University Press, 1999), 40–73.

5. David Landreth, *The Face of Mammon: The Matter of Money in English Renaissance Literature* (Oxford: Oxford University Press, 2012), 72–73.

6. Andrew Marvell, "A Dialogue between the Soul and Body," in *The Complete Poems*, ed. Elizabeth Story Donno, 103–4 (London: Penguin Books, 2005), l.4.

7. Schoenfeldt, *Bodies and Selves*, 55.

8. Ibid., 61.

9. Landreth, *The Face of Mammon*, 73, 74, 72.

10. Georges Bataille, "Base Materialism and Gnosticism," in *Visions of Excess: Selected Writings, 1927–1939*, ed. and trans. Allan Stoekl, 45–52 (Minneapolis: University of Minnesota Press, 1985), 45.

11. While this conception of sexuality extends throughout Bataille's work, see in particular *Erotism: Death and Sensuality*, trans. Mary Dalwood (San Francisco: City Lights Books, 1986).

12. Again, Bataille's notions of materiality and sexuality are always political and stretch throughout his career, but see, in particular, early essays like "The 'Old Mole' and the Prefix *Sur* in the words *Surhomme* and *Surrealist*" and "The Psychological Structure of Fascism," both in *Visions of Excess* (Bataille, *Visions of Excess*, 32–44 and 137–60), as well as the later *The Accursed Share, An Essay on General Economy*, vol. 1, *Consumption*, trans. Robert Hurley (New York: Zone Books, 1988).

13. Unless otherwise specified, all biblical citations are to the King James Version.

14. Goldberg, *The Seeds of Things*, 77.

15. Rudolf Bultmann, *Theology of the New Testament*, vol. 1, trans. Kendrick Grobel (New York: Charles Scribner's Sons, 1951), 235.

16. Landreth, *The Face of Mammon*, 73.

17. Qtd. in Edmund Spenser, *The Works of Edmund Spenser: A Variorum Edition*, vol. 2, ed. Edwin Greenlaw, Charles Grosvenor Osgood, and Frederick Morgan Padelford (Baltimore, MD: Johns Hopkins Press, 1933), 288–89.

18. Herodotus, *Herodotus*, ed. A. D. Godley (Cambridge, MA: Harvard University Press, 1920), 1.179.

19. Diodorus of Sicily, *Library of History*, vol. 1, trans. C. H. Oldfather (Cambridge, MA: Harvard University Press, 1933), 2.12.

20. John Milton, *Paradise Lost*, in *John Milton (The Oxford Authors)*, ed. Stephen Orgel and Jonathan Goldberg, 355–618 (Oxford: Oxford University Press, 1991), 7.238–39; Gordon Teskey, *Delirious Milton: The Fate of the Poet in Modernity* (Cambridge, MA: Harvard University Press, 2009), 39.

21. Teskey, *Delirious Milton*, 40.

22. Landreth, *The Face of Mammon*, 73.

23. Virgil, *Virgil's Georgics*, trans. Janet Lembke (New Haven, CT: Yale University Press, 2005), 4.309–13.

24. Qtd. in Spenser, *Variorum*, 288–89.

25. Teskey, *Delirious Milton*, 39.

26. Michel Foucault, *The History of Sexuality*, vol. 1, *An Introduction* (New York: Vintage Books, 1990), 101. See Goldberg's analysis of Foucault's term in Jonathan Goldberg, *Sodometries: Renaissance Texts, Modern Sexualities*, 2nd ed. (New York: Fordham University Press, 2010), 1–26.

27. Bataille, *Erotism*, 11.

28. Schoenfeldt, *Bodies and Selves*, 61.

29. Grille originates in a dialogue of Plutarch's where he is written back into the *Odyssey*'s Circe episode; Spenser perhaps knew the story from Gelli's *Circe*. Plutarch's Grille speaks for animal kind, upholding their life as morally superior to human life for, among other reasons, being more temperate. In alluding to Plutarch, Spenser raises the possibility that this common dungy life is not opposite to the virtue of temperance, nor to its hero, Guyon, who shares with Grille a primary letter. See the discussion of the passage in Spenser, *Variorum*, 394–95.

30. Giorgio Agamben, *Homo Sacer: Sovereign Power and Bare Life*, trans. David Heller-Roazen (Stanford, CA: Stanford University Press, 1998), 15–29, 81–86.

31. Bataille, "The Psychological Structure of Fascism," 140–48.

32. Diodorus, *Library of History*, 2.11. Justin, *Epitome of the* Philippic History *of Pompeius Trogus*, trans. J. C. Yardley (Atlanta: Scholars Press, 1994), 1.2.

33. Ovid, *Metamorphoses*, ed. John Frederick Nims, trans. Arthur Golding (New York: Macmillan, 1965), 4.67–68.

34. See Maureen Quilligan's account of Pizan's recuperation of Semiramis in "Allegory and Female Agency," in *Thinking Allegory Otherwise*, ed. Brenda Machosky, 163–87 (Stanford, CA: Stanford University Press, 2010).

35. Justin, *Epitome*, 1.2.

36. Qtd. in H. David Brumble, "Semiramis," in *Classical Myths and Legends in the Middle Ages and Renaissance: A Dictionary of Allegorical Meanings* (Chicago: Fitzroy Dearborn Publishers, 1998), 307–9; Dante, *Inferno*, trans. Mark Musa (Bloomington: Indiana University Press, 1995), 5.55, 60.

37. Justin, *Epitome*, 1.2.

38. See Jeffrey Jerome Cohen's work on the ambivalencies that surround cultural depictions of giants from the Middle Ages onward in *Of Giants: Sex, Monsters, and the Middle Ages* (Minneapolis: University of Minnesota Press, 1999).

39. Harry Berger Jr., *The Allegorical Temper: Vision and Reality in Book 2 of Spenser's* Faerie Queene (New Haven, CT: Yale University Press, 1957), 97.

40. Jacques Derrida, "Des Tours de Babel," trans. Joseph F. Graham, in *Acts of Religion*, ed. Gil Anidjar, 104–34 (New York: Routledge, 2002), 106.

41. Walter Benjamin, "The Task of the Translator," in *Illuminations*, trans. Harry Zohn, 69–82 (New York: Schocken Books, 1968), 78.

42. Ibid., 74.

43. I draw here on Barbara Johnson's insightful commentary that, in Benjamin's essay, the relation between translation and pure meaning has the structure of the imperfect subjunctive, what would have been. Barbara Johnson, *Mother Tongues: Sexuality, Trials, Motherhood, Translation* (Cambridge, MA: Harvard University Press, 2003), 57.

44. Paul de Man, "'Conclusions': Walter Benjamin's 'The Task of the Translator,'" in *The Resistance to Theory*, 73–105 (Minneapolis: University of Minnesota Press, 1986), 92.

45. Edmund Spenser, "Epistle," in *The Shepheardes Calender*, in *The Shorter Poems*, ed. Richard McCabe, 23–156 (London: Penguin Books, 1999), line 60. Further citations given in the text.

46. Bataille, *Erotism*, 15.

CHAPTER 2

Extreme Cary

David Glimp

In a brief addendum to "Graphina's Mark," the final chapter of *Desiring Women Writing*, Jonathan Goldberg concludes his discussion of Elizabeth Cary's *The Tragedy of Mariam* by observing that Cary's play possesses a "dramatic sensibility more Marlovian than Shakespearian."[1] What does it mean to suggest that a given work displays a Marlovian dramatic sensibility? In the immediate context of the argument in "Graphina's Mark" the claim builds on Cary's association with texts that share subjects with Christopher Marlowe (specifically, a history of Edward II she may have written and a biography of Tamburlaine she did write but that now is lost). If we turn to chapter 4 of *Sodometries*, focused primarily on Marlowe's plays *Edward II* and *Dido, Queen of Carthage*, it becomes clear that in Goldberg's lexicon, attributing to someone a Marlovian dramatic sensibility ranks as high praise indeed; Goldberg's admiration for Marlowe derives in large measure from the way this playwright understands how sodomy—the complete dissolution of social order—is imbricated in the very structures of power, logics of rule, conceptual resources, modes of association, and institutions organizing Renaissance England's social and political life. By inhabiting, indeed relishing, the terms of abjection and execration through which Renaissance English society attempted to regulate behavior, ground and maintain its hierarchies, and police its foundational exclusions, Marlowe's characters render visible the instability of those hierarchies and of the conceptual distinctions through which the world becomes thinkable and actionable. Goldberg's sense that it is "imperative" for his readers "to recognize in Marlowe a site of political resistance"[2] resides not only in the destabilizing effect of Marlowe's deployment of cultural categories but also in the forms of critical awareness and agency such destabilization enables for characters otherwise excluded from the workings of power. For instance, Goldberg shows how the voicings of power make available forms of agency and precedents for action to characters—primarily, Queen Isabella from *Edward II* and Dido from *Dido, Queen of Carthage*—within a world otherwise bent on subordinating or abjecting them. Though *Desiring Women Writing* is less concerned with the category of sodomy than his previous book, this aspect of Goldberg's analysis makes visible elements the two works share. For present purposes, we can note how his virtuoso reading of the character Graphina demonstrates how her puzzling, almost gnomic, speech in *Mariam* strategically mimes and undermines the gender and status hierarchies informing the play's narrative world. In so doing, Graphina's utterances create a deconstructive perspective from which it is possible to read the "utopic and egalitarian desires," and the possibilities for resistant thought and female agency, Cary's play inscribes even in its most stridently patriarchal formulations.[3]

In this essay, I seek to build on Goldberg's insight about Cary's Marlovian sensibilities. Specifically, what follows works to extend this insight to Cary and Marlowe's staging of geopolitical states of emergency. In her representation of international conflict and crisis, Cary demonstrates her commitment to and adaptation of what we might understand as Marlovian extremophilia. In characterizing Marlowe's work in this way, I mean that Cary and Marlowe share a deep interest in what happens under the extreme pressure of a world immersed in crisis, how characters act and interact when their ordinary routines for understanding and negotiating the world are thrown into spectacular disarray. In *Sodometries* and elsewhere, Goldberg works hard to make clear that the texts he examines are not extremist, cannot be dismissed as the utterances of marginal figures, outliers, or cranks, but have to be recognized as articulating concepts and perspectives central to English Renaissance culture. With that caveat in place it is also the case that Marlowe pushes governing logics, hierarchical structures, and available conceptual vocabularies to the extreme point at which they strain and buckle beneath the pressure of their internal contraditions. Like Marlowe, Cary evidences an extremophilic interest in what happens to characters in the moments of the dissolution of the social bonds and forms of personhood that confer and constrain the intelligibility of existence. Such scenarios of heightened vulnerability and deep suffering foreground how states of emergency possess the capacity to reorganize collective life radically, momentarily to throw balances of power into disarray, to disrupt quotidian routines, and to render temporarily obsolescent most of the available ways of justifying action. My primary concern in what follows is to demonstrate how, through her adaptation of and response to Marlovian extremophilia, Cary foregrounds the ways a polarizing logic of security diminishes ethical possibilities—truncates the available modes of relating to oneself and to others—and thereby compromises resources for worldmaking. To begin showing how this is the case, I turn now to Marlowe's play, *The First Part of Tamburlaine the Great*, as a valuable place to identify the extremophilic strategies he deploys for depicting the world falling apart.

The first point to note here is that Marlowe's representation of states of emergency draws on the resources of what Richard Tuck describes as "ruthless humanism."[4] For present purposes, Tuck's term encompasses a more or less heterodox mode of framing moral and political thought that situates personal and collective security as a—and frequently the—central organizing concern of governance. Marlowe's extremophilic version of ruthless humanism understands security to center on the relation of friend and enemy and, in turn, on capacities to exercise violence in order to create, manipulate, or operate within such relations.[5] A brief moment from act 5 of Marlowe's *Tamburlaine* shows how this is the case. The particular scene focuses on Tamburlaine's assault on the city of Damascus and the panic-stricken efforts at crisis management that assault prompts. Faced with Tamburlaine's demand for surrender, the rulers of Damascus initially refuse; according to his "custom," Tamburlaine's negotiating strategy involves a three-day process.[6] On the first day, furnished in white, he demands peaceful surrender; on the second day, sporting red tents and armor, he promises to kill all of the soldiers and men of the age of military service; the third day, outfitted in black, he promises to annihilate everyone in the town. Characteristically for Marlowe, this scene depicts a highly polemicized world. Relations between people exist in a kind of hyper-clarified realm of allegiance and enmity, with sociality defined in terms of the interaction between friends—which is how the play figures the relationship between Tamburlaine and his generals (see, for instance, 2.3.30–32 and 2.7.34)—and enemies. In showing Tamburlaine imposing this basic logic on his relations to others as he moves across the globe, thereby exploiting for his own ends the antagonism inherent in this security logic, Marlowe dramatizes social worlds falling apart but also provisionally coming back together again in surprising ways. After Tamburlaine's third and final siege has begun, the Governor of Damascus seizes on a plan to "offer our safeties to his clemency" (5.1.12) by sending an envoy of "harmless virgins" (5.1.18) to beg for mercy. Prior to the doomed meeting, one of the women responds as follows to the governor's plan and request of them:

> First Virgin. If humble suits or imprecations
> (Utter'd with tears of wretchedness and blood
> Shed from the heads and hearts of all our sex,
> Some made your wives, and some your children,)
> Might have entreated your obdurate breasts
> To entertain some care of our securities
> Whilst only danger beat upon our walls,
> These more than dangerous warrants of our death
> Had never been erected as they be,
> Nor you depend on such weak helps as we. (5.1.24–33)

In this passage, the extreme pressure of threatened annihilation strikingly reorganizes Damascan political life and creates a kind of radical democracy, though one sustained for only the briefest of moments. The "harmless" and "lovely" Virgins, previously excluded from the political sphere proper, actively ignored as objects of care, now occupy a drastically redefined role as political subjects who need to be convinced to act in ways the country's rulers understand to be vital to the survival of Damascus. In her sharp response to the governor, the First Virgin renders evident the hierarchies, structures of subordination and exclusion, and criterion of evaluation that organize Damascan political existence and turns those elements of life in Damascus against the fratrocentric order that finds itself suddenly deeply vulnerable. Though the virgins agree to the plan, the First Virgin's analysis of the governor's "device" (5.1.52) criticizes both their prior exclusion from the political domain and the unlikely success of their proposed strategy of appealing to Tamburlaine's sympathy. Why should the virgins' affective intensity work on Tamburlaine, she implies, if all the women of the city were unable to move the city fathers' "obdurate breasts" to surrender in the first place? Marlowe casts the First Virgin as the more astute political analyst and overturns political and social hierarchies by demonstrating her superior grasp of Tamburlaine's approach to the world and the workings of the Tamburlaine murder and accumulation machine.

In a polity that narrowly defines her and other women's roles, the First Virgin improvises authority in a complex simulation both of Tamburlaine and of the critique of Tamburlaine. For, in her speech to the Governor of Damascus and in the speech she reports, she situates herself and the other women of Damascus as both extraordinarily attuned to Tamburlaine's demands on an affective level, viscerally aware of his plans for those he counts as enemies, and a vehicle for communicating his threats. In her framing of recent events and their present circumstances, the First Virgin both relays and intensifies Tamburlaine's message to the Damascan governors, amplifying the Scythian's demands and plans in the form of "tears of wretchedness and blood." Their simultaneous fear of Tamburlaine and miming of his threats place them in a position of both opposition to and identification with Tamburlaine, thereby occupying a contradictory position, a point of logical incoherence that both registers and forges a critical agency from within their extreme circumstances. The First Virgin leverages her simulation of Tamburlaine in a way that calls into question the Damascan polity's foundational exclusions and suggests that the fratrocentric republic of Damascus is not strongly differentiated from its other—the Tamburlaine accumulation machine—but holds to many of the same values that motivate Tamburlaine and thereby lead to the slaughter of its people. The First Virgin points out that the circumstance in which they find themselves has arisen because the Damascan governors, in their insusceptibility to pity, acted like Tamburlaine, with "obdurate breasts" indifferent to the "securities" of others. The extremity of circumstances has the effect of bringing into being an awareness of the arbitrariness and inadequacy of existing hierarchies and practical routines securing quotidian existence. For a brief moment, the concept of what defines collective security, how it is produced, who it encompasses, what values it enshrines, and who bears the costs of safety comes into question, becomes visible as something that might be defined in other terms.

The First Virgin has the unfortunate distinction of being right about Tamburlaine's diminished capacity for sympathy. In the subsequent scene he listens to the Damascan virgins' speech, toys with them for a few lines, and then sends them offstage to be slaughtered (5.2.1–65). We are no doubt meant to be horrified by Tamburlaine's brutality, his unwillingness to create an exception to his military ritual. But by the same token, pity for the Damascan virgins does not fully exhaust the effects the episode is designed to produce. Marlovian extremophilia manifests in the disorganization of experience his play sponsors, the way his characters confront the hyper-polemicized realm of a world structured by the face-off between allegiance and enmity. One further example will help prepare the way for seeing how Cary adapts Marlowe's extremophilic staging of geopolitical states of emergency and treatment of questions of collective security. Like the Damascan First Virgin, who is both critical of her governor and attached to her leader enough to agree to his plan, Tamburlaine's captive and eventual wife, Zenocrate, experiences her circumstances as a matter of, strictly speaking, ambivalence. Immediately after Tamburlaine's destruction of Damascus, Zenocrate comes on stage to find the dead bodies of the virgins and of the empress and emperor of Turkey, Zabina and Bajazeth, the last of whom Tamburlaine has kept as captives and tortured for several scenes until they kill themselves. She responds to the tragic spectacle in front of her by processing it through the lens of a standard *de casibus* theme of the rise and fall of the great—"Those that are proud of fickle empery / And place their chiefest good in earthly pomp, / Behold the Turk and his great emperess!" (5.2.290–92). This last comment attempts to rewrite the play as a morality drama, to frame its horrifying actions in a way that make sense of the terrible violence on display or narrated.[7] It also seeks to appeal to a conceptual framework for defining security as ultimately a theological issue, displacing the instability of "earthly pomp" with the assurances to be found in a supramundane sphere.

Viewed in this way, Zenocrate's observations strive to provide some kind of epistemological clarity, imagining that Tamburlaine might learn from his own lesson by developing sympathy for the dead Turkish rulers, might adopt the right perspective on the action enabling a modified stance toward the world by recognizing his own implication in their story, the possibility that he might one day find himself in their position. This is obviously not what happens, and in fact she never delivers this speech to Tamburlaine; her remarks are more of a wish that her betrothed might understand the scene in the way she narrates. The point is not just that Zenocrate's attempt to construct a critical position of epistemological clarity fails to have any impact on the protagonist. The point is that the play incorporates multiple intersecting and interfering perspectives on the actions it narrates and that Zenocrate is a perfect example of this phenomenon. Zenocrate is both repulsed by her betrothed's actions and drawn to his magnificence. Even as she strives to generate a kind of epistemological detachment and sense of moral clarity about the unfolding of events, she is powerfully drawn to Tamburlaine and thereby embodies the highly complex, highly disorienting effects this play strives to produce. The ambivalence itself—the presence of two competing capacities for action and thought, of contradictory values and responses—speaks to the way Marlowe pushes the security logic structuring this play to the point of paradox, that is, to the point at which the hyper-polarized, hyper-polemicized world comes to be both compelling and horrifying, fascinating and unbearable.

To be sure, Cary's *The Tragedy of Mariam* differs from Marlowe's *Tamburlaine* in important ways. For one, it directly presents no single figure capable of organizing the world in the way that Tamburlaine does, no single character whose movement across the globe orients readers' or viewers' attention.[8] That said, the world Cary narratively projects is, like Marlowe's world, immersed in a state of emergency, organized around the plight of characters confronting radically unfamiliar circumstances, striving to improvise agency within the volatile flux of unpredictable events. *The Tragedy of Mariam* centers on inter-dynastic struggles in Palestine in the immediate wake of Octavius Caesar's consolidation of imperial power after his victory over Antony and Cleopatra at Actium. The play follows the actions of a number of characters as they respond first to what is taken to be certain news about the death of Herod, the tyrannical ruler of Palestine, and second to his surprise return. The main plot line follows the titular character, King Herod's wife, and her reaction to the news of Herod's death, her interactions and struggles with her mother, Alexandra, her husband's ex-wife, Doris, and her sister-in-law, Salome. This last character successfully frames Mariam for conspiring to kill Herod after his return and then convinces Herod to execute his wife for her supposed treason. This brief description of the primary narrative arc suggests the way Cary's play exists to explore the permutations of how people inhabit emerging circumstances, negotiate the confusion of extreme worldly contingency, respond intellectually and affectively to the unfolding events on a geopolitical stage, and strive to find ways of achieving a secure existence in an otherwise uncertain and inhospitable world.

Cary's representation of geopolitical states of emergency, like Marlowe's, takes place in the context of a highly polemicized world, one characterized by sharp distinctions between friend and enemy and by the way friendship necessarily entails enmity. As Goldberg observes, the language of friendship in Cary's play is used to characterize a wide variety of attachments, "same-sex alliances" and "consanguine and marital relationships."[9] Indeed, to develop this insight in the direction of the reading of Marlowe offered above, just about every relation in this play—between men and women, between men, between people of different status, between peoples of different nationality or race—is explicitly or implicitly operatively organized around the friend/foe distinction. The geopolitical relevance of this conceptual matrix is evident in the observation of Herod's brother-in-law,

Constabarus, about the actions of Caesar: "For who can think that in Anthonius's fall,/Herod his bosom friend should scape unbruis'd?"[10] Constabarus's assumption is that if Herod was "bosom friend" to Antony, such intimacy automatically makes him the enemy of Caesar. That Constabarus is wrong about Caesar's behavior—Caesar embraces Herod as a friend, heaping upon him more honors than he had received under Antony—shows that Constabarus underestimates the fluidity of political relations in the Roman Empire. But his error does not change the fact that the terms rendering the world intelligible and governing association and enmity remain operative. This assumption about the immanent principles structuring political existence in turn attempts to regulate the interplay of sameness and difference, generates a schema people use to comprehend and to orient themselves within the complex unfolding of volatile events on a highly fraught geopolitical stage.

One of Cary's primary concerns is to show the insecurity and unsustainability of the friend/enemy schema. The play's protagonist, Mariam, demonstrates Cary's reservations about such an account of security in the ambivalence of Mariam's response to the unfolding of events within the hyper-polemicized world she inhabits. In particular we may note the soliloquy that opens the play, a response to the recent news of Herod's death. Mariam's lengthy speech confronts both the "joy" she feels at being rid of her tyrant husband and her surprised experience of "grief" at the news of his death. In response to her initial wave of grief, thoughts occur to Mariam that counter her feelings, specifically the thought that Herod killed her brother (Aristobulus) and her grandfather (Hircanus) and had left an order for her to be killed in the event of his own death, an order obviously ignored by his counselor, and Mariam's friend, Sohemus. As she states,

> These thoughts have power, his death to make me bear,
> Nay more, to wish the news may firmly hold:
> Yet cannot this repulse some falling tear,
> That will against my will some grief unfold.
> And more I owe him for his love to me,
> The deepest love that ever yet was seen:
> Yet had I rather much a milkmaid be,
> Than be the monarch of Judea's queen.
> It was for nought but love he wish'd his end
> Might to my death but the vaunt-courier prove:
> But I had rather still be foe than friend,
> To him that saves for hate, and kills for love.

Hard-hearted Mariam, at thy discontent
What floods of tears have drench'd his manly face!
How canst thou then so faintly now lament
Thy truest lover's death, a death's disgrace:
Ay, now, mine eyes, you do begin to right
The wrongs of your admirer and my lord. (1.1.51–68)

Though critics have noted perceptively the ambivalent quality of these lines, they have also read the opening soliloquy as "half"-hearted, insincere, or "intemperate"—in any case, as a position to be overcome.[11] Rather than dismiss Mariam's opening performance or side with those voices in the text that seek to judge or regulate Mariam, I propose to read this speech in the context of the passages from Marlowe I have addressed, especially the discussion of Zenocrate's ambivalent response to her husband's actions. The Marlovian context helps make sense of Mariam's speech as an instance of Cary foregrounding certain limitations of the scene of politics as a basic matrix governing personhood, sociality, and the unfolding of events in the conflictual space of the Roman Empire, precisely the overorganized scene in which geopolitical relations and personal affection operate by the same basic friend/enemy logic. Mariam's effort to constitute herself as an object of attention and action—her highly focused meta-level awareness of the play between her thoughts and her affective responses, and her various ongoing attempts to calibrate and recalibrate what she thinks and how she feels to the circumstances in which she finds herself—effectively forestalls any stable resolution into a single state. This aspect of her observation of, and conversation with, herself determines the oscillation that characterizes the soliloquy, its dynamic restlessness and refusal to settle into one of what Mariam sees as the only two available ways of feeling about the situation in which she finds herself.

Refusing to settle into either of these perspectives constitutes a way of refusing the world as it is presently constituted. That is, Mariam performs ambivalence in a way that in its oscillation expresses a longing for something for which only minimal vocabulary or conceptual equipment is available. In such a situation, the oscillation itself represents a more or less inchoate desire to be able to inhabit another world. To draw on Lauren Berlant's account of more contemporary texts and circumstances, we can say that, faced with the awareness that her basic attachments—both to a particular person and to a structure of political existence—are "obstacles to [her] flourishing," Mariam strives to mobilize what resources her circumstances afford in order to imagine forms of personhood and collective life not relentlessly structured in such highly polemical ways.[12] In this regard, I take the fantasy of being a milkmaid rather than the "monarch of Judaea's queen"—a kind of non sequitur that pops up in the midst of the back and forth between Mariam's love and hate—to function in several ways. As Donald Foster has noted, the pastoral fantasy alludes to a similar wish of Queen Elizabeth, who voiced a desire to be a milkmaid rather than Queen.[13] Though in lines immediately before those quoted above Mariam references Julius Caesar's mixed emotions about the death of Pompey as a precedent for her ambivalence (1.1.1–14), in this brief couplet she appeals to the words of a royal female counter-source, citing Queen Elizabeth at the moment at which the monarch strategically articulates a desire not to be monarch, to occupy some other kind of existence. In the context of its utterance, the desire to be another kind of person also signals a rejection of the world as presently constituted, confronts her world as inhospitably impoverished in the resources it does not make available for assembling a viable life.

Framed in this way, the milkmaid fantasy echoes another literary precedent, Homer's account of Achilles in the underworld from book 11 of *The Odyssey*. When Odysseus questions Achilles about the afterlife and muses that death cannot be so bad for one of such high status among the dead, Achilles answers: "Better . . . to break sod as a farm hand/for some poor country man, on iron rations,/than lord it over all the exhausted dead."[14] Inhabiting an existence he does not recognize and within which there are no forms of recognition he could value, Achilles longs for the briefest experience of a world that is intelligible to him. In his extreme circumstance, it doesn't matter to him where in his society's hierarchy he should be placed, just that he can belong to a world that makes sense. Mariam's—and Queen Elizabeth's—statements revise that wish suggestively by aligning their own world with that of the dead, occupying the place of Achilles in the underworld in order to formulate a critical gesture that renders the present world hellish, intolerable. But in comprehending the world of the living to be unviable, expressing the desire to be a milkmaid makes reference to another genre of being as a placeholder for some alternative dispensation, another world organized otherwise, along less highly polarized lines. The ever so momentary emergence of the potential for some other kind of existence signals a heterotopic wish for alternative types of personhood and collectivity, some other ways of inhabiting the world, and indeed some other world to inhabit, a world to which it might be worthwhile to attach.[15]

To read Mariam's opening speech in such terms suggests how the play as a whole archives a wide array of modes of inhabiting a world organized around the friend/enemy distinction. For instance, to catalog a few of the primary strategies, characters create isolated microcosms in which they can safely dwell as friends (Babas's sons in hiding on Constabarus's estate), negotiate and renegotiate lines of amity and enmity via intrigue in order to enable serial friendships (Salome and, to a certain extent, Mariam's mother, Alexandra), structure an entire life around scorn for one's enemies (Herod's ex-wife Doris), forge experimental, hybrid modes of sociality and interaction (as do Salome's estranged husband, Constabarus, and her new love, Silleus, who in the course of dueling become something like frenemies). Mariam's opening ambivalence is one among many possible ways of moving through the hyper-polemicized world of Palestine and the greater-Mediterranean geopolitical landscape, though it is not an especially viable form of securing an existence. When her mother, Alexandra, arrives on stage, the phenomenon quickly disappears, as mother castigates daughter for having any ambivalence whatsoever about the unfolding events. News of Herod's death can only for her and members of her family be a cause for celebration. Following suit as the narrative moves forward, Mariam occupies many of the positions mentioned immediately above. In so doing, she effectively embraces the scene of political existence as I have described it and struggles to identify and enact forms of critical agency within that scene. But what she learns, and indeed what most characters learn in the play, is the difficulty, if not impossibility, of taking the world on anything other than its own terms.

Such an insight informs Mariam's final soliloquy, in which she ponders her impending execution at the command of her husband. Confronting her approaching death, she asks:

> Am I the Mariam that presum'd so much,
> And deem'd my face must needs preserve my breath?
> Ay, I it was that thought my beauty such,
> As it alone could countermand my death. (4.8.525–28)

These two sentences narrate Mariam's experience as one of enlightenment. She began the play thinking that she possessed an attribute—her beauty—that would exempt her from the rules of the geopolitical game. Experience has proven her wrong, and she now knows the truth of her vulnerability. But in the process of articulating this insight, she gives voice to the extremity of the tensions structuring the world she is about to leave. I take this to be the point of the question she raises about herself, the striking way that momentarily Mariam is unsure if she is the same person from earlier in the play. One way to read the words immediately following her question, the homonymic "Ay, I," is as suggesting at the level of sound a self-splitting, a differential repetition that linguistically underscores a profound uncertainty about her status as a person. Specifically, such uncertainty foregrounds how Mariam's experience disrupts her understanding of what constitutes the grounds of personhood across time. Mariam's initial thought about herself and her ability to persist turns out to be so incompatible with the schema of power organizing political life and its basic categories of intelligibility—again, the basic opposition between friend and enemy—that it challenges, at least momentarily, Mariam's identity. Her questioning whether or not she is the same person, in effect become a stranger to herself—as if inhabiting a Derek Parfit thought experiment testing the conditions of personal identity through time and space—registers the degree to which it is not possible for Mariam to exempt herself from the organizing schema of geopolitical life and still remain recognizable as a person.[16]

The uncertainty Mariam voices lasts only momentarily, and that moment is quickly followed by a redefined sense of personal continuity and coherence. This retroactive clarification rests on an alternative sense of the words "Ay, I it was," read as an emphatic affirmation. This statement displaces Mariam's initial account of understanding her beauty as that which will allow her to persist in the world (despite her husband's power to put people to death) with a revised account of personhood as a matter of "thought." Her renewed sense of personal continuity derives from precisely the enlightenment noted above, the process of reflecting on her thinking and correcting that thinking in light of experience. But however certain Mariam may be that she is in fact the same character from the beginning of the play, the grounds of that continuity rest on a contradiction of sorts. She is the same person, but that sense of continuity rests on her awareness that she was wrong about possibilities for safety in the world. If for Mariam being the same person from one moment to the next rests on a meta-level awareness of being certain about oneself and one's beliefs as they relate to the world, to acknowledge having been wrong about the world reintroduces the problem by underscoring her susceptibility to being mistaken. In this light, and in the particular world of Cary's play and the volatility and uncertainty of geopolitical life it depicts, the instability of existence foregrounds the inherent challenge of maintaining a coherent sense of personhood across time.

Cary reinforces this abstract account of the contradictions informing her protagonist's understanding of personhood in her depiction of Mariam's actions after this moment. Another way to understand the statement "Ay, I it was" is as Mariam's simultaneous recognition that her personal qualities do not make her special and as her recommitment to the world she inhabits. From here on out, forced to take the governing realities of geopolitical existence on their own terms, Mariam plays the game masterfully. And she does so in a way that exploits the available resources of personhood and demonstrates the limits of the schema organizing personhood and political life in Palestine and beyond. I take this to be the burden of her response to Alexandra who, in an effort to display her profound commitment to Herod's rule, "loudly rail[ed]" (5.1.36) against her daughter for her perceived disloyalty as Mariam walks to her execution. As Nuntio providing the details of her death reports, Mariam refuses to respond to her mother in kind. "She made no answer, but she look'd the while, / As if thereof she scarce did notice take, / Yet smil'd, a dutiful, though scornful, smile" (5.1.50–52). Mariam's dutiful scorn performs a simultaneous allegiance and enmity, deference to her mother and defiance as she mimes the scornful forms of enmity she has used and encountered before in her interactions with Salome and Doris. The final gesture toward her mother performs a paradox, both as a critique of her mother's actions—demanding enmity toward Herod at the beginning of the play and criticizing her daughter for opposing him in any way—and as a kind of diagnostic event.

To describe Mariam's actions in such terms is to follow Niklas Luhmann's lead in understanding paradox as a circumstance in which conflict within a given system cannot be adjudicated within the terms that organize that system. Paradox thus serves as an impetus to constitute a second-order perspective from which it is possible both to see the larger unity that organizes the conflict and to access the "unsaid" that is excluded when a set of distinctions are introduced to make sense of the world.[17] With such an understanding of paradox in mind, we can turn to the play's final Chorus, which participates in the diagnostic appeal to paradox. Throughout the play the Chorus's interventions are frequently among the most reactionary and misogynist in their articulation of patriarchal ideology. Their speeches are generally obnoxious, sententious, at times confused—talking about characters who have not been onstage—speaking with extreme moral authority in ways that are over the top and not that useful, outraged about things that seem beside the point.[18] The beside-the-pointness of their interventions, as much as the increasing stridency of their patriarchal bromides, signals the degree to which they are in the same boat as everyone else in the play, responding to a highly polarized and deroutinized existence thrown into absolute disarray, an existence over which they, no more than anyone else, can claim any kind of control.

Cary marks the limits of the Chorus's capacity to encompass this world on its own terms with their final intervention.

> Whoever hath beheld with steadfast eye,
> The strange events of this one only day:
> How many were deceiv'd, how many die,
> That once today did grounds of safety lay!
>   It will from them all certainty bereave,
>   Since twice six hours so many can deceive. (5.1.259–64)

The effect of the play is to undermine certainty, and the mechanism of this undermining is the experience of characters who discovered that they were not safe. Their summary account of the epistemological effects the play produces implies that safety is not a concept that serves to organize action in the world so much as a source of error. They continue:

> This day's events were certainly ordain'd,
> To be the warning to posterity:
> So many changes are therein contain'd,
> So admirably strange variety.
>   This day alone, our sagest Hebrews shall
>   In after times the school of wisdom call. (5.1.289–94)

On the one hand, the Chorus's statements could be read as an effort to functionalize the events that have transpired, in the way that one of Cary's primary sources—Thomas Lodge's translation of Josephus's *Antiquities of the Jews*—frames the history it offers as what I have elsewhere referred to as a "technology of experience."[19] Lodge instructs his readers to use the text as a repository of the catastrophic experiences of others from which they can shape their own future experience; the purpose of works like Josephus's *Antiquities* is to "awaken mans idlenes, and arme them against casualties."[20]

On the other hand, we might view their concluding statement not as articulating some functional insight or truth about how best to inhabit the world as presently constituted, but via the rhetorical trope of paradox articulating the limits of that world. Naming "This day alone . . . the school of wisdom" is a paradoxical gesture to the extent that the content of this wisdom is that everyone is mistaken, that the only certainty is that no one is certain. If we take the Chorus to understand itself as included among the category of those "with steadfast eye" who have observed the day's events, the statement has the effect of logically canceling their insights, including their various comments throughout the play about proper action and safety. Enlisting safety in its concluding paradox, the Chorus effectively renders safety a problem, signals the inadequacies of the security doxa—the hegemonically reductive ways in which safety is conceived via the friend/foe distinction—and constructs a perspective from which it is possible to see the limits of this particular dispensation of security. To be sure, neither the Chorus nor anyone else in the play offers any kind of affirmative vision for an alternative understanding of safety, either personal or collective. All this collection of characters provides is an open-ended, underspecified process of cultural transmission, already falsified since I am not aware of any sage Hebrews who have identified "this day alone" as the "school of wisdom." Cary's intervention in contemporary political discourse is to use the resources of precursor drama, written history, and moral and political thought to raise the question of what it means to be safe, a minimal gesture to be sure, but a careful opening nevertheless onto the possibility of imagining a world otherwise.

This essay has sought to understand Elizabeth Cary as possessing a Marlovian dramatic sensibility. Goldberg's claim about Cary's relation to Marlowe helps account for crucial aspects of the geopolitical scenography of *The Tragedy of Mariam, Fair Queen of Jewry*, specifically how Cary leverages Marlovian representational strategies to disrupt hegemonic understandings of security. By way of conclusion I wish to note how the understanding of Cary's play advanced above also connects to aspects of Goldberg's argument in his recent book, *The Seeds of Things*, and, in particular, his engagement with Foucault's work on ethics. Foucault's interest in the ethical formulations of Greek and Roman antiquity, he observes, was the occasion for a reflexive effort to articulate and to live an ethics of inquiry. Such an ethic constituted an act of ongoing "self-cultivation," "a continual self-scrutiny and self-examination" linked to "a political practice that seeks to remake the world in a manner that might reconnect individual and collective life to life in the largest sense."[21] Here is Foucault in the introduction to the second volume of his *History of Sexuality*, *The Use of Pleasure*:

> What would be the value of the passion for knowledge if it resulted only in a certain amount of knowledgeableness and not, in one way or another and to the extent possible, in the knower's straying afield of himself. There are times in life when the question of knowing if one

> can think differently than one thinks, and perceive differently than one sees, is absolutely necessary if one is to go on looking and reflecting at all. . . . In what does [philosophy] consist, if not in the endeavor to know how and to what extent it might be possible to think differently, instead of legitimating what is already known?[22]

Rather than legitimating what is already known, the particular ethics Foucault performs in his work is an intellectual practice grounded on problematizing what we think we know, a more or less permanent inquiry that takes its goal an ongoing "ascesis": "an exercise of oneself in the activity of thought."[23] For Foucault, problematizing something makes it possible to shift from the dominant terms any given discourse imposes on thought and action into another perspective that refuses to take those terms for granted, as obvious or self-evident. So doing, such an approach enables, in Paul Rabinow's words, "a 'modal change from seeing a situation not only as a given but equally as a question.'"[24] The Foucauldian ethos of scholarship is critical—a discourse about constraints on thought and action—and about possibilities, about cultivating an awareness of openings and potential, about the resources for understanding and inhabiting the world otherwise in a way not constrained by things as they are, the work of reimagining the world and of "making a life worth living and loving."[25]

NOTES

1. Jonathan Goldberg, *Desiring Women Writing: English Renaissance Examples* (Stanford, CA: Stanford University Press, 1997), 190.

2. Jonathan Goldberg, *Sodometries: Renaissance Texts, Modern Sexualities* (Stanford, CA: Stanford University Press, 1992), 141.

3. Goldberg, *Desiring Women Writing*, 181.

4. Richard Tuck, *Philosophy and Government, 1572–1651* (Cambridge: Cambridge University Press, 1993), 36.

5. An obvious point of reference here is Carl Schmitt's definition of the "concept of the political" in terms of the friend/enemy distinction, though Schmitt's post-Westphalian understanding of geopolitical interaction strives to distinguish between the enemy who has to be chased back to his borders and the foe who has to be destroyed. Carl Schmitt, *The Concept of the Political*, trans. George Schwab (Chicago: University of Chicago Press, 1996). Also relevant is Étienne Balibar's discussion of how nation-states, as a defense against their compromised authority, reassert their sovereignty by expanding and reenergizing the category of the public enemy. Étienne Balibar, "Strangers as Enemies: Further Reflections on the Aporias of Transnational Citizenship," *Globalization Working Papers* 06/4, Institute on Globalization and the Human

Condition, McMaster University, Canada (May 2006), 1–17, available online at http://socialsciences.mcmaster.ca/institute-on-globalization-and-the-human-condition/documents/IGHC-WPS_06-4_Balibar.pdf. The power of Balibar's analysis of contemporary states is also fraught by its recommitment to the liberal state as the primary framework for preserving the rights of strangers, which he would make into citizens.

6. Christopher Marlowe, *The First Part of Tamburlaine the Great*, in *The Complete Plays*, ed. J. B. Steane (Harmondsworth, UK: Penguin Books, 1969), 5.2.4.

7. For Marlowe's relationship to morality traditions, see David Bevington, *From Mankind to Marlowe: Growth of Structure in the Popular Drama of Tudor England* (Cambridge, MA: Harvard University Press, 1962). For a more recent reading that argues for strong lines of continuity between the mystery cycles and Marlowe's work, see John Parker, *The Aesthetics of Antichrist: From Christian Drama to Christopher Marlowe* (Ithaca, NY: Cornell University Press, 2007), 183–245.

8. The closest we get is the somewhat hazy and obscure figure of Octavius Caesar, who has just defeated Antony and Cleopatra and, in the wake of his victory at Actium, is in the process of re-establishing Roman control over the empire, rearticulating and re-establishing alliances in the newly stabilized circum-Mediterranean space of Roman rule. Though the plot hinges on the obscurity of his sovereign decision about whether or not Herod lives or dies, Caesar is in the background, off stage, setting the basic terms for the moment of existence in Palestine, certainly, but not commanding readers' attention in the same way as Tamburlaine.

9. Goldberg, *Desiring Women Writing*, 186, 227n20. I also register here my indebtedness to Laurie Shannon's reading of Cary's play in "Chaste Associations in Cary's *Tragedy of Mariam*," chapter 2 of *Sovereign Amity: Figures of Friendship in Shakespearean Contexts* (Chicago: University of Chicago Press, 2002), 54–89.

10. Elizabeth Cary, *The Tragedy of Mariam*, ed. Barry Weller and Margaret W. Ferguson (Berkeley: University of California Press, 1994), 2.2.169–70. All references will be to this edition and noted in the text.

11. For "half"-hearted, see Maureen Quilligan, "Staging Gender: William Shakespeare and Elizabeth Cary," in *Sexuality and Gender in Early Modern Europe: Institutions, Texts, Images*, ed. James Grantham Turner, 208–32 (Cambridge: Cambridge University Press, 1993), 225; for insincere, see Donald W. Foster, "Resurrecting the Author: Elizabeth Tanfield Cary," in *Privileging Gender in Early Modern England*, ed. Jean R. Brink, 141–73 (Kirksville, MO: Sixteenth Century Journal Publishers, 1993), 148–49; for "intemperate," see Marta Straznicky, "'Profane Stoical Paradoxes': *The Tragedie of Mariam* and

Sidneian Closet Drama," *ELR* 24 (1994): 104–34, 125. Margaret Ferguson offers an important exception to this critical inclination to dismiss the opening speech in *Dido's Daughters: Literacy, Gender, and Empire in Early Modern England and France* (Chicago: University of Chicago Press, 2003), 292.

12. Lauren Berlant, *Cruel Optimism* (Durham, NC: Duke University Press, 2011), 1. I also derive from this work an emphasis on the potentials for "immanent world making" (8) that reside in even the most fraught ordinary existences.

13. Foster, "Resurrecting the Author," 148. My thanks to Laurie Shannon and Lara Bovilsky for inviting me to think further about Mariam's fantasy of being a milkmaid.

14. Homer, *The Odyssey*, trans. Robert Fitzgerald (Garden City, NY: Anchor Books, 1963), 201.

15. My account of Mariam's brief pastoral fantasy draws on Julian Yates's understanding of pastoral as metaplasmic genre, offering affordances for rearticulating the basic terms of existence. Julian Yates, "What Was Pastoral (Again)? More Versions," in *The Return of Theory in Early Modern English Studies: Tarrying with the Subjunctive*, ed. Paul Cefalu and Bryan Reynolds, 93–118 (New York: Palgrave Macmillan, 2011). Dympna Callaghan may be right that this figure is appealing to Mariam because racially (un)marked, and such a possibility should be kept in mind as a limit on the metaplasmic world-making efficacy we might attach to this gesture. Dympna Callaghan, "Re-reading Elizabeth Cary's *The Tragedie of Mariam, Faire Queene of Jewry*," in *Women, 'Race,' and Writing in the Early Modern Period*, ed. Margo Hendricks and Patricia Parker, 163–77 (London: Routledge, 1994).

16. Derek Parfit, *Reasons and Persons* (Oxford: Oxford University Press, 1984).

17. Niklas Luhmann, "Deconstruction as Second-Order Observing," *New Literary History* 24, no. 4 (1993): 769–70.

18. Here I follow Ferguson and Weller's observation that though the Chorus assumes the "appearance of impersonal authority" voicing and applying a set of normative criteria to the characters in the play, "their gnomic, conventional utterances seem somewhat off the mark, not only capricious and volatile in the application of general precepts but also inadequate to the psychological, spiritual, or even practical situation of the protagonist." Barry Weller and Margaret W. Ferguson, introduction to their edition of *The Tragedy of Mariam*, 1–59, 35.

19. David Glimp, *Increase and Multiply: Governing Cultural Reproduction in Early Modern England* (Minneapolis: University of Minnesota Press, 2003), 32.

20. Thomas Lodge, "To the Courteous Reader, As Touching the Use and Abuse of Historie," in *The Famous and Memorable Workes of Josephus*, trans. Thomas Lodge (London: G. Bishop, S. Waterson, P. Short, and Tho. Adams, 1602), sig. 4v.

21. Jonathan Goldberg, *The Seeds of Things: Theorizing Sexuality and Materiality in Renaissance Representations* (New York: Fordham University Press, 2009), 56.

22. Michel Foucault, *The History of Sexuality*, vol. 2, *The Use of Pleasure*, trans. Robert Hurley (New York: Vintage Books, 1990), 8–9, quoted in Goldberg, *The Seeds of Things*, 67.

23. Foucault, *The Use of Pleasure*, 9.

24. Paul Rabinow, *Anthropos Today: Reflections on Modern Equipment* (Princeton, NJ: Princeton University Press, 2003), 18–19, quoted in Stephen J. Collier, Andrew Lakoff, and Paul Rabinow, "Biosecurity: Towards an Anthropology of the Contemporary," *Anthropology Today* 20, no. 5 (October 2004): 3–7, 3.

25. Goldberg, *The Seeds of Things*, 57.

CHAPTER 3

Marlowe's Footstools

Aaron Kunin

Adrian's Footstool

Does a chair sit or stand?

A body can sit in a chair. Bodies are different, though, and sitting can look like a lot of things: You can sit on the edge of the seat with your back straight, letting the chair support your body in just one place; or, alternately, you can slouch and sink into the chair; you can draw your legs up and let them dangle over the sides, or cross one over the other, or fold them together in a lotus. You can do other things that look sort of like sitting: you can kneel, squat, or curl up in a ball. You can also stand on the chair's seat to reach an item on a high shelf, or climb onto a higher platform.

The chair seems to have fewer options. But what is it doing? Its limbs (not its seat and back) rest on the ground, so it is standing. However, insofar as the posture of the seat and back mimic that of the body it supports, it is sitting. And then, with all four limbs pressed to the ground, it seems to be doing something else. Maybe its expression is suppliant. Praying, maybe. Or crawling?

Chairs are quasi-human in that human workers make them and in that they have some features in common with human form: they have legs and a seat and may also have a back and arms. From this point of view, the number of limbs in a chair's body seems excessive. Four legs and two arms add up to an insect body; and, as with insects, the chair's skeleton tends to be exposed. If you include a human sitter as part of the package, then you might have two more legs and two arms, which, if you imagine the latter as pedipalps, could make a spider-like body. Three legs might be just enough to make a rooted tree or a plant that propels itself by its roots, such as a triffid.

(There are chairs in the world that have only one leg, which is a human possibility. Is there an example of a chair with two legs, standing or walking upright? How many legs do you count on Gerald Summers's lounge chair [Figure 1], made of a single ingeniously molded piece of plywood, where the legs, arms, back, and seat are not distinct but a unified surface? Maybe that is more of an amoeba body.)

I will return to the question of chairs in the second section of this essay. I want to begin by focusing on footstools, which are either a primitive kind of chair or an adjunct to chairs. In a remarkable motif in Marlowe's verse plays, a footstool has two positions, standing and stooping. The following passage is from *Doctor Faustus*.

> Pope Adrian. Cast down our footstool.
> King Raymond. Saxon Bruno, stoop,
> Whilst on thy back his holiness ascends
> Saint Peter's chair and state pontifical.
> Pope Bruno. Proud Lucifer, that state belongs to me!
> But thus I fall to Peter, not to thee.
> Pope Adrian. To me and Peter shalt thou groveling lie
> And crouch before the papal dignity.
> Sound trumpets then, for thus Saint Peter's heir
> From Bruno's back ascends Saint Peter's chair.
> (*Doctor Faustus*, B Text, 3.1.88–97)[1]

Pope Bruno, the footstool, has to be "cast down," because he was not originally in the down position. He has to "stoop" from an upright position and—because, left to his own devices, he would not always be waiting by the throne to be used—for that to happen, someone has to tell him to stoop. Pope Adrian cannot tell him. An elaborate chain of command separates Adrian from direct communication with the furniture. The chain of

Figure 1. Gerald Summers, Bent Plywood Armchair; image courtesy of Peter Petrou Gallery, London

command links elite political operators: Adrian, a spiritual power, gives the command to Raymond, King of Hungary, a temporal power, who passes it to Bruno, a rival spiritual power. Here the chain breaks. The footstool resists. He thinks he is the pope; he says so distinctly and eloquently.

From a design perspective, Bruno's service as footstool is impractical. His use could never be ordinary and is, on the contrary, ritualistic. Surely some clever engineer could imagine a smoother, more comfortable path to the throne. Bruno's ritual function is something more important than comfort, which is the opposite of comfort. Adrian sacrifices his own comfort to enhance Bruno's discomfort.

I deliberately use the word *discomfort* rather than *dehumanization*. The footstool in this scene has everything in common with human form, because Bruno's is a human body, living and whole. His other human attributes include a gender (masculine), a name (Bruno), and an ambition (to enjoy the state of the papacy) and its verbal expression: "That state belongs to me!"

(Some readers think that he might be Giordano Bruno. I would like to think so too, because this identification would give him the additional human attribute of participation in intellectual history. Giordano Bruno, victim of the persecution of Clement VIII, and a sort of animist thinker, might have appreciated the image of a defiant stool talking back to the pope. However, since the character is called Saxon Bruno rather than Nolan Bruno, I doubt it.)

This list of attributes is overspecific if I am merely trying to establish Bruno's humanity, and that is the point: this footstool is overspecific. When Adrian intones, "Cast down our footstool," he refers to one footstool only. No other article of furniture in the Vatican collection, no matter how practical or costly, will do. (Note that there are *two* popes but only *one* footstool. Common and proper nouns have traded places.)

Adrian and Raymond do not conspire to strip Bruno of his individuality or his human attributes. They refer to him as a footstool, but they also address him as Bruno and allow him some freedom to express his views. They even listen and respond to what he says. (Adrian studiously refuses to give Bruno direct commands, but he does address him directly.) They never dispute Bruno's human dignity. They only disagree on the political question of whether he should also enjoy "papal dignity."

Thus the primary audience for their performance is Bruno, whom they treat as a negligible utility but never take for granted. They want to convince him that he is not the pope. To a lesser degree, Adrian may be his own audience. He may need to hear himself declare his ascension so that he can remember that he is actually the pope—because it is confusing when someone else makes the same claim. Bruno's short speech has the same logic: he wants Adrian to hear that he does not acquiesce, and he wants to hear it too, particularly in circumstances that are destructive to his self-image.

There is another audience within the scene. This third audience is an anomalous figure. It has no lines—an extraordinary omission for a character in a play by Marlowe. Others talk to it and about it, but it does not talk, although it does have a human identity, a gender, and a name. I am referring to Saint Peter's chair. In the setting designed by Bernini several decades after Marlowe's death, the chair has become almost inaccessible. To ascend to its seat, you would need something more than a footstool;

you might have to stand on the shoulders of both John Chrysostom and Augustine, the church fathers who stand to the right of the chair and who are made of the same materials.

Christopher Wood and Alexander Nagel have studied the logic by which St. Peter's Basilica retains its identity during a period in which it is being destroyed and rebuilt.[2] Their account ends before Bernini intervenes, but the "chain of substitutions" they uncover is useful for understanding the association of the chair with Peter. The gilded bronze chair that Bernini designed encloses a much older chair that Peter may or may not have actually sat in; or the older chair may include wood fragments from a chair that Peter once sat in. However old the older chair may be, it takes its chronology not from the epoch of its origin but from the ancient epoch to which it refers.

Further, by synecdoche, the chair refers to its traditional sitter in the ancient epoch, Peter, who is the antitype of the two rival popes. Bruno clarifies that he "falls" only "to Peter," and thus to himself, because Peter is his model; while Adrian further clarifies that Bruno, in falling to Peter, cannot help falling "to Peter's heir" (meaning Adrian) as well. The chair has no lines because it has nothing to add to this exchange. Links on the same chain of substitutions, each of the rival popes refers to the same type as the chair.

There is a fine symmetry in the composition of this scene. A man acting as a footstool declares his submission to a chair acting as a man.

Tamburlaine's Footstool, Part 1

Marlowe was fascinated by the image of a man stepping on another man's back to climb into a chair. The short scene from *Faustus* revises and condenses a relationship that Marlowe explores more thoroughly in two acts of *Tamburlaine the Great, Part 1*. Here is a relevant sample.

> TAMBURLAINE. Bring out my footstool.
> . . .
> Fall prostrate on the low, disdainful earth
> And be the footstool of great Tamburlaine,
> That I may rise into my royal throne.
> BAJAZETH. First thou shalt rip my bowels with thy sword
> And sacrifice my heart to death and hell
> Before I yield to such a slavery.
> TAMBURLAINE. Base villain, vassal, slave to Tamburlaine,

Unworthy to embrace or touch the ground
That bears the honor of my royal weight,
Stoop, villain, stoop, stoop, for so he bids
That may command thee piecemeal to be torn
Or scattered like the lofty cedar trees
Struck with the voice of thund'ring Jupiter.
BAJAZETH. Then, as I look down to the damnèd fiends,
Fiends, look on me, and, thou dread god of hell,
With ebon scepter strike this hateful earth
And make it swallow both of us at once!
TAMBURLAINE. Now clear the triple region of the air
And let the majesty of heaven behold
Their scourge and terror tread on emperors. (4.2.1–32)

Adrian's footstool and Tamburlaine's footstool are the only footstools in Marlowe's theater. This means that they are normal, in a sense. Marlowe never writes about stools made of wood—not discrete pieces nailed to one another by a carpenter, nor interlocking pieces fitted together by a joiner, nor a single piece shaped on a turner's lathe. Instead, a great ruler, a pope or a king, makes a footstool out of another great ruler, a pope or a king. He does it with his voice.

Think of it this way: when Adrian calls for his footstool, he wants a unique object, Bruno. When Tamburlaine calls for his footstool, he wants a unique object, Bajazeth. Comparing the two passages, I learn something about footstools as a species. When Marlowe calls for a footstool, he wants a living man's body.

In the last two sections of this essay, I argue that the footstools in these scenes are normal in two other senses—political and dramaturgical. The argument will take me far beyond a consideration of Marlowe's imagination. However, I do not want to lose sight of the special (that is to say, not normal) meaning that footstools have for Marlowe. The image of the human footstool fascinated and delighted him. This is a fact about him and not about all people or all poets. (He was a major influence on the generations of poets and playwrights who followed him, and they repeated many of his discoveries, but they left the footstools alone, for the most part.)

POLITICS

In the section titled "Aspects of Power" in *Crowds and Power*, Elias Canetti discerns a hidden meaning in the careers of all soft chairs.

> An upholstered chair is not only soft, but also obscurely gives the sitter the feeling that he is sitting on something *living*. The give of the cushions, their springiness and tension, has something of the quality of living flesh and may conceivably be the cause both of the aversion which many people feel for chairs that are too soft, and of the extraordinary importance which others, not generally self-indulgent, attach to this form of comfort.[3]

When you sit in a chair, you are sitting on a person. You can pretend that this is not so by sitting in a hard chair. Or you can remind yourself of this relationship, luxuriate in your power over others, by using an especially comfy chair. Or you can make the point clear to everyone by making use of a person's actual body. Even the body of an extraordinary person, such as the Ottoman emperor!

If Canetti is right, everyone wants to do what Tamburlaine does to Bajazeth. Tamburlaine's footstool is an unnecessarily graphic representation of what people want from furniture. Tamburlaine seems to agree that his treatment (he calls it his "handling") of Bajazeth responds to a basic, universal, unspoken desire. At first, he is uncharacteristically laconic in announcing what he is going to do with Bajazeth after defeating him, inevitably, in battle: "I will not tell thee," he tells Bajazeth, "how I'll handle thee" (3.3.84), because the idea is so good that he does not want to ruin it by anticipation. Everyone will appreciate it, though. They will "smile to see thy miserable state" (3.3.86). Even the stars in the sky will "Smile . . . / And dim the brightness of their neighbor lamps" (4.1.33–34). Tamburlaine's soldiers and the stars above are smiling because they have now satisfied a desire they did not know they had. They would not have imagined it, but when they see it, they like it. Maybe the spectators in Marlowe's theater wear the same smile.

Canetti's account of the power of sitting is inadequate to Tamburlaine's handling of his footstool in at least one way: Tamburlaine talks to his footstool. What is more, the footstool talks back. It does not consent to its use as a footstool. Canetti could not have imagined that.

> The thing sat on is no longer even animate. Its function is settled forever and it has less volition even than a slave; its state is the quintessence of slavery. Its user is free to do exactly as he likes with it. He can come and sit down and remain sitting for as long as he pleases, or he can get up and go away without giving it a thought.[4]

There is some trouble in this account even before I test it against the example from *Tamburlaine*. A chair has "less volition than a slave" but is nonetheless "the quintessence of slavery." These two forceful statements do not go together. Canetti seems to say that the chair typifies slavery—that is its symbolic meaning, which the sitter either unconsciously relishes or unconsciously avoids—without being an example of slavery. Because it is impossible to enslave a piece of wood. You cannot even enslave a horse. The wood can be property, and the horse can be tamed, but enslavement only happens when people are treated as property.

According to Canetti, people are naturally free. They have a special gift of self-transformation, which "is clearly expressed in the mobility of the face. . . . It is inconceivable how many changes a face can undergo in the course of a single hour."[5] Objects, however, are governed by necessity. Treating a person as property, a slave, violates human freedom. Treating a person as an object cancels human freedom entirely.

(Since he does not particularly value human freedom, Canetti does not seem to be disturbed by its loss. Both enslavement and objectification appear as relatively benign forms of violence in an account of human civilization in which power relationships more frequently look like one person eating another. For example, Canetti defines "family" not in terms of genealogy but rather as an occasional, exceptional grouping: people eating together but not eating one another.)[6]

The first thing Canetti notices about a chair is that it is "not even animate." By contrast, Julia Reinhard Lupton views mobility as the essential fact in a chair's existence. She is commenting on a passage from Shakespeare's *Taming of the Shrew*:

> Kate. . . . I knew you at the first
> You were a movable.
> Petruchio. Why, what's a movable?
> Kate. A joint-stool.
> Petruchio. Thou hast hit it. Come, sit on me. (2.1.192–96)

> Kate calls Petruchio "a movable" (a piece of furniture, or *meuble*), which she then specifies as a "joint-stool," the lowest form of seating in medieval and Renaissance houses. Denying him the dignity of a chair, she reduces him to an object designed to bear the rump of anyone in the house, and to be moved about at will for the frequent rezonings of shared space that characterized the minimalist choreography of Renaissance furnishing. Joint-stools afford sitting; they also afford rapid transport from one space to another; and they can, under certain circumstances, afford hurling.[7]

So. Another stool. A joint-stool, to be precise, but not interlocking pieces of wood: rather, Petruchio's human limbs. Like all furniture, as Lupton shows, this footstool with human joints is a "movable" and therefore not attached to a place as a house or a rooted tree would be. It moves around the room, and into other rooms, and can be carted away to other buildings. Different people can sit on it, step from it to a higher seat, play cards on it, lay out tomorrow's shirt on it.

Lupton calls these various options "affordances." The term, which comes from design, is strategic. Designers talk about the affordances of objects and environments, whereas engineers talk about uses and abuses. A tool has a use, which is the activity for which an engineer intended it. The stool's use is sitting, and anything else, such as hurling, would be tool abuse.[8] But designers do not necessarily intend just one use. They design for living, which is to say, for freedom.

Affordances are the measure of freedom available to furniture. You cannot restrict the possible uses of a piece of furniture any more than you can design a perfectly safe piece of furniture. Anything a footstool can do is an affordance. Because it has options, the footstool is not entirely subject to necessity.

What about Bajazeth? While acting as a footstool, he does not have "less volition than a slave." His will to rule the Ottoman Empire remains intact. His volition is exactly that of a slave: he wants something, and meanwhile he is being used for what someone else wants. "Slavery" is his name for this condition, and "slave" is one of Tamburlaine's names for him, along with "villain, vassal," and "footstool."

Maybe he would rather have less volition. Unlike Petruchio, who declares a wish to be used as an object, he does not say, with obscene suggestion, "Sit on me." Instead he says, "Rip my bowels with thy sword/And sacrifice my heart to death and hell." In other words, kill me and make furniture out of my skeleton. The bowels and heart are crucial elements of a human organism that have no purpose in a footstool. In asking to have them eliminated, Bajazeth, who really wants to be emperor, prefers objecthood to slavery.

Should he prefer it? There is some question as to whether being "the footstool of great Tamburlaine" is an honor or a degradation. The very ground that he walks on is honored to receive Tamburlaine's "royal weight." Tamburlaine calls the same ground "the low, disdainful earth," and Bajazeth calls it "this hateful earth," which I take to be names for the same feeling at greater and lesser degrees of intensity. The disdain that the ground feels for Bajazeth may be compared to that of the washroom attendant who notes the unfashionable appearance and poor fit of your clothes and icily calls you "ma'am."

The ground's affordances include bearing Tamburlaine's weight and receiving Bajazeth's embrace, but it experiences the former as an honor and the latter as a kind of abuse. Bajazeth does not even deserve the ground's support and is therefore doubly unworthy of the honor of stooping to insert his body between the ground and Tamburlaine's foot.

If Bajazeth's nomination as footstool—but royal footstool—is simultaneously insult and honorific, Tamburlaine's position is similarly ambivalent. I do not so much mean that his glory in this exchange depends on the neck of the emperor on which he treads. Rather, that his power derives from a different source of which he is the honored but undeserving instrument. In the formula that he repeats obsessively throughout both five-act plays, he is the "scourge of heaven" or "scourge of God."

Isn't the pope also conceived as a similar kind of instrument? In the traditional formula, "Servant of the servants of God"? "Of all titles ever assumed by prince or potentate," as Henry Adams observes, "the proudest."[9]

Tamburlaine's Footstool, Part 2

Dramaturgy

"Stoop, villain, stoop, stoop" (*Tamburlaine the Great, Part 1*, 4.2.22–23). Marlowe liked the sound of the vowel in *stoop* so much that he wanted to hear Tamburlaine say it three times. Then he wanted to hear it again in *Faustus*: "Saxon Bruno, stoop" (*Doctor Faustus*, B Text, 3.1.89). But this was not enough! Adrian says the word another time—a fifth repetition—just seventy lines later: "Then thou and he and all the world shall stoop" (3.1.158).

Maybe it was the final "p," the only sound that *stoop* does not share with *stool*, that Marlowe really wanted to hear. In any case, the frequent returns of the simple command to stoop suggest a frustration of someone's desire. No matter how many times you indulge this desire, it is still not enough. Maybe the command simply is not working except as a sound effect. (You might say that Tamburlaine has to give the command a third time because Bajazeth has not carried it out after the second.)

The fact that Tamburlaine is talking at all is somewhat gratuitous. The entire exchange could be replaced by a short stage direction: "Bajazeth kneels before the throne. Tamburlaine steps on his back and climbs into the seat." The scene does not go like that. Instead, they command, reply, curse, and wrangle, for thirty-two lines. Marlowe wanted to hear all of the words. The king and the footstool have to be talking the entire time.

Tamburlaine's counselors observe the inefficiency of the play's language and try to correct it. "You must devise some torment worse, my lord," Techelles offers, "to make these captives rein their lavish tongues" (*Tamburlaine the Great, Part 1*, 4.2.66–67). Techelles has a point. The efficient political solution would be the destruction of Tamburlaine's enemies. Recall Bajazeth's preferred solution: "First thou shalt rip my bowels with thy sword . . . " (4.1.16). He will be a footstool only when Tamburlaine has him killed and fabricates a useful object from his skeleton.

This is not a solution about which Tamburlaine ordinarily has any scruples. In *Part 1*, Marlowe dramatizes this solution in Tamburlaine's unflinching destruction of the city of Damascus, starting with the slaughter of four virgins ("O, pity us!" "Away with them, I say, and show them Death!" [5.1.119–20]); in *Part 2*, in Tamburlaine's murder of his son Calyphas.

That would be one way of handling the problem of Bajazeth. A less efficient but equally effective solution would be to use brute strength to enforce Bajazeth's unfree status. Punish his body. Take away his voice. Teach him the consequences of disobedience. Curiously, Tamburlaine is far less disciplined in handling his enemy emperor than in handling enemy towns. For although he threatens to have Bajazeth torn to pieces, which he fancifully compares to shavings from a cedar tree struck by a thunderbolt, the threat is empty. He has no intention of doing any such thing. Why does he make so many allowances for the eccentricities of his furniture? "My lord," Queen Zenocrate wonders, "how can you suffer these outrageous curses by these slaves of yours?" (*Part 1*, 4.4.26–27).

Tamburlaine's answer is instructive: "I glory in the curses of my foes" (4.4.29). He wants the footstool to be a living, conscious, willful man. He wants him to have a voice. He wants to hear his curses. He wants to step on his back—an emperor's back—while he resists. The political point of the command was never to conquer the object's resistance. The point is for the object and the speaker to hear the command and the curse over and over.

The political point has a dramaturgical explanation. According to Hannah Arendt, making a world usually means making things; maintaining a world usually means making things that last.[10] Marlowe, even when writing about pieces of furniture, and even when writing about human bodies used as furniture, does not rely on objects and bodies. As always, he emphasizes voice.

Marlowe's theater typically uses sonorous diction and extravagant imagery to create action and spectacle. All of Marlowe's readers must confront this tendency eventually. As Harry Levin succinctly puts it, "Driven by an impetus towards infinity and faced with the limitations of the stage, the basic convention of Marlovian drama is to take the word for the deed."[11] Important elements of drama are narrated but not quite in the manner of Greek chorus or Shakespearean soliloquy. A peculiar sort of dialogue sets lyric utterances against one another.

Think of the psychomachia in *Faustus*.

> —O Faustus, lay that damnèd book aside. (1.1.69)
> —Go forward, Faustus, in that famous art. (1.1.73)
> —Settle thy studies, Faustus, and begin
> To sound the depth of that thou wilt profess. (1.1.1–2)

These commands are spoken by the Good Angel, the Bad Angel, and Faustus, each a different aspect of the same character. Three actors appear onstage to represent a single voice talking to itself, translating action into lyric utterance and fragmenting lyric into dialogue.

The scene in Vatican City is more complicated, because there are three distinct characters, two of whom believe themselves to be the one and only pope. The dramaturgy, however, is the same. Adrian declares his papal state by loading his entrance with commands—first directed to his retainer, then to his furniture, and finally to himself. When Tamburlaine ascends the throne, he and Bajazeth trade impossible commands: Bajazeth tells the "dread god of hell" to make the earth swallow both kings, and Tamburlaine calls on some of the stars to outshine other stars (4.2.27, 4.2.33–34). Psychologically, the effect may be compared to that of whistling a sprightly tune on a walk through an unfamiliar neighborhood. You are announcing your presence and your nonchalance to the residents and convincing yourself that you exist. Here I am. Listen to my soundtrack. Come inside my head where that tune is always playing.

According to the enigmatic pronouncements of Allen Grossman's *Summa Lyrica*, lyricism is an ideal special effect for showing majesty.

> In the lyric "space of appearance," all being is celebratory. . . . The speaker in lyric has mastered the process of manifestation, and endured the tragic losses which manifestation entails, without being destroyed. The speaker in lyric has not lost heart. To go on speaking, not to lose heart, is an occasion of celebration and an attribute of majesty.[12]

In the story that Grossman tells, all people were originally invisible. Early civilizations developed poetry as a technique for making special people, kings, visible. As a result, almost anything that appears in a poem looks more or less like a king. For modern poets with democratic ambitions, the tendency of poetic language to multiply images of kings might sound like a problem. For Marlowe, it sounds like the solution to a problem.

At least, Levin makes it sound like a solution. According to Levin, Marlowe uses poetic language as a compensatory mechanism reconciling "an impetus towards infinity" with "the limitations of the stage." This formula echoes Barabas's entrance in *The Jew of Malta*, which takes the form of an impossible command addressed to his wealth: "Give me," he says, carriers of wealth with greater value than gold pieces, so as to "enclose/Infinite riches in a little room" (1.1.19, 1.1.36–37) and obviate scenic representation. Elsewhere Levin expresses his appreciation for this line, remarking that "nothing could be more Marlovian. . . . It is hard to imagine how a larger amount of implication could be more compactly ordered within a single pentameter."[13] To Tamburlaine's political advisors, poetry seems to be a needless expenditure; to a literary critic (putting aside the rarity of Marlowe's genius, even within the cultural flowering of the Elizabethan period), it seems a thrifty allocation of resources. On a practically bare stage, using only human voices, Marlowe shows infinite wealth and absolute power. Very economical.

Jonathan Goldberg has a different interpretation of this tendency. In a reading of *Edward II*, Goldberg highlights a speech by Gaveston that "defines in advance precisely the kind of theatricalization *Edward II* will not offer."[14] Gaveston imagines seducing Edward by producing entertainments in which boys wear women's clothing, playing on the fears of Puritan antitheatrical writers, and anticipating the hopes of some modern readers, for the effects of this Elizabethan stage convention. However, Goldberg points out, Gaveston seduces Edward using his own body, without cross-dressing performers, and, in fact, without professional entertainers of any kind. Gaveston does not need to wear a dress in order to become sexually interesting to Edward.

What if this interpretation—lyric majesty undone by performance—were the model for Marlowe's dramaturgy? Rather than constituting action, the speeches would be fictions even within the fiction of the play, providing a view into a world distinct from the scene in which they are spoken. This is how the impossible commands seem to work in one of Marlowe's most celebrated set-pieces, Faustus's descent into hell. As the time of his spiritual contract runs out, Faustus calls on all the stars to stand still, for the sun to "make/Perpetual day," and for his body to be sublimated into a cloud. As though Faustus's wishes to slow time have the effect of making it run faster, an hour passes before he has finished reciting a speech of fewer than sixty lines (with more of the lines spoken before the clock strikes the half-hour than after).

Stephen Greenblatt concludes that Faustus's desires are ultimately objectless: "Faustus speaks endlessly of his appetite, his desire to be glutted, ravished, consumed, but what is it exactly that he wants?"[15] It is true that Faustus is rarely satisfied with what he gets, but Greenblatt's question only makes sense if Faustus is allowed to want exactly one thing. I assume that Faustus wants everything that he says he wants—in other words, he wants to see the stars stand still *and* he wants to experience being a cloud—and is not obligated to seek a common principle unifying his desires. The objects Faustus wants are easy to grasp, starting with this one:

> I'll have them fill the public schools with silk,
> Wherewith the students shall be bravely clad. (1.1.89–90)

I work in a school myself and can testify that it would be cool to have the entire campus wrapped in layers of silk like a Christo and Jeanne-Claude project. I would also appreciate new kimonos for the students and faculty to wear as uniforms. Is it really necessary to explain these desires?

The shape of the political hierarchy finally depends on dramaturgy. (Which of the incompatible verbal cues do you follow? One can imagine stagings of *Faustus* in which Adrian defiantly asserts his ascension from beneath the foot of the Elector of Saxony, or stagings of *Tamburlaine* in which Bajazeth makes Tamburlaine his eunuch, or in which the mouth of hell swallows both of them.) The problem lies not in determining what the characters want, since their desires are spoken in "high astounding terms" (*Tamburlaine, Part 1*, prologue), but in conforming them to what others want, since they tend to view one another as objects of desire, instruments that will help them get what they want, or obstacles. Only in *Hero and Leander* does Marlowe suggest "mutual appetence" even as a possibility.

Everyone onstage looks like a king, even the furniture, because everyone onstage, including the furniture, is voicing wildly unreasonable commands.

NOTES

1. Christopher Marlowe, *Doctor Faustus and Other Plays*, ed. David Bevington and Eric Rasmussen (Oxford: Oxford University Press, 1995). All quotations from Marlowe's plays will refer to this edition.

2. Christopher Wood and Alexander Nagel, *Anachronic Renaissance* (Cambridge, MA: MIT Press, 2010), 313–19.

3. Elias Canetti, *Crowds and Power*, trans. Carol Stewart (New York: Farrar, Straus, and Giroux, 1984), 390.

4. Ibid., 389.

5. Ibid., 374.

6. Ibid., 221.

7. Julia Reinhard Lupton, *Thinking with Shakespeare: Essays on Politics and Life* (Chicago: University of Chicago Press, 2011), 55.

8. See Luke Wilson, "Renaissance Tool Abuse and the Legal History of the Sudden," in *Literature, Politics, and Law in Renaissance England*, ed. Erica Sheen and Lorna Hutson, 121–45 (Basingstoke, England: Palgrave, 2005). Wilson's examples are limited to tools used as weapons, but the concept has a broader application.

9. Henry Adams, *Democracy: An American Novel* (New York: Penguin, 2008), 101.

10. Hannah Arendt, *The Human Condition* (Chicago: University of Chicago Press, 1958), 167–74.

11. Harry Levin, *The Overreacher: A Study of Christopher Marlowe* (Boston: Beacon Press, 1952), 62.

12. Allen Grossman with Mark Halliday, *The Sighted Singer: Two Works on Poetry for Readers and Writers* (Baltimore, MD: Johns Hopkins University Press, 1991), 21.

13. Levin, *The Overreacher*, 87.

14. Jonathan Goldberg, *Sodometries: Renaissance Texts, Modern Sexualities* (Palo Alto, CA: Stanford University Press, 1992), 115.

15. Stephen Greenblatt, *Renaissance Self-Fashioning: From More to Shakespeare* (Chicago: University of Chicago Press, 1980), 217.

PART II

Sociality

CHAPTER 4

"Who Is Speaking Here?": Shakespeare's Sonnets, Modern Authorship, and the Contemporary University

Robert Matz

The question posed by Roland Barthes in *S/Z*, "who is speaking here?," raises this essay's three areas of concern: problems of source and authorship in Shakespeare's sonnets, the modern idea of the author occasioned by Shakespeare's self-representation in them, and the way in which historical circumstances shape our ideas of authorship.[1] This shaping includes our historical present, defined by economic and political pressures on the university in general, and the humanities and social sciences in particular. Since my argument advocates treating the author as a particular person, I might add a bit about "who is speaking" in this essay: I am a reader of Shakespeare's sonnets, a literary critic, and, most recently, a university administrator, part of whose charge is to explain the activities of a college of humanities and social sciences to sometimes skeptical audiences. The criticism I offer in this essay of an antihumanist critique of authorship comes out of that experience. This essay represents my effort to think through a position on authorship that fits my personal and professional commitment to a model of education that requires an interest in the individual student and, hence, genuinely wants to know "who is speaking here."

I take it as read that the answer to "who is speaking here?" is not simple, because identity is fluid. Identity is expressed and shaped in language, and because language is something inherently repeatable and exchanged, appropriated and transformed, identity is repeatable and exchanged, appropriated and transformed as well. Moreover, language disperses identity between the speaker and a pre-existing language and, at any moment, across the course of the speaker's enunciation. Nonetheless, I also take it as read that "who is speaking here?" is a question about the position from which someone is speaking as much as it is about the unfixing of that position. The author always speaks from somewhere, from particular identity positions (social status, gender, religion, etc.) and from a particular historical moment. The challenge is to recognize the fluidity of identity without treating that fluidity as transcendent free play.

In the first part of this essay I try to answer the question "who is speaking here?" with regard to Shakespeare's sonnets and their sources. There is an unsettled debate about which literary sources are most important to the sonnets—who is speaking there? Shakespeare answers in the sonnets that his words are his own: Shakespeare is speaking there. That answer hardly decides it—the sonneteer's claim that his words are his own itself has its sources, most notably for Shakespeare in Sidney's *Astrophil and Stella*. But Shakespeare's answer is remarkable for its insistence on the uniqueness of his voice and name, an insistence that ramifies through later source criticism of the sonnets, as well as our representations of Shakespeare as author. Broadening the scope of the argument, I turn in the second part of this essay to Foucault's "What Is an Author?" as a locus for a familiar critique of modern authorship, defined by its assumptions of authorial unity and autonomy. Sonnet 76 anticipates this modern authorship and the reasons for its antihumanist Foucauldian critique. At the same time, the repetition with difference in Shakespeare's sonnets points to the limits of the critique and recalls instead Shakespeare's indebtedness to early modern understandings of authorship. In the third part of this essay I argue that the antihumanist critique of modern authorship is not only inadequate to this early modern understanding of the author but also inadequate to the challenge of our contemporary moment. I focus on the contemporary shift from modern authorship to what might be called—in a couple of senses—a corporate one. This new conception of authorship, characteristic of much current discussion and policy in higher education—especially in the humanities and social sciences—suggests that the end of modern authorship may have dystopian rather than emancipatory effects.

"Every Word Doth Almost Tell My Name"

Shakespeare's sonnets are singular among English early modern sonnet sequences for being titled with their author's proper name rather than the loves to whom the sonnets are addressed.[2] The closest precedent is *Astrophil and Stella*, called in their first, pirated 1592 edition "Syr. P. S. His Astrophel and Stella. Wherein the excellence of sweete Poesie is concluded." A second printing that year adds to its title and content "sundry other rare Sonnets of diuers Noble men and Gentlemen." These titles nearly name Sidney, but allusively through initials or puns, and the second iteration further absorbs Sidney's identity into that of "diuers Noble men and Gentlemen," whose discourse in turn converges around a universalizable topos—"the excellence of sweete Poesie"—rather than a particular desire for a sweet beloved. Contrast the title page to the 1609 quarto, "Shakespeare's Sonnets, never before imprinted." The only addition in this title to the proper name, "never before imprinted," underscores the sonnets as more intimate expression, being made available for the first time for public consumption. We have no way of knowing whether Shakespeare had any part in the choice of this title, but as I will detail below, even if he did not, the title follows the lead of the sonnets themselves in stressing that they are the unique expression of their author—Shakespeare's Sonnets.

Still, the fact that this title might be the publisher's rather than Shakespeare's points to the problems in the title's claim to Shakespeare's ownership of his words. To the intervention of pirates and publishers we could add the most obvious, the famously conventional form of the sonnet itself.[3] Hence, the title "Shakespeare's Sonnets," which sounds unexceptional in a post-Romantic world, makes a more tendentious claim in Shakespeare's early modern one, given its pedagogy and aesthetic of imitation, its habits of common placing, and its lack of established copyright protection for authors. It is also a more tendentious claim for our postmodern world, which sees in the invocation of the author's proper name a desire, as Foucault put it, to stem "the proliferation of meaning" by turning the contingent circulations of discursive fictions into the inevitable truths of authorial genius.[4]

Some readers of Shakespeare's sonnets have limited this proliferation of meaning by seeing them as personal expressions of their author. Though Geoffrey Bullough included *Venus and Adonis* and *The Rape of Lucrece* in his *Narrative and Dramatic Sources of Shakespeare*, he thought the sonnets did not require the same excavation of source material. As direct expressions of

Shakespeare's experience, the sonnets instead became a source themselves, for Shakespeare's plays: writing of the "difficulties of young people in love and friendship" portrayed in *Two Gentlemen of Verona*, Bullough turns to the sonnets (in particular number 40: "Take all my loves, my love, yea take them all") to suggest that "by now Shakespeare himself has had bitter experience of both."[5]

However, there is a long critical tradition that views the sonnets as conventional rather than personal. This tradition is driven not only by the actual conventionality of much early modern sonneteering but also by the desire to depersonalize the sonnets' homoerotic, adulterous, or obsequious content, and so separate it from Shakespeare's proper name.[6] These emphases on the dependence of the sonnets on earlier sources often have an effect similar to arguments that treat the sonnets as autobiographical. For example, though Gordon Braden notes that there are almost no direct echoes of Petrarch's *Canzoniere* in Shakespeare's sonnets—no clear evidence that Shakespeare even read Petrarch—he nonetheless maintains that "Shakespeare's sequence is in certain ways one of the most Petrarchan of the age."[7] And by "Petrarchan" Braden means specifically rather than generically so. Other commentators could be adduced to suggest Shakespeare's significant indebtedness to Daniel, du Bellay, Spenser, or Sidney, among others.[8] Whatever the validity of these claims, they are also motivated by a particular interpretation of Shakespeare as author and person. Thus Braden finds Shakespeare—despite evidence to the contrary—most in the tradition of the great tradition. Or consider the obvious absence, until relatively recently, of Barnfield's homoerotic poetry from most studies of Shakespeare's sources—though one might think that "other men's poetry about love for a male beloved" would be a key desiderata in this effort. Sonnet writing was iterative and multifarious. Source criticism, when it fails to acknowledge the intertextual proliferation of sources in the sonnets, produces a stable set of poems and a stable identity mediated through a singular or dominant source, in a way not very different from the stable author imagined in biographical readings.

This idea of the stability and unity of Shakespeare's authorship goes back to the sonnets themselves, not only in their title but also in particular sonnets, such as 76:

> Why is my verse so barren of new pride,
> So far from variation or quick change?
> Why with the time, do I not glance aside
> To new-found methods and to compounds strange?

Why write I still all one, ever the same,
And keep invention in a noted weed,
That every word doth almost tell my name,
Showing their birth and where they did proceed?
O know, sweet love, I always write of you,
And you and love are still my argument;
So all my best is dressing old words new,
Spending again what is already spent:
For as the sun is daily new and old,
So is my love, still telling what is told.[9]

Sonnet 76 echoes later understandings of Shakespearean authorship as expressive biography ("you and love are still my argument") or unitary voice ("so is my love still telling what is told"). Although supporting these understandings of Shakespeare's authorship, Shakespeare's emphasis on a poetry in which "every word doth almost tell my name" derives from motives different from later constructions of Shakespearean genius. One motive of this sonnet is moral. "Quick change" is not only, as Shakespeare has already glossed it, rhetorical variation but also faithlessness. Glancing aside to "new-found methods and to compounds strange," though figuring rhetorical innovations, suggests broader infidelities. Shakespeare instead insists on his rhetorical and emotional faithfulness, to himself and to his beloved: "So is my love still telling what is told."

A second, related motive is literary. Shakespeare is asserting the kind of laureate authorship described by Richard Helgerson, in which the author locates his authority in "an ethically normative and unchanging self." Stephen Dobranski argues that this notion of authorship was buttressed by printers using the singular author as a selling point for books by, for example, including images of a book's author in its frontispiece.[10] An emergent idea of singular authorship might go hand-in-hand with a title—Shakespeare's Sonnets—supplied by the printer. Dobranski argues that conditions that we often see as counter to the birth of the author, such as the dominance of printers over writers, could in the early modern period also collaborate in that birth. Possibly too, the sonnet's rejection of its contemporary "time" of "new found methods" and "compounds strange" in favor of "old words" suggests a rejection of the modern poetaster in favor of a more authoritative literary tradition, a rejection that echoes in Braden's wish to connect Shakespeare to Petrarch rather than some contemporary whom Shakespeare does clearly and regularly echo, such as Daniel or, no doubt worse, Constable.

Finally, Shakespeare makes these moral and possibly literary claims in relationship to a strong and anxious social claim, most obviously in his defense of his words' legitimate and transparent "birth"—this from a man whose parvenu claims to gentility became part of a complaint against William Dethick, Garter King of Arms, who provided the Shakespeare family with its coat of arms, a coat of arms probably also mocked by Jonson in the motto "not without mustard."[11] Likewise the poem glances toward a deprecated sumptuary spending by those with "new pride" during a "time" (early modern London) of "quick change" in which Shakespeare does not participate: his "weed" fits his name. Moreover, the sonnet is not newfangled but rather "dressing old words new." The economic vocabulary of the sonnet's conclusion, "spending," "telling," likewise points to the social horizon of the poem.

Unsurprisingly, Shakespeare's claim to original rather than imitative authorship is not original. Sidney's *Astrophil and Stella* includes several sonnets that make the same kind of claim. What is striking about Shakespeare's version, however, is its dour intensity. When Sidney brags about his "inward touch" he too makes a social claim—he has the sprezzatura of one to the manner born—but his challenge to all to "behold Stella" if they seek "to nurse at fullest breasts of fame" has an exuberance that looks outward—certainly to other men who compete over Stella.[12] Shakespeare's sonnet (with the exception of its address to the young man, which I will consider below) is notable for the extent to which it draws inward, toward stasis and solipsism. The writer is "still all one, ever the same." And to repeat: "you and love are still my argument." If the "old words" dressed "new" are not those of other older poets but Shakespeare's own, then the writer who refused to be a plagiarist of others becomes, in turn, a plagiarist of himself. This poverty of originality results in a poet who finds he is only "spending again what is already spent." The unity of Shakespeare's authorship is so strongly urged, and so defensive, that it becomes mere repetition of the same. Shakespeare only somewhat retrieves himself from this sheer repetition by switching metaphors—from money to time—in which a sun both "new and old" promises some fertility—some difference within the same. Likewise, the final phrase "still telling what is told" includes some forward movement in its gerund and in a "still" that is continual movement. But it also continues the sense of stasis, conveyed particularly in the repetition of "telling" and "told" and heard perhaps as well in the contrary meaning of the word "still." Perpetually doing the same, it is not clear the writing is getting anywhere.

It is easy to guess at the source of this nearly relentless drive toward unity of voice and name. Divided by his birth and his class aspirations, appropriating a poetic form at once the property of others and, in early modern England, his betters (such as Sidney), Shakespeare insists all the more crazily that he is an undivided self. The obsession with authorial singularity, one that transforms even the repetition of one's own words into plagiarism by merely dressing up old words or spending the already spent, glances at the very fear it defends against, that of an inauthentic repetition of others' books by those who lack "the inward touch," the sprezzatura of those "Noble men and Gentlemen" who define Sidney's identity.

Shakespeare's fame, especially as a poet, depended on the great popularity of *Venus and Adonis* and the *Rape of Lucrece*, not on membership in an aristocratic community. Shakespeare models his authenticity on Sidney's. But he eschews the possibility of communal authorship in which the shared identity of "Noble men and Gentlemen" trumps individual identity and makes less pressing, even uninteresting, the claim to individual authorship. To be sure, no community is ever so happily whole, and Sidney certainly asserted himself against competing elites from above, or commoners from below, competitions that motivate the bragging about his "inward touch." Nonetheless, Shakespeare's sonnets sound different from Sidney's in their extreme reliance on Shakespeare's proper name, whether in the title to the sonnets or in the every word that almost tells it. Shakespeare may invoke his words' true birth, but he lacks interest in directly addressing a group of similarly ambitious "Noble men and Gentlemen." Bereft of this community we find Shakespeare full only of himself.

Or rather, Shakespeare would be full of himself, and empty too, if it were not for the fair young man who secures the authenticity and value of Shakespeare's words: "O know, sweet love, I always write of you, / And you and love are still my argument." The importance of the young man to this sonnet significantly qualifies any conflation of its claims to authorial self-sufficiency with a modern idea of the author. In quoting himself Shakespeare quotes someone else: "I always write of you." That someone else, moreover, seems to be a person of high social status. However much sonnet 76 may in other ways appear to engage in or at least predict a modern idea of authorship, the centrality of the young man to the sonnet reminds us of the limits of Shakespeare's self-assertion. Shakespeare depends on a man who likely has a real name—that is, a noble one—in order to prop up his own name as an author.

"Old Words New"

If sonnet 76 does not really provide an anticipation of modern authorship, it seems just as well. For the authorship that sonnet 76 nonetheless in large part asserts, that of a writer whose every word "doth almost tell my name," suggests the qualities that discommend it to the Foucault of "What Is an Author?" and to the critique of authorship as individual genius in general. This authorship denies its dependence on a wider discourse—Petrarchan, Sidneyean—even as it speaks it. In its refusal to allow the outside in, it further discounts any discordant notes within the writer's work or self. As Foucault puts it, the author is "only a projection, in more or less psychologizing terms, of the operations we force texts to undergo, the connections we make, the traits we establish as pertinent, the continuities we recognize, or the exclusions we practice."[13] Such is the projection of authorship that Shakespeare seems to engage when in sonnet 76 he presents his authorship as always the same even when, like the sun, it changes its position. Finally, Shakespeare's emphasis on his true love for the young man effaces another outside, the social circumstances that drive Shakespeare to insist on his constancy and truth even as—or rather because—new gentility marks him as part of the social world of "new pride" and "quick change." The affirmation of selfhood in sonnet 76 may posit itself against this world, but it also recalls Foucault's comment that the modern author is "characteristic of our era of industrial and bourgeois society, of individualism and private property."[14] In this last claim I am perhaps allegorizing too much, making the Shakespeare of sonnet 76 too much a figure of a kind of authorship that Foucault claims comes later. I think, however, that the general point can be made: read as an assertion of Shakespearean authorship, sonnet 76 suggests all the reasons to be skeptical of that authorship and of the self that it implies, in the lack of recognition of the dependence of the writer or the self on others and on history, and the related reduction of writing or selfhood to a simple and self-directed unity. In the case of authors, and of the author Shakespeare in particular, this unity has special access to the truth. More concretely, this view leads to the unfortunate emphasis on Shakespeare over other early modern writers in the classes we most often teach.

This critique of modern authorship itself requires qualification, however. For starters, my identification of Sidney's sonnet sequence as a source for Shakespeare's has not led to me doing away with the names of Sidney or Shakespeare. Rather, the identification of a source has led me to count the differences between the two poets in their related sonnets about originality. I think sonnet 76 is right when it asserts that "every word doth almost tell my name." Without insisting that every sonnet Shakespeare wrote was Shakespearean or every sonnet Sidney wrote was Sidneyean, I think most of us most of the time could identify a sonnet by Shakespeare versus one by Sidney without the author's name. If not every word, "almost every word." Further, Foucault's critique of authorship entails this conclusion. To be sure: we could argue that Sidney's sonnets are the essential source for Shakespeare's or, more likely, that the stylistic variations between the sonnets are superficial "compounds strange" that do not reflect their basic, shared Petrarchan discourse, which is notoriously always the same: "pronounce but love" and we know that "dove" is sure to follow. Yet either to reduce sonnet 76 to its origin in a single earlier writer (Sidney) or in a single discourse (Petrarchanism) would be exactly to limit the author's "proliferation of meaning" by anchoring it to a source. At its hypothetically reductive extreme, the treating of Shakespeare and, as a corollary, every other author, as an instance of a generalized discourse creates the mirror opposite of the stable author who is always the same, "still telling what is told."

Worth noting in this respect is that we cannot tell whether sonnet 76's "dressing old words new" refers to Shakespeare's old own words in other sonnets or to the old words of other sonneteers. Given sonnet 76's emphasis on self-repetition the former seems more likely, but other sonnets, such as 106, are certainly aware of their repetition of the words of older poets and old words, such as 106's "fairest wights." Even if that phrase could be decided one way or the other, similarly ambiguous words, phrases, and sentences are about the most common thing in Shakespeare's sonnets, more common even than *dove* following *love*. The nonidentity that opens up even in the minutest ambiguities of a line from the sonnets—say in a line that seems to stress unproblematic iteration—may also be seen as the nonidentity that opens up between two writers who share the same discourse. If the writer is never self-same, neither is the discourse. Old words new are repetition with difference.

Shakespeare—his sonnets and plays—are certainly more various, porous, and dependent than his authorship has often been represented. But we can blur these edges without fully subsuming Shakespeare's role as author. The classical and Renaissance idea of *imitatio*, after all, did not generally mean the identical repetition of someone else's words but their refashioning for the present time—"old words new"—along with the synthesis of many previous authors' words, as bees gather honey.[15] This idea of writing, dependent, among other kinds of dependencies, on its sources but not reducible to them, seems like a good start for a description of authorship, one that recognizes individual agency and expression without reducing authorship to it.

Such agency and expression might be viewed as an illusion of bourgeois subjectivity. Richard Halpern, for example, argues that early modern writing pedagogy produced "empty heterogeneity," a circulation of meaningless difference that keeps the machinery of social distinction going while occluding its action. Courtly in origin, this difference without meaning would find its highest expression in the bourgeoisie.[16] Yet as Elizabeth Hanson has observed, early modern pedagogies and schools never simply aligned themselves with the aims of one class.[17] Moreover, Halpern's comparison of writing style to the empty difference of sartorial fashion depends on its satirical force: learning from other authors to write well is just like learning from fashion magazines to dress well![18] The joke distracts from the inadequacy of this position. On the one hand, by comparing early modern writing instruction to the superficiality of fashion, Halpern implies that some more serious, authentic authorship must be available elsewhere. On the other hand, the idea that the author's writing style is just like sartorial style provides no basis on which to argue for the importance of authorship or education as the cultivation of self more generally. In the final part of this essay I argue that the very vulnerability of individual authorship to forces outside itself, rather than entailing a critique of the author as individual subject, requires its defense.

"What Does It Matter Who Is Speaking?"

Foucault observes in "What Is an Author?" that the author function "does not affect all discourses in the same way at all times and in all types of civilization."[19] The sources, activities, meanings, and even definitions of authorship change over time—hence not "author" but "author function." Describing authorship through any single frame—for example, that of literary history, society, discourse, or textuality—forecloses our understanding of authorship in the same way that attributing the work of the author to the self-directed "I" does—as when Shakespeare's sonnets are reduced to a mere instance of sonnet discourse. Moreover, because the frame is singular it may come to seem self-evident, natural, and universal rather than time-bound, particular, and precarious. Foucault observes this substitution of one unitary and all-explanatory source for another when, referring to Barthesian celebration of writing as textuality, he remarks in "What Is an Author?" that "in current usage, however, the notion of writing seems to transpose the empirical characteristics of the author into a transcendental anonymity."[20] As the god-like author once transcended historical circumstance, so, in this version of authorship, does the play of the text.[21] Because there are author functions but not authors—each identification of the meaning and source of authorship complicating the other—the definition of the author is inevitably a boundary problem, which means it is a historical one. Historical in two senses: first, because there is no natural circumscription of the sources of authorship, the boundary changes over time. And second, those changes are not autogenous but shift according to historical pressure, including the pressure of nonliterary forces. The young man of the sonnets, to allegorize him even further, but I hope not without warrant, occupies the role in the sonnets of the historical, nonliterary context in which Shakespeare writes. He is the nonwriting other on which Shakespeare's conception of his self and his authorship depends.

How we construct authorship likewise depends on nonliterary contexts. It is not a problem to be resolved once and for all but an argument by particular people within determinate historical conditions. "What Is an Author?" identifies both the historical conditions of authorship and the limits of a humanism that celebrates the author as self-creating genius. Written over forty years ago, however, the essay is unlikely to provide us with a historically sensitive answer to what definition of the author in present circumstances best replaces a flawed humanist one. If "What Is an Author?" is read further as simply a critique of the humanist subject—a reading that Foucault in the essay often seems to encourage—then the essay seems not merely out of step with our current historical situation as writers and intellectuals but inadequate to it. In particular, that critique of authorship offers no effective challenge to prevailing market-oriented opinion in the United States and elsewhere as it shapes contemporary discussion about the purposes of education, particularly at the university level.

At the end of "What Is an Author?" Foucault writes,

> I think that, as our society changes, at the very moment when it is in the process of changing, the author function will disappear, and in such a manner that fiction and its polysemous texts will once again function according to another mode, but still with a system of constraint—one that will no longer be the author but will have to be determined or, perhaps, experienced.[22]

There is a utopian quality to Foucault's prediction of the disappearance of the modern author, a hopeful "wait and see." True, Foucault insists that this new author function will operate within "a system of constraint," but the mysterious futurity of this system and Foucault's singling out of "fiction and its polysemous texts" seems to open out to a realm of greater possibility rather than of limit. But what if this future makes the author disappear in ways that do not seem liberatory?

Along with long-held political animus in the United States against universities and their faculty, more recent economic conditions and political decisions, including rising tuitions, a recessionary job market, and the retreat of states from the financing of public higher education, have driven especially strong antipathy toward the study of the humanities and social sciences. Because these fields deal with politically charged issues and are often conceived of as economically unproductive, political and economic objections to them frequently coalesce.[23] In Virginia, the state in which I work, these attitudes have expressed themselves in the promotion of teaching with Massive Open Online Courses (MOOCs) and in the pressure on university undergraduates to pursue Science, Technology, Engineering, Math, and Health (STEM-H) degrees. Ignorance about or antipathy toward the humanities and social sciences plays a role in championing MOOCs and STEM-H, but the primary motive is economic. Both MOOCs and STEM-H are seen as solutions to the rising cost of higher education: MOOCs by teaching more students with less labor and STEM-H by offering, it is presumed, a higher return on the investment in education—higher personal incomes, higher tax revenues, and, most tendentiously, greater social utility. The drive toward using MOOCs to decrease education costs came to particular prominence in Virginia in the summer of 2012, when the president of the University of Virginia was nearly ousted by the university's politically appointed trustees (known as its Board of Visitors) in part because the trustees did not think the president, Teresa Sullivan, was moving quickly enough to get the university into the business of online education. The drive toward STEM-H is structurally enshrined in Virginia education policy. It is now part of state law to favor STEM-H, including by exploring the possibility of granting incentives to students to major in STEM-H fields (by providing special scholarships or tuition discounts, for example) and by encouraging funding models for Virginia's state universities that favor academic programs or facilities in STEM-H.[24]

I hasten to add that neither MOOCs nor STEM-H, in the abstract, require a narrowing of educational goals. As a form of inexpensive delivery of educational content, MOOCs surely have the potential to open up new educational interests for a great number of people. And study in STEM-H certainly requires creative and critical energies, just as study in the social sciences or the humanities does. The economic forces driving these MOOC and STEM-H initiatives, however, are shaping them in the opposite direction, toward provision of technocratic instruction rather than an education that engages students' creative and critical capacities. Within the current economic context, MOOCs are championed primarily as providers of inexpensive and deracinated content that crowds out more personal and interactive study, and STEM-H becomes job training, in which students learn no more than they need to fill current or anticipated employment opportunities.

One of the essays influencing members of the Board of Visitors in their attempt to oust University of Virginia president Sullivan was an opinion piece in the *Wall Street Journal* by John E. Chubb and Terry M. Moe on the important place of MOOCs in the future of higher education. ("Good piece in WSJ today—why we can't afford to wait," the University of Virginia's rector wrote to her vice-rector.)[25] According to Moe and Chubb's article, it is time to stop fetishizing individual differences in classroom instruction when such instruction can be done much more efficiently as a MOOC taught by a single professor:

> Colleges and universities, whatever their status, do not need to put a professor in every classroom. One Nobel laureate can literally teach a million students, and for a very reasonable tuition price. Online education will lead to the substitution of technology (which is cheap) for labor (which is expensive)—as has happened in every other industry—making schools much more productive.[26]

Of course, the authors of this column observe that some courses require "person to person" contact and that universities will continue to provide these courses. But it is not hard to see that in this model the preference will be for courses that do not require individual "persons" but instead reproducible discourses and the technologies that enable them. The constraints that shape authorship in this model are efficiency and productivity. If one Nobel laureate can limit the proliferation of meaning in the discourse, that works nicely. Even if MOOCs at present—the enthusiasm of the University of Virginia Board of Visitors in 2012 now seems especially misguided—have disappointed their backers, it is unlikely that they will disappear from the educational scene. Still more unlikely to disappear is the underlying hope to transform education into a more cost-effective transfer of fixed and standardized knowledge.[27] Meanwhile, the circulation of ideas without much respect for the authority of particular authors means that accomplished university presidents can be fired on the basis of any pundit's columns. "What does it matter who is speaking?"[28] I think most of us in the University of Virginia situation would reply, "It matters a lot."

When Foucault speculates at the end of "What Is an Author?" about what it would look like to write or speak in a world in which these activities "develop in the anonymity of a murmur" I confess I have a hard time imagining such a world, in part because Foucault's evocation of it seems to involve a set of meta questions ("What are the places in it where there is room for possible subjects? Who can assume these various subject functions?") rather than the experience of this anonymous discourse itself.[29] I do agree with Foucault, however, that all ideas of authorship depend on some limiting authority. The anonymity of medieval authorship depended on the word of God or on that of a writer's auctores. The communal sharing of coterie poetry depended on a shared sense of writing like "Noble men and Gentlemen." For Chubb and Moe authorship is both hyperbolized and diminished. There is one Nobel-Prize winner and the rest of us. If the author with which we are most familiar is a product of bourgeois private property, the author function of the MOOC seems to coincide with the disappearance of that middle class: there are the super rich and the rest. This fantasy of the Nobel laureate delivering wisdom to the masses seems well suited to a society experiencing growing economic inequality.

This hyperbolized and diminished authorship conforms as well to a pattern that Seán Burke identifies as a product of critiques of the modern author. The announcement of the death of the author as individual human subject coincides with or leads to a return of a transcendent super Author—the very sort of return for which Foucault takes Barthes to task in the celebration of a transcendent textuality. Burke argues that Foucault follows the same pattern in his celebration of Nietzsche, with whom Foucault himself identifies, and of authors such as Freud and Marx, who define an entire discourse. This return of the repressed is inevitable, Burke argues, because the author who announces the death of the subject cannot himself be a subject in the conventional sense: he or other, privileged authorial substitutes for him, must somehow transcend the mystified subjectivity denounced: "Any radical eschatology of the subject would require the constitution of a subjectivity beyond man and time, as the disappearance of man in time."[30] Another way to put this point is that antiauthorialism has two different but sometimes conflated targets, the biographical and the transcendent author. Yet the implications of the criticism of these two kinds of authors are different: the biographical author—rich or poor, ducated one way or another, burdened with this experience or that, living, that is, in time—is the antidote to the transcendent author. Indeed, the shift from 1970s poststructuralism to 1980s New Historicism played out at large this shift from language to the author, often uncomfortably matching Foucauldian critique of the autonomous self with an interest in the lives and art of particular writers (Greenblatt) and sometimes turning in the other direction altogether to announce the tremendous power of authorship (Montrose).

The fantasy of the MOOC is likewise one in which a single transcendent author—the Nobel prize winner who can say all that needs to be said about a subject—sucks all the subjectivity out of the room, since there are presumably no other views of the subject to be had, either from students or from other instructors. Likewise, the advocates of STEM-H-only education find their great transcendent subject in the invisible hand of the market, while students' interests, creativity, critical capacities—the qualities that would enrich their subjectivities—are diminished in the name of job training. The derogation of the subject in the contemporary university and in the antihumanist reading of Foucault come from completely different places and different motives. The parallels are just coincidental. But a historicist account of authorship should take stock of the coincidence, the merely contingent circumstances that challenge positions held as abstract universals. Biographical attention to authors, far from elevating their authority, puts them in their place. Likewise, an emphasis on the historical context in which debates about authorship take place challenge a reading of Foucault that flattens an analysis of the author function into a universalizing critique of the subject or a utopian release from the trammels of identity.

Part of the current historical context driving debates around education is the substantial improvements in productivity new technologies make possible. However, these productivity increases, which depend on automation and standardization, do not affect many kinds of education, which, as Chubb and Moe put it, require "person to person" interaction. Such education, which encompasses much teaching in the humanities and social sciences, becomes increasingly expensive because it cannot match new economies of scale that standardization and automation enable—hence the push for MOOCs or for students who can be trained in STEM fields in order to further increase and benefit from new advances in these technologies.[31] Instruction in English, and in the humanities and social sciences more generally, however, requires communication, creativity, and critical dialogue. Much of this instruction has to be person to person: it assumes that information comes from particular authors, not from anonymous authority; it claims to help develop all its participants' own capabilities as authors as well as consumers of knowledge; and it adjusts itself to the needs of particular students through relatively personal instruction (small classes, office hours), as opposed to factory-scale content delivery. The kind of author most challenged in Foucault's essay—not the student- or teacher-author in the classroom but the (by definition) canonized author who is often the subject of a class—is equally important to defend. English studies in particular cannot afford to give away the cultural capital of the celebrated author—whether long or more recently canonical.[32]

The notion of self-generating authorship is a mystificatory fantasy. I do not think the same can be said for the advocacy of authorship as part of a generative conversation that develops the individual expression of its participants. The notion that an individual's creative and deliberative capacities are developed by the regular exercise of this kind of authorship is surely not simply false or fictive. Further, because writing and reading demand our engagement with the language of others while alienating our own, it is not at all inevitable that such experiences of authorship are conservative or calcifying. Stressing authorship as rooted in part in individual selves does not entail ignoring all that challenges and shapes that self. But it does suggest that we cannot regard the question "what difference does it make who is speaking?" as a dismissive rhetorical one.

When Shakespeare declares in his sonnets that "every word doth almost tell my name," it may strike us as a boast and a forecast of the future lionization of his authorship. Yet the debt of his words to those of other sonneteers, and the ever-shifting feelings expressed in those words, hardly reveal a stable, self-composed author. Indeed, as a whole the sonnets are less boastful about the author's name than full of reflections on its vulnerability, as in Shakespeare's advice to the young man to forget him after his death, so that "my named be buried where my body is / And live no more to shame nor me nor you" (sonnet 72). Putting a name on writing makes the author responsible for it and opens him up to all kinds of criticism: it is Shakespeare's "name" that "receives a brand" of public shame (sonnet 111)—the brand itself being a kind of naming experienced with pain and offering only restriction. Moreover, to be a name in the sonnets—for the young man as well as Shakespeare—is to find oneself vulnerable to larger forces, to slander, time, and death. Authorship is, in every way, precarious.

NOTES

1. Roland Barthes, *S/Z: An Essay*, trans. Richard Miller, preface by Richard Howard (New York: Farrar, Straus and Giroux, 1975), 41, 140, 151, 172.

2. Thomas P. Roche, *Petrarch and the English Sonnet Sequences*, AMS Studies in the Renaissance 18 (New York: AMS Press, 1989), 386.

3. A form about which Sidney complained in the *Defence of Poesy*, "truly many of such writings as come under the banner of unresistible love, if I were a mistress, would never persuade me they were in love: so coldly they apply fiery speeches, as men that had rather read lover's writings" (*Sir Philip Sidney: The Oxford Authors*, ed. Katherine Duncan-Jones [Oxford: Oxford University Press, 1989], 246). Sidney could have been describing Thomas Watson's early sequence *Hekatompathia, or Passionate Centurie of Love*, whose sonnets provide their source poems along with additional helpful glosses to the sonnets' vocabulary and allusions. The name Petrarch comes up in Shakespeare's plays only as a joke, a byword for the conventional poses of the lover.

4. Michel Foucault, "What Is an Author?," in *Aesthetics, Method, and Epistemology*, vol. 2, *Essential Works of Foucault*, ed. James D. Faubion, trans. Josué V. Harari and James D. Faubion, 205–22 (New York: New Press, 1998), 221.

5. Geoffrey Bullough, *Narrative and Dramatic Sources of Shakespeare*, vol. 1 (New York: Columbia University Press, 1957), 210; see also 164.

6. See Robert Matz, "The Scandals of Shakespeare's Sonnets," *ELH* 77 (2010): 477–508.

7. Gordon Braden, "Shakespeare's Petrarchism," in *Shakespeare's Sonnets: Critical Essays*, ed. James Schiffer, 163–83 (New York: Garland, 1999).

8. See, for example, A. Kent Hieatt, "The Genesis of Shakespeare's Sonnets: Spenser's *Ruines of Rome: By Bellay*," *PMLA* 98 (1983): 800–14; Patrick Cheney, "Shakespeare's Sonnet 106, Spenser's National Epic, and Counter-Petrarchism," *English Literary Renaissance* 31 (2001): 331–64; J. B. Leishman, *Themes and Variations in Shakespeare's Sonnets* (London, Hutchinson, 1961); and Anne Ferry, *The "Inward" Language: Sonnets of Wyatt, Sidney, Shakespeare, Donne* (Chicago: University of Chicago Press, 1983).

9. Quoted from Stephen Greenblatt, ed., *The Norton Shakespeare: Based on the Oxford Edition*, 2nd ed. (New York: W. W. Norton, 2008), 1971–72. All quotations of Shakespeare's Sonnets in this essay are from this edition.

10. Stephen B. Dobranski, "The Birth of the Author: The Origins of Early Modern Printed Authority," in *DQR: Studies in Literature*, ed. Stephen Donovan, Danuta Fjellestad, and Rolf Lunden, 23–45 (Amsterdam: Rodopi, 2008), 40–41. Helgerson quoted in Dobranksi (40). For a more assertive case for Shakespeare pursuing a self-conscious project of authorship, based on classical models, to become the "national poet-playwright," see Patrick D. Cheney, *Shakespeare, National Poet-Playwright* (Cambridge: Cambridge University Press, 2004). Cheney attributes more coherence and control to Shakespeare's authorship than I find persuasive, as when he writes, with the

sonnets as his example, that the "final telos of Shakespearean poetry, we may speculate, is to prepare the soul" for salvation (227). The sonnets end, however, with a pretty spectacular dying fall, whether one considers their end the subsequence about the black mistress, the two final anacreontics, or sonnet 126, with its missing quatrain and missing theological consolation.

11. Katherine Duncan-Jones, *Ungentle Shakespeare: Scenes from His Life* (London: Arden Shakespeare, 2001), 96.

12. *Astrophil and Stella* 15, in *Sir Philip Sidney*, 158–59.

13. Foucault, "What Is an Author?," 213–14.

14. Foucault, "What Is an Author?," 222.

15. See Thomas M. Greene, *The Light in Troy: Imitation and Discovery in Renaissance Poetry*, Elizabethan Club Series 7 (New Haven, CT: Yale University Press, 1982), esp. 72–75.

16. Richard Halpern, *The Poetics of Primitive Accumulation: English Renaissance Culture and the Genealogy of Capital* (Ithaca, NY: Cornell University Press, 1991), 44.

17. Elizabeth Hanson, "The Interiority of Ability," *Dalhousie Review* 85 (2005): 260–70.

18. Halpern, *The Poetics of Primitive Accumulation*, 42–43.

19. Foucault, "What Is an Author?," 216.

20. Foucault, "What Is an Author?," 208. Adrian Wilson, "Foucault on the 'Question of the Author': A Critical Exegesis," *Modern Language Review* 99 (2004): 339–63, 346. See also Seán Burke, *The Death and Return of the Author: Criticism and Subjectivity in Barthes, Foucault, and Derrida*, 2nd ed. (Edinburgh: Edinburgh University Press, 1998), 110.

21. Burke, *The Death and Return of the Author*, 110.

22. Foucault, "What Is an Author?," 222.

23. See, for example, Kevin Kiley, "North Carolina Governor Joins Chorus of Republicans Critical of Liberal Arts," *Inside Higher Ed*, January 30, 2013. http://www.insidehighered.com/news/2013/01/30/north-carolina-governor-joins-chorus-republicans-critical-liberal-arts.

24. Virginia Code § 23–38.87:19. Creation of STEM public-private partnership; duties and responsibilities.

25. Scott Jaschik, "The E-Mail Trail at UVa," *Inside Higher Ed*, June 20, 2012. http://www.insidehighered.com/news/2012/06/20/e-mails-show-uva-board-wanted-big-online-push.

26. John E. Chubb and Terry M. Moe, "Chubb and Moe: Higher Education's Online Revolution," *Wall Street Journal*, May 30, 2012, sec. Opinion. http://online.wsj.com/article/SB10001424052702304019404577416631206583286.html.

27. Tamar Lewin, "After Setbacks, Online Courses Are Rethought," *New York Times*, December 11, 2013, page 1. "Whatever happens at San Jose," where a first MOOC-for-credit experiment was a failure, "even the loudest critics of MOOCs do not expect them to fade away." The author goes on to assert that they will be reshaped. The question is how much the drive to "efficient" instruction will continue that reshaping. On this point see also Audrey Watters, "The MOOC Revolution That Wasn't," The Kernel, *Daily Dot*, August 23, 2015, http://kernelmag.dailydot.com/issue-sections/headline-story/14046/mooc-revolution-uber-for-education/.

28. Foucault, "What Is an Author?," 205, quoting Beckett.

29. Foucault, "What Is an Author?," 222.

30. Burke, *The Death and Return of the Author*, 99; see also 103.

31. This problem is a version of the economists William Baumol and William Bowen's analysis of the economics of art production, which becomes more expensive relative to production that benefits from technology improvements. See Robert B. Archibald and David H. Feldman, *Why Does College Cost So Much?* (Oxford: Oxford University Press, 2011), 38–41, 117. If the human mind is a machine, it turns out be a not very productive one compared to the computer, at least where regular and quantitative data are concerned.

32. John Guillory, *Cultural Capital: The Problem of Literary Canon Formation* (Chicago: University of Chicago Press, 1993), 41–45, 52–55.

CHAPTER 5

Hamlet and the Truth about Friendship

James Kuzner

Just after *The Mousetrap* is performed and the deeply perturbed Claudius has fled, Hamlet refers to Horatio as "O Damon dear." "This realm," he remarks, "dismantled was / Of Jove himself; and now reigns here / A very, very—paiock" (3.2.265–77).[1] In calling Horatio "Damon," Hamlet presumably alludes to a classical legend of friendship and kingship, adapted at length in Richard Edwards's 1564 comedy, *Damon and Pithias*.[2] In this essay, I consider why the allusion might matter: what the comic example, by comparison, tells us about friendship's potential in *Hamlet*. I begin, then, by briefly recounting the story of Damon and Pithias as Edwards portrays it.

Reputedly the truest friends in all of history, these two arrive in Syracuse, ostensibly to learn its customs, but almost immediately their servant, Stephano, perceives an atmosphere of tyranny and terrified servility: "I lyke not this Soyle," he says, "for as I go ploddynge, / I marke there two, there three, their heads always nodding, / In close secret wise, styll whispering together."[3] "The soyle is suche," he concludes, "that to liue heare I can not lyke" (B4). True friendship, we quickly discover, cannot flourish on blood-soaked Syracusan soil; in its place are false friendships held together by deception, flattery, and fear.

Dionisius, the tyrant accountable for such degradation, hears a report that Damon dreamed of killing him and sentences his visitor to death as an aspiring regicide. Damon, who has some things to take care of, is not yet ready to die; he asks that the king would "prolonge my lyfe therby . . . to set my thynges in a stay" (C1). Dionisius asks for a pledge, and when Damon's word is not sufficient, Pithias offers to be his friend's pledge and die in his place, should the allotted time expire—as, of course, it does. Yet Pithias remains unruffled. "I am not loth to doo what so euer I sayde," he assures us, "Ne at this present pinch of death am I dismayed . . . They [the Gods] have reserued me to this passynge great honour, / To die for my frind, whose faith, euen now, I do not mistruste." Before Pithias is done this honor Damon hurries in and tells his friend to stand aside: "Geue place to me, this rowme is myne," he says, "on this stage must I play, Damon is the man." At this a disappointed Pithias chastises the hangman Gronno for being slow with his noose: "thou cruell minister, why didst not thou thine office, / Did not I bidde thee make hast in any wyse? / Hast thou spared to kill me once that I may die twyse: / Not to die for my friend, is present death to me" (D1). Pithias continues to claim that he, not Damon, should still be executed in light of his friend's tardiness. Damon is unconvinced; true, he did not arrive exactly on time, but it is not yet noon, so he should still be allowed to lose his life.

Damon acknowledges that this disagreement, after a lifetime of consensus, is a bit odd. "Ah my Pithias," he asks, "shall we now breake the bondes of Amitie?" Dionisius, who has been quiet all the while, is utterly overcome by the scene before him—"my spirites are soddenly appauled, my limes waxe weake / This straunge friendship amaseth me so, that I can scares speake"—but Pithias, perhaps unaware of this change, keeps asking to be killed. Damon, also oblivious, abuses Gronno: "Thou coward minister, why doest thou not let me die?" (D2). Gronno's hand quivers with fear, during which interval Pithias again begs to be hanged. Dionisius remains astonished by this wrangling over who gets to be executed: "Were there euer such frindes on earth as were these two?" he asks. "What harte is so cruell that would deuide them asunder? O noble friendship, I must yeld, at thy force I wonder: / My hart, this rare frindship hath pearst to the roote, / And quenched all my fury" (D2). Their example so overwhelms Dionisius that he forswears tyranny and asks to be admitted to their rare fellowship. Damon and Pithias grant his wish, promising to instruct the erstwhile tyrant in the ways of true friendship.

In revealing friendship's truth—its virtuous basis in unbreakable trust, total open-heartedness, and willing self-sacrifice—Damon and Pithias also expose the truth of Syracusan politics. While monarchy might be permissible, tyranny—driven by the ruler's self-interest, unfathomable distrust, and desire to induce fear—is an abomination. At the end of Edwards's play, the form of ideal friendship promises to be replicated in the structure of Syracusan polity. (Included among the converts are not only Dionisius but also Gronno and the onetime flatterer and false friend, Aristippus.) The story of Damon and Pithias is so idealized as to seem merely fanciful, yet stories such as theirs—in early modernity and today—fuel the notion that classical friendship is scalable and that it is not oxymoronic to speak of a politics of friendship founded on classical ideals. Damon and Pithias's story, for example, shares with the politics of friendship outlined by Thomas Spragens, wherein many of friendship's principles—trust, loyalty, counsel, criticism, receptivity to new friends and ideas—are translatable to the wider social realm and wherein an initial relinquishment of a possessive self-conception ultimately serves to bolster, protect, and strengthen the self.[4] The movement from seeming self-loss to ultimate self-aggrandizement appears ridiculous in the purified version that is *Damon and Pithias*,[5] but the procedure is elaborated commonly not only in early modern England, as I have shown elsewhere, but also among contemporary theorists across a broad spectrum, including Francis Fukuyama, John Rawls, and Jürgen Habermas.[6]

This procedure is harder to observe in a tragedy like *Hamlet*, which ends not with a renewed polity but with a pile of corpses, a play in which corrupt kings cannot change; in which those who die in another's place do so involuntarily; and in which the closest thing to self-sacrifice is Horatio's attempted suicide. So why does Hamlet refer to Horatio as Damon? Surely he is too intelligent merely to allude ineptly. But surely, too, it is odd for Hamlet to imply that he is akin to Pithias: How does he offer to sacrifice himself for Horatio, manage to take his place, or, for that matter, do him any sort of service? Some critics—for instance, Christopher Warley—are indeed dubious about the play's central friendship, while others have praised that friendship as either an embodiment or at least an approximation of classical standards.[7] Agnes Heller, for example, writes that their "friendship is an absolute friendship—first friendship in the Aristotelian tradition," that Hamlet "confirms himself as a man, as a whole soul, through Horatio's friendship."[8] In fact, Heller goes so far as to say that there is no beauty in the play "except in the friendship between the dead hero and the living storyteller who resurrects him."[9] Julia Reinhard Lupton, in the same vein but more modestly, writes that "the Hamlet-Horatio couple draws its energy from the classical discourse of friendship" and that Horatio forms part of a "fellowship of friends who lighten and lessen" Hamlet's isolation.[10]

Such accounts are hardly as idealizing as *Damon and Pithias*—for Heller, friendship is the one solid object in an otherwise shattered world, and while Lupton locates liberal possibilities in the play's friendships, she does not posit any causal or promissory relationship between the play's friendships and democracy to come as Shakespeare imagines it. Still, Heller and Lupton's *Hamlet* resembles the classical legend in that friendship offers major safeguards for selfhood and even progressive political potential. Their work forms part of a much broader trend in recent studies—including the work of critics as disparate as Annabel Patterson, Laurie Shannon, and Andrew Hadfield—wherein Shakespearean friendships and selfhoods anticipate the protections and entitlements of early modern republicanism and modern democracy.[11]

In this essay I offer a different set of terms by which to compare and contrast Hamlet and Horatio's case with that of Damon and Pithias. Particularly, I show how *Hamlet* explores relationships among friendship, truth, and the unsettling of self. As the above description implies, *Damon and Pithias* nearly ends in darkness; without Dionisius's intervention, the dispute over who shall die in proving friendship's truth threatens to go on forever, to result in a double hanging, or even to devolve into lurid murder-suicide. There is an element in excess of the wish to preserve the friend that fuels Damon and Pithias's desires to be the one who dies first—as though neither could be a true friend, could prove friendship's truth, without perishing, as though friendship's essence is more in death than in life.

In the next two sections of this essay, I consider closely related issues as they arise in *Hamlet*. In the first, I present a disagreement early in the play about what true friendship is—specifically, about whether it can or should strengthen the self's integrity (as it does in *Damon and Pithias*) or erode that integrity (as it threatens to do in Edwards's play). This tension, between self-aggrandizing and self-shattering models of friendship, has never been so elegantly outlined as in Jonathan Goldberg's *Endlesse Worke*. There, Goldberg illustrates how early modern friendship, despite its classical trappings, produces "a society of loss," how friendship functions as "an otherness that overwhelms and subverts the self."[12] For Goldberg, as well as a host of recent theorists—such as Judith Butler, Maurice Blanchot, Jacques Derrida, and Jean-Luc Nancy, who emphasize friendship's precarious, unavowable, aneconomic, and inoperative dimensions—unsettled selfhood is friendship's truth.[13] It is also, the first section concludes, Hamlet and Horatio's truth.

Classical friendship discourse foregrounds willing self-sacrifice in order to distinguish true friendship from lesser, merely instrumental friendships, even though this discourse also acknowledges that friends happen to be emotionally, socially, and materially improved as a result of friendship. In *Hamlet*, by contrast, Shakespeare imagines a world where friendship has little instrumental value and where friends are undone irrespective of their will. In the second section, accordingly, I explore the pitfalls as well as the possibilities of friendship whose truth is loss. Here I look at Hamlet and Horatio's graveyard exchange and the exchanges that surround Hamlet's death. The first of these illuminates why friendship exists—what it can do when it cannot strengthen the self or the state—while the second shows how this truth about friendship means that the value to be found in Hamlet and Horatio resides elsewhere than in the modeling of a stable politics, and resides instead in an intensity, even a sublimity, that lasting political forms could never accommodate.

The Grounds of Friendship

The question of friendship's essence arises right away in *Hamlet*, on the guard platform at Elsinore. Horatio and Marcellus approach Bernardo and Francisco, who calls out "Stand, ho! Who is there?" "Friends to this ground," Horatio answers (1.1.14–15). He appeals to territorial identity, but his utterance also conjures the idea that one might be a friend, in the first place, to a ground rather than a person, or at least that friendship inheres in establishing grounds on which friends might stand. Horatio implies not only that friendship depends on shared ground of one kind or another—that there can be no friendly community between those with nothing in common—but also, most crucially, that being a friend to a ground means being unthreatening to those who share the ground. (This is why Dionisius, at the opening of *Damon and Pithias*, is incapable of friendship; he is a threat to all with whom he shares Syracuse.)

A dispute about the grounds of friendship, though, soon arises. When the Ghost beckons Hamlet in act 1, Marcellus counsels him not to follow: "Look with what courteous action / It waves you to a more removed ground. / But do not go with it" (1.4.60–62). Implicit in Marcellus's warning is that friendship's shared ground offers safety whereas ground set apart offers only danger, and that he acts as a friend by keeping Hamlet close. Horatio seconds Marcellus, but Hamlet ignores them both: "I do not set my life at a pin's fee," he remarks (4.65). Nevertheless, Horatio persists:

What if it tempt you toward the flood, my lord,
Or to the dreadful summit of the cliff
That beetles o'er his base into the sea,
And there assume some other horrible form,
Which might deprive your sovereignty of reason
And draw you into madness? Think of it:
The very place puts toys of desperation,
Without more motive, into every brain
That looks so many fathoms to the sea
And hears it roar beneath. (4.69–78)

In response to this Hamlet threatens his friends' lives.[14] To hinder him—to prevent him from confronting risk—is a dereliction, one that would render his friends worthy of his sword's edge. Being a friend, in Hamlet's view here, means to master worry and allow him to leave shared ground for a perilous space that might well induce suicide.[15]

Horatio and company assume what seems commonsensical: that friends offer protection, safety, and stability. Hamlet assumes otherwise, without love for life or a wish to preserve it. Insofar as he is capable of friendship, its basis would have to be quite different from the basis of the story of Damon and Pithias and, more broadly, of the Aristotelian and Ciceronian models that deeply influenced early modern discourse and that Horatio here seems to adopt. Aristotle writes that the good man (the only sort of man capable of friendship to begin with) "wishes for himself what is good and what seems so, and does it . . . and does so for his own sake . . . and he wishes himself to live and be preserved, and especially the element by virtue of which he thinks. For existence is good to the virtuous man . . . ."[16] Cicero, following Aristotle, writes that "every one loves himself . . . every one is dear to himself, and unless the same principle be transferred to friendship, no true friend will be ever found, for a friend is, as it were, a second self . . . [man] both loves himself, and seeks out another whose soul he may blend so intimately with his own, as to make almost one person out of two."[17]

Aristotle's own, earlier conception that a friend is like a second self is so encompassing that one cannot even perceive one's own existence without also perceiving the friend's existence.[18] The Aristotelian train of thought proceeds as follows:

> . . . if perceiving that one lives is in itself one of the things that are pleasant (for life is by nature good, and to perceive what is good present

> in oneself is pleasant); and if life is desirable, and particularly so for good men, because to them existence is good and pleasant (for they are pleased at the consciousness of the presence in them of what is in itself good; and if as the virtuous man is to himself, he is to his friend also (for his friend is another self)—if all this be true, as his own being is desirable for each man, so, or almost so, is that of his friend. Now his being was seen to be desirable because he perceived his own goodness, and such perception is pleasant in itself. He must, therefore, perceive the existence of his friend together with his own . . . . [19]

Hamlet's existence is remote from this. Often, he seeks neither to preserve himself nor to act virtuously, so he cannot form a friendship that approximates classical ideals. Hamlet remarks to Ophelia that he is "very proud, revengeful, ambitious; with more offences at my beck than I have thoughts to put them in, imagination to give them shape, or time to act them in. What should such fellows as I do crawling between earth and heaven?" (3.1.123–29). His claim might not be so sweeping in its applicability or so precise in its enumeration of his own faults, but still—and without wishing to be moralistic—Hamlet has a point. He is, to cite but one example, about to slaughter Polonius by accident and react with utter insouciance upon discovering his error.[20] Hamlet is not and cannot be good; his perception of his existence is not and cannot be pleasant. He is not enamored of the element by which he thinks and in relation to Horatio can hardly make one out of two, his claim to keep Horatio in his heart's core notwithstanding.[21] ("Give me that man/That is not passion's slave," Hamlet says, "and I will wear him/In my heart's core, ay, in my heart of heart,/As I do thee" [3.2.61–72].)

Given Hamlet's antic disposition, his propensity for abstraction, and his edginess to a lethal degree, we might justly ask how Horatio manages to be his friend at all.[22] Shakespeare ratifies, at any rate, the commonplace notion that friendships such as the one between Damon and Pithias are—at least—exceedingly rare. Aristotle writes that "it is natural that such friendships should be infrequent; for such men are rare,"[23] while Cicero observes that "in all the ages that have elapsed, scarcely three or four pairs of friends are enumerated."[24] Montaigne goes even further: "So many coincidences are needed to build up such a friendship," he claims, "that it is a lot if fortune can do it once in three centuries."[25] "In the practice of ordinary and customary friendships," Montaigne avers with reference to a possibly apocryphal quote, "we must use the remark that Aristotle often repeated: 'O my friends, there is no friend.'"[26]

Certainly this is so for *Hamlet*, if we employ classical standards. Yet it seems undeniable that the play contains friendship. Hamlet's case raises the question of what friendship is possible when classical grounds not only are unattainable, as is exceedingly common, but also cannot even be approximated. What form can friendship take when so many of its supposedly cardinal features—exemplary virtue and encouragement, sage counsel and sanctuary—are forced outside friendship's bounds? Horatio, of course, could be and has been said to embody or offer many of these things: he attempts to protect Hamlet, advising him about the Ghost and the likelihood that he will lose the wager against Laertes; he even (if Hamlet is at all to be believed)[27] embodies Stoic ideals of rational self-control. But Hamlet, for much of the play, bars Horatio from performing friendship's usual offices. Counsel, save in one instance, is anathema to him, and he vociferously dismisses efforts at saving him. Cicero writes that "most men preposterously . . . aspire to have a friend such as they themselves can never be; and expect from their friends allowances which they do not extend to them."[28] Hamlet has this aspiration, perhaps, yet does not demand special allowances from Horatio. He and Horatio are not equals, and so from an Aristotelian perspective their friendship could be equalized through a certain proportion, with Hamlet offering more material reward and Horatio more honor, but this is simply not what either is after.[29] Hamlet seemingly wants friendship—wants to wear Horatio in his heart—yet wants their relation grounded in something other than classical models for which friendship and selfhood are mutually reinforcing. With Horatio he seeks some other, more vexed ground on which friendship might exist.

Before I trace this ground's outlines, we should probably pause over the moment when Hamlet does accept counsel: when his friendship with Horatio might bear some resemblance to classical models. This moment occurs when Hamlet, thinking the Ghost may be a devil, stages *The Mousetrap*. "I'll have grounds," he insists, "More relative than this" and tasks Horatio with helping secure those grounds. "Observe my uncle," Hamlet asks him. "Give him heedful note; / For I mine eyes will rivet to his face; / And, after, we will both our judgments join / In censure of his seeming" (3.2.72–84). The play is performed, Hamlet calls Horatio "Damon," and they agree to "take the ghost's word for a thousand pound" (3.2.280–81). Horatio lends friendly support of a readily recognizable kind; as in the story of Damon and Pithias, an act of friendship secures a truth that promises to thwart political villainy, here by deposing Claudius and righting historical record. Critics have noted the complexity and variety of Hamlet's aims in staging the play but observation is, at the least, what he asks of Horatio and what the latter offers.[30] The reason the episode fits the classical model rather poorly is that it neither grants Hamlet much stability nor does much to reform the Danish polity—that, if anything, it accelerates the unraveling of both. So while this act of friendship perhaps has the possibility of being operative, that possibility remains unrealized.

The Truth about Friendship

Hamlet and Horatio's graveyard exchange indicates why friendship is bound to be inoperative. As Hamlet picks up Yorick's skull, the two continue a discussion about death: "Let me see," he says. "Alas, poor Yorick! I knew him, Horatio: a fellow of infinite jest, of most excellent fancy; he hath borne me on his back a thousand times. And now how abhorred in my imagination it is. My gorge rises at it . . ." (5.1.179–83). Hamlet's surprise suggests that he has, until now, assumed that memory preserves, that it can compensate for death and withhold the dead from oblivion through collective memory. From this vantage, memory matters, as does setting historical memory straight; but the moment he confronts Yorick's skull Hamlet abandons this vantage, abhorring the memory of having been borne on Yorick's back. Remembrance itself—the deception of preservation that it induces—becomes contemptible, a betrayal of truth.

Hamlet then asks Horatio about Alexander's fate, ruling out the possibility that it is only for base figures that physical rot also erodes the realms of memory. Hamlet negates imperial grandeur with the darkly humorous image of the loam Alexander became stopping a beer barrel:

> HAMLET. . . . Prithee, Horatio, tell me one thing.
> HORATIO. What's that, my lord?
> HAMLET. Dost thou think Alexander look'd a this fashion i' th' earth?
> HORATIO. E'en so.
> HAMLET. And smelt so? Pah!
> [*Throws down the skull.*]
> HORATIO. E'en so, my lord.
> HAMLET. To what base uses we may return, Horatio! Why may not imagination trace the noble dust of Alexander till 'a find it stopping a bung-hole?
> HORATIO. 'Twere to consider too curiously to consider so.
> HAMLET. No, faith, not a jot; but to follow him thither with modesty enough, and likelihood to lead it, as thus: Alexander died, Alexander was buried, Alexander returneth to dust; the dust is earth; of earth we make

> loam; and why of that loam whereto he was converted might they not stop a beer barrel?
> Imperious Caesar, dead and turn'd to clay,
> Might stop a hole to keep the wind away.
> O, that that earth which kept the world in awe
> Should patch a wall t'expel the winter's flaw!
> But soft! but soft! awhile. Here comes the King. (5.1.190–211)

This exchange is full of peculiarities. One is the terseness of Horatio's replies, almost as though Hamlet is Socrates and he an interlocutor, such that he, not Hamlet, is the one undergoing a realization. A second, related oddity is that Horatio bothers to respond once Hamlet casts away Yorick's skull; surely by now a question about the likely odor of Alexander's remains is rhetorical. "E'en so, my lord" is a strange affirmation—an instigation, even. Damon and Pithias's friendship inoculates against death both when they live and in posterity, when they exist as ideals. The graveyard exchange could hardly serve a more opposed purpose. Horatio, eschewing the protective rhetoric he employed on the ramparts at Elsinore, enables and even hastens Hamlet's morbid train of thought, to the point that his tepid objection about considering too curiously proves no impediment at all. For Damon and Pithias, proving friendship's truth secured their identities; here friendship's pursuit of truth dissolves all identity, indeed dissolves all boundaries save those that keep beer from flowing freely.

Of community's—a subset of which is friendship's—relationship to death, Jean-Luc Nancy writes that the former cannot work on the latter by negating or compensating for death. Rather,

> community is calibrated on death as on that of which it is precisely impossible to *make a work* . . . . Community occurs in order to acknowledge this impossibility, or more exactly—for there is neither function nor finality here—the impossibility of making a work out of death is inscribed and acknowledged as "community." . . . A community is the presentation to its members of their mortal truth.[31]

Blanchot, in broad accord with Nancy about what human relations can and cannot do with death, believes I err if I say, "I do not die because the community of which I am part (or the fatherland, or the universe, or humanity, or the family) goes on."[32] The graveyard scene bears out a similar insight: namely, that Hamlet and Horatio cannot make of death a work—as, in investigating Old Hamlet, they perhaps felt able to do. Yorick's identity is no less ruined in having passed away because Hamlet's Elsinore goes on;

Alexander's own fame cannot keep him from plugging a bunghole. Friends are unable to redeem mortal truth by transforming it into something else, unable to temper it in any way with pleasant or amazed reminiscence. Friendship in the graveyard indeed consists in a prolonged acknowledgment of this inability—in tracing Alexander's transformation from one dead thing into another.

That friendship operates in utter inoperativity is evident in a third peculiarity of the graveyard exchange: that Hamlet seems not to reach the end of the line of thought that he himself has set in motion. When he exclaims "O, that that earth which kept the world in awe / Should patch a wall t'expel the winter's flaw!" he seems not only distressed but even newly surprised by renown's futility in the face of decay, and wholly unaware of the paradox in his own description of Caesar as "that earth which kept the world in awe"; it is more strange that Caesar (earth) should awe a thing of which he was part (the world)—and from which he would have to be apart in order to awe—than that Caesar should become a patch in a wall. Through Hamlet's renewed amazement, Shakespeare discloses that their friendship cannot make a work of death by inducing a recognition that lasts, cannot do even this modest good.

Commenting on this scene, William Kerrigan writes that "what is peculiar, I think, is that [Hamlet] seems to be learning the most elementary truth about death (it comes to all, no matter how great) for the first time."[33] Here Kerrigan draws on A. C. Bradley's insight that for Hamlet the "fixed habitual look which the world wears for most men did not exist," that he "was for ever unmaking his world and rebuilding it in thought" and thus that for him "there were no old truths."[34] In thinking through death, to be sure, friendship cannot foster self-development—cannot create a store of wisdom—but instead forms part of what Goethe long ago saw as Hamlet's failed *Bildungsroman*.[35] Further, while Horatio's position formally resembles that of a Socratic interlocutor—that is, of someone developing—the position is evacuated; he betrays no surprise, seems to assent not to an idea newly brought to consciousness but to what he already believes and has ignored for quotidian existence. Their shared acknowledgment of oblivion fails to yield the calm that Hamlet later evinces in the "Let be" speech, fails even to yield an improved knowledge state. Friendship means only that they do not have to confront the grim truth alone and that the truth of final ruin always will feel new; realization of this "fine revolution"—of each fine pate full of fine dirt—will not shed its intensity (5.1.88).

Hamlet and Horatio's friendship occurs in, not in spite of, their perishing and their imperfection. In the play's final scene, this truth about friendship raises a question about whether a choice between truth and friendship is inevitable, the answer to which conditions the politics of friendship imaginable in *Hamlet*. As Hamlet dies of poisoning and asks his friend to influence how he is remembered, his knowledge state still seems stunted, as if the graveyard scene never occurred. "Horatio," he declares, "I am dead: / Thou livest; report me and my cause aright / To the unsatisfied" (5.2.330–32). This first request may or may not be ethically unsavory; reporting Hamlet's cause "aright" could mean reporting that cause truthfully—dispelling vicious rumors that are sure to circulate—but also could mean reporting the cause as though it were righteous, suppressing repellent elements of Hamlet's character and action.

Shakespeare discourages any immediate puzzling through of this ambiguity, though, by giving Horatio some surprising lines—"Never believe it," he answers, "I am more an antique Roman than a Dane; / Here's yet some liquor left" (5.2.332–34)—that raise other, connected questions. First, what is the "it" that Hamlet ought never to believe? Simply that Horatio is willing to outlive his friend? That anyone will be unsatisfied with Hamlet's behavior or that, contrariwise, anyone could believe an account of that behavior that does not include an element of censoriousness? Shakespeare does not clue us in. "Never believe it," so vaguely declarative, after numerous readings can acquire the resonance of a proverb akin to "Question Authority." But, considering the vacuity of Polonius's earlier precepts ("Neither a borrower nor a lender be," "to thine own self be true," etc.), "Never believe it" is unlikely to appear on page one of my personal diary.

Horatio, in any case, believes friendship requires of him something other than what Hamlet asks. It requires not a Danish form of life, focused on court politics, circuits of rumor, and so on, but an ancient Roman one fixated on noble self-killing. Horatio wants to practice a friendship purified of the corrupt flattery of a court quickly filling with corpses; he wants to lose himself in friendship. As he sees it, the choice is between a degraded form of decay and an exalted one. Friendship is an acknowledgment of mortal truth and as a friend Horatio means to embody that truth.

The changed Horatio of the graveyard scene again appears—this, despite the recurrence, some moments earlier, of a protective gesture ("If your mind dislike anything," he advises Hamlet prior to the duel, "obey it. I will forestall their repair hither, and say you are not fit" [5.2.209–10]). While Hamlet is dying there also recurs a stark opposition between his understanding of friendship and Horatio's, only now their places are exchanged. Hamlet champions friendship as serving preservative purposes (he wants Horatio to shield his name against wounds) whereas Horatio seeks to prove friendship by sending himself into the oblivion from which, earlier, he sought to save Hamlet. But Hamlet insists; with strength enough to wrest the poisoned cup from Horatio's hand, he reiterates his request:

> As th'art a man,
> Give me the cup. Let go. By heaven, I'll ha't.
> O God! Horatio, what a wounded name,
> Things standing thus unknown, shall live behind me!
> If thou didst ever hold me in thy heart,
> Absent thee from felicity awhile,
> And in this harsh world draw thy breath in pain,
> To tell my story . . .
> (*Hamlet dies.*) (5.2.334–41)

Hamlet, a regicide, does not want to be remembered as a traitor and villain. He wants an unknown truth—Claudius's own treason—made known. Whether he wants Horatio to tell all that he knows is a separate question. Given the blithe unconcern with which Hamlet kills Polonius, the brutality with which he verbally assaults Ophelia, and the ease with which he dispatches Rosencrantz and Guildenstern, I cannot imagine how Horatio could tell Hamlet's story in good faith without wounding his friend's name. Hamlet asks not that Horatio tell as unbiased a story as he is able but that he tell "my story"—his version of that story, in which he is not responsible for the demise of Polonius, Ophelia, or his old friends. "If Hamlet from himself be ta'en away," he earlier explains, "And when he's not himself that does wrong Laertes, / Then Hamlet does it not" (5.1.226–28).[36] Hamlet asks Horatio to prove friendship, and preserve his friend's legacy, at least partly through deliberate dishonesty. Commitments to friendship and to truth seem very much at odds.

Earlier I invoked the pseudo-Aristotelian utterance "O my friends there is no friend!" as pertinent to *Hamlet*. Given this, it is unsurprising, and perhaps even inevitable, that a tension would exist between friendship and truth, that Hamlet in his imperfection would ask Horatio to choose between the two. If good—close—friends need not be good men, friends might well ask friends to distort the truth about each other and to disregard the import of mortal truth. In asking Horatio to ensure the integrity of his friend's identity, Hamlet also asks Horatio to undergo a rather disreputable self-sacrifice.

Horatio thus must decide whether to adhere to another pseudo-Aristotelian utterance: namely, "Plato is my friend, but truth is my better friend." Heller, who also invokes these utterances, claims *Hamlet* as an example of how no choice need be made between friendship and truth—a claim, I think, not very amenable to the text.[37] Aristotle's choice of truth over his teacher, Plato, implies the inevitability of the sort of choice now faced by Horatio. Heller points out that the history of philosophy can be understood as the history of betrayal—of choosing truth and so of exposing the flaws of one's predecessors—and Horatio also faces a choice in relating his friend's history. Hamlet frames the situation such that Horatio can commit to truth or to friendship but not to both.

Horatio's penultimate speech best indicates where his commitments lie. An English ambassador enters and, having related that Rosencrantz and Guildenstern are dead, asks from whom they will have thanks. "Not from his mouth," Horatio replies,

> Had it th-ability of life to thank you:
> He never gave commandment for their death.
> But since, so jump upon this bloody question,
> You from the Polack wars, and you from England,
> Are here arrived, give order that these bodies
> High on a stage be placed to the view;
> And let me speak to th' yet unknowing world
> How these things came about. So shall you hear
> Of carnal, bloody, and unnatural acts;
> Of accidental judgments, casual slaughters;
> Of deaths put on by cunning and forc'd cause;
> And, in this upshot, purposes mistook
> Fall'n on th' inventors' heads—all this can I
> Truly deliver. (5.2.364–78)

Perhaps Horatio can truly deliver all of this, though it is unclear if this is truth. Horatio says nothing obviously false, but he does begin with some obfuscation; he remarks only that Claudius did not order the deaths of Rosencrantz and Guildenstern—and thus conceals Hamlet's role in their execution. Yet as he continues Horatio appears to side less wholeheartedly with his friend.[38] While he emphasizes Claudius's unnatural murder, and while he uses twenty words to note the cunning by which Laertes and the king inadvertently did in almost everyone, Horatio also mentions "accidental judgments" and "casual slaughters"—which, of course, conjures the death of Polonius.[39]

Horatio may absolve Hamlet on several scores, but he does draw attention to Hamlet's culpability in at least one instance. Horatio implies he knows that Hamlet mistook Polonius for Claudius and deems the slaughtering "casual." According to the *Oxford English Dictionary*, "casual" in the seventeenth century can mean "accidental" or "produced by chance" but also "unmethodical, haphazard, 'happy go lucky.'"[40] Horatio suggests that Hamlet's pass through the arras was both; presumably "casual" does not mean only "accidental," which Horatio has just used, and his words bring to mind Hamlet's unconcern about his error as well as suggest that this unconcern somehow changes the nature of a killing not initially intended as casual in any sense. Hamlet ascribes so little value to Polonius's life that Polonius effectively *is* dead in the prince's mind: the Lord Chamberlain's literal death merely manifests what Hamlet thinks of him to begin with. Killing Polonius by accident does not make the killing any less the expression of a flawed character. Horatio's speech registers this. Indeed, given that Polonius's death is listed as but one element in a heap of violent acts, none of which Horatio assigns to discrete agents, it is unclear with what degree of clarity—let alone in what condition—Hamlet's identity will emerge in Horatio's telling.

Thus I strain to resolve the issue of whether Horatio chooses friendship or truth and I can only imagine how vexed a full accounting of Hamlet's history would be. To the degree that Horatio conceals his friend's ill deeds, he chooses Hamlet, and to the degree that he brings these deeds to light, he chooses truth. Horatio moves between models of friendship, seeking to safeguard Hamlet's name yet also wounding that name. If truth is paramount, it seems unconscionable that Horatio would absolve Hamlet for sending old friends to their deaths, and Hamlet might well turn in his grave, were he in one, to hear Horatio describe his casual slaughter. Rather than achieving a just balance between friendship and truth, Horatio vitiates his commitments to both.[41]

In so doing, Horatio is undone.[42] These commitments have held Horatio's identity together—indeed, has that identity had another element of much significance?—so that now he seems wildly destabilized. Even drinking from the poisoned cup would have left his identity less unsettled; cementing his unexplained transformation from the prudent, risk-averse Horatio of act 1, drinking would also cement his identity as so devoted a friend as to have no existence in that friend's absence. As Michael Neill observes, "it is part of the play's cruelty (or Hamlet's egotism) . . . that Horatio is not allowed to proceed to the extremity of sentimental consolation promised by suicide."[43]

We know so little about Horatio that, figuratively speaking, he has seemed to exist for Hamlet—to exist in relation to him; by keeping Horatio from figural oblivion, in one respect Hamlet *is* a kind of Pithias.[44] After the cup is taken from him, Horatio becomes incoherent, not filled with conflicting ideas or emotions, as complex Shakespearean characters are said to be, but instead broken by a psychic caesura. Horatio is hardly flat in the sense that Damon and Pithias are, but his subjectivity does not seem rich so much as riven.

For him, brokenness is friendship's consequence. Cicero, in one sense unlike Aristotle, often remarks on how friendship can be overwhelming. Friendship, for him, "will inevitably involve distress, and quite often at that," though the distress here is that of shared suffering, not of thorny ethical situations such as the one that Horatio is in; for Cicero, too, only good men can be good friends.[45] In our own context Judith Butler also writes that vulnerability is friendship's inevitable—but also its potentially valuable—outcome. We are, she writes, "attached to others, at risk of losing those attachments, exposed to others, at risk of violence by virtue of that exposure"; "we're undone by each other . . . and if we're not, we're missing something."[46]

Horatio's career shows how attachments pull us apart and how any politics of friendship must account for this: for the extreme difficulty involved in friendship itself and in making friendship scalable, indeed in combining personal and more broadly social commitments—here, to Hamlet and to justice—in any way whatsoever. Horatio does not provide a perfect model for such combination and Shakespeare seems unsure as to the form a more operative combination might take. After all, his interest in *Hamlet* is in the inoperative. The play's central friendship thereby implies an indefinite politics, one definitely unlike the politics suggested by the story of Damon and Pithias, unlike the politics that Lupton finds intimations of in *Hamlet* and that others find more fully in Shakespeare. The story of Damon and Pithias implies a certain, and certainly an optimistic, political style—one in which, for instance, a monarch should submit to counsel and should not arbitrarily exercise emergency power. The politics of their friendship is one of protection and empowerment, one that assumes friendship's boundless force as well as our own infinite capacity for improvement. Hamlet and Horatio's story implies nothing so confident or definite.

Butler argues that when we fail to see how we undo each other—and how a politics of friendship must accommodate undoing—we overlook the opportunity to reflect on how to inhabit our vulnerability rather than construct imaginary worlds, such as that of Damon and Pithias, in which friendship by its power suffuses the polity and in so doing rules vulnerability out. Politics, for Butler, instead should proceed under the assumption that vulnerability cannot be eradicated; for her, politics fails so long as its project is to minimize our susceptibility to others. The political project suggested by *Hamlet* cannot be of this kind, as the play's world is a wound that will always be open.

The intimations we have are of a much more basic project. There is undeniable sublimity in Horatio's still living, in his speaking at all so soon after seeking to kill himself. In a lacerated state, he asks to appear before an as yet unknowing world, to do so "even while men's minds are wild, lest more mischance / On plots and errors happen" (5.2.386–87). His wish to appear amid devastation staggers me. Shakespeare gives no reason to think that his speech will heal Denmark's wounds in any lasting sense, but he does give cause to admire Horatio's wish to forestall needless violence. In a tragic world, such a modest wish—such a minimal politics—may be the only kind imaginable.

For Hamlet and Horatio, friendship is the presentation of mortal truth in all its intensity, is their facing how impossible it is to make of death a work. Horatio stands as an example of life that goes on, broken, burdened by Hamlet's dying request that he deny this impossibility while in its very midst. Horatio's example forces me to take seriously the precariousness of all human lives and political forms and prompts me to imagine how precarious lives might be lived because they must be lived.

NOTES

1. All quotations of the play are from William Shakespeare, *Hamlet*, ed. R. B. Kennedy (London: Harper Press, 2011).

2. Robert C. Evans makes this point in "Friendship in Hamlet," *Comparative Drama* 33, no. 1 (1999): 88–124, 112. Evans notes, rightly if briefly, that both Damon and Pithias and Hamlet and Horatio are working against a tyrant, then moves on.

3. All quotations of Edwards's play are from the 1571 version, *The Excellent Comedie of Two the Moste Faithfullest Freendes, Damon and Pithias*, held at the Huntington Library in San Marino, California.

4. See Thomas A. Spragens Jr., "Civic Friendship in Liberal Society," in *Civic Liberalism: Reflections on Our Democratic Ideals*, 175–212 (Oxford: Rowman and Littlefield, 1999).

5. Robert Stretter points out that when ideals of classical friendship made their way onto the early modern stage, those ideals became the subjects of "often scathing mockery." See Robert Stretter, "Cicero on Stage: *Damon and Pithias* and the Fate of Classical Friendship in English Renaissance Drama," *Texas Studies in Literature and Language* 47, no. 4 (2005): 345–65, 346.

6. See James Kuzner, *Open Subjects: English Renaissance Republicans, Modern Selfhoods, and the Virtue of Vulnerability* (Edinburgh: Edinburgh University Press, 2011), esp. 44–56.

7. See Christopher Warley, "Specters of Horatio," *ELH* 75, no. 4 (2008): 1023–50.

8. Agnes Heller, "The Beauty of Friendship," *South Atlantic Quarterly* 97, no. 1 (1998): 5–22, 19, 21.

9. Ibid., 22.

10. Julia Reinhard Lupton, "The Hamlet Elections," in *Thinking with Shakespeare: Essays on Politics and Life*, 69–95 (Chicago: University of Chicago Press, 2011), 80, 86.

11. The list here is quite long, but some principal texts are Annabel Patterson, *Shakespeare and the Popular Voice* (Oxford: Basil Blackwell, 1989); Laurie Shannon, *Sovereign Amity: Figures of Friendship in Shakespearean Contexts* (Chicago: University of Chicago Press, 2002); and Andrew Hadfield, *Shakespeare and Republicanism* (Cambridge: Cambridge University Press, 2005).

12. Jonathan Goldberg, *Endlesse Worke: Spenser and the Structures of Discourse* (Baltimore, MD: Johns Hopkins University Press, 1981), 86, 103.

13. Blanchot, Butler, and Nancy I discuss below. The most relevant text of Jacques Derrida's is *The Politics of Friendship*, trans. George Collins (London: Verso, 1997).

14. The text forces readers to take the threat particularly seriously because, as Karen Newman points out, "Horatio is the one character in the play with whom Hamlet does not contend." See Karen Newman, "Two Lines, Three Readers: *Hamlet*, TLN 1904–5," *Shakespeare Quarterly* 62, no. 2 (2011): 263–70, 269.

15. Peter Holbrook argues that it is through being outside shared space that Hamlet, in a way worth praising, achieves selfhood: "Hamlet's self is not the passive product of an intersubjective discourse (and therefore nugatory and contemptible). Instead it is remote, dignified and precious and, as a result, *worth fighting for*." Holbrook implicitly positions friendship and selfhood as antithetical, though in a way that valorizes selfhood and that, thus, is not particularly interested in relationships such as Hamlet and Horatio's. See Peter Holbrook, *Shakespeare's Individualism* (Cambridge: Cambridge University Press, 2010), 68.

16. Aristotle, *Nicomachean Ethics*, 2nd ed., trans. David Ross (Oxford: Oxford University Press, 2009), 168.

17. Cicero, *De Senectute et De Amicitia*, trans. William Lewers (Dublin: William B. Kelly, 1850), 63–64.

18. For a fascinating take on the perception of the friend and its consequences for politics, see Giorgio Agamben, "The Friend," in *What Is an*

Apparatus?, trans. David Kishik and Stefan Pedatella, 25–37 (Stanford, CA: Stanford University Press, 2009).

19. Aristotle, *Nicomachean Ethics*, 178.

20. G. Wilson Knight is not wrong to say, as others have, that Hamlet "takes a devilish joy in cruelty towards the end of the play." See G. Wilson Knight, "The Embassy of Death: An Essay on *Hamlet*," in *The Wheel of Fire: Interpretations of Shakespearian Tragedy with Three New Essays*, 17–46 (London: Methuen & Co., 1949), 27.

21. Stanley Cavell suggests that we can even find in Hamlet a "refusal of participation in the world." See "Hamlet's Burden of Proof," in *Disowning Knowledge: In Seven Plays of Shakespeare*, 179–91 (Cambridge: Cambridge University Press, 2003), 188.

22. Margreta de Grazia, in a well-known recent study, shows how Hamlet can be and has been likened to the roustabout clown of the medieval folk tradition. Roustabout clowns tend not to have close friendships. See Margreta de Grazia, *"Hamlet" without Hamlet* (Cambridge: Cambridge University Press, 2007).

23. Aristotle, *Nicomachean Ethics*, 146.

24. Cicero, *De Amicitia*, 41.

25. Michel de Montaigne, *The Complete Essays of Montaigne*, trans. Donald Frame (Stanford, CA: Stanford University Press, 1958), 136.

26. Ibid., 140.

27. And perhaps he is not, as Warley points out. "Hamlet's words certainly cannot be construed as an objective account of who Horatio really is." Warley, "Specters of Horatio," 1033.

28. Cicero, *De Amicitia*, 64.

29. Aristotle, *Nicomachean Ethics*, 161.

30. Paul Kottman, for example, has argued that Hamlet "wants a scene" as much as he wants proof, while Lars Engle writes that Hamlet aims to "cease trying to anchor [his] behavior on either inner or outer certainties, and instead will seek to ground it on observation, probability, morality, desire, and so forth." See Paul Kottman, *A Politics of the Scene* (Stanford, CA: Stanford University Press, 2008), 161, and Lars Engle, *Shakespearean Pragmatism: Market of His Time* (Chicago: University of Chicago Press, 1993), 70.

31. Jean-Luc Nancy, *The Inoperative Community*, trans. Peter Connor (Minneapolis: University of Minnesota Press, 1991), 15.

32. Maurice Blanchot, *The Unavowable Community*, trans. Pierre Joris (Barrytown, NY: Station Hill Press, 1988), 10.

33. William Kerrigan, *Hamlet's Perfection* (Baltimore, MD: Johns Hopkins University Press, 1994), 12.

34. A. C. Bradley, *Shakespearean Tragedy* (New York: Meridian Books, 1955), 98.

35. See the excerpt from *Wilhelm Meister* in *Hamlet: Critical Essays*, ed. Joseph G. Brice (New York: Garland Publishing, 1986), 503–6.

36. For an excellent account of how Hamlet, in saying this, may or may not be sincere and of "Shakespeare's sense of the lack of access that persons normally have to the actual springs of their own behavior," see Richard Strier, "Excuses, Bepissing, and Non-being: Shakespearean Puzzles about Agency," in *Shakespeare and Moral Agency*, ed. Michael Bristol, 55–68 (London: Continuum, 2010).

37. Heller writes that

> Horatio is telling his best friend's story while placing that friend in the draft of being where truth appears. What is the truth of Hamlet's story? It is what Horatio presents as the truth about Hamlet. He loves Hamlet, so his truth is the truth of love; he is a just man, so his truth is also the truth of justice. He does what the dying Hamlet asks him to do. After Hamlet's death, Horatio takes on the greatest of burdens—the burden of surviving his best friend. And the only thing that makes him carry this burden for a little longer is the need to tell Hamlet's story, truthfully, as his friend has asked him to do. (Heller, "The Beauty of Friendship," 21)

38. "To judge by this summary," David Lucking writes, "the tale that Horatio intends bears little resemblance to what the prince has in mind," a tale in which Hamlet is likely to be "an agent of destruction swept up in a whirlwind of fortuitous happenings." While I think Lucking overstates the case a bit here, his point has merit. David Lucking, "*Hamlet* and the Narrative Construction of Reality," *English Studies* 89, no. 2 (2008): 152–65, 155.

39. Of lines 373–78, James Shapiro writes that "Horatio's words underscore much he has failed to grasp about his friend," that "the same could as easily be said of *Titus Andronicus*." That Horatio is incapable of presenting a full or even an accurate account of his friend's story I would never deny. The question is whether he intends to aspire toward such an account. See James Shapiro, *1599: A Year in the Life of William Shakespeare* (London: Faber, 2005), 299.

40. *Oxford English Dictionary Online*, s.v. "casual."

41. Lars Engle argues that Horatio does embody a balance of this kind, that he is possessed of a "detached attachment": that Horatio is "able to take a disinterested, nonstakeholder's attitude toward what one is thinking about"—not in any absolute sense but as a "relative virtue." See Lars Engle, "How Is

Horatio Just?: How Just Is Horatio?," *Shakespeare Quarterly* 62, no. 2 (2002): 256–62, 259, 262.

42. Timothy Wong, in an argument similar to Lupton's, argues that "Horatio ends up as the most sovereign character in the kingdom when the curtain falls," because he "take[s] charge of the only remaining sovereign right at the end of the play, the dying voice of the prince." This formal sovereignty may exist, but I would maintain that Horatio feels nothing of it. See Timothy Wong, "Steward of the Dying Voice: The Intrusion of Horatio into Sovereignty and Representation," *Telos* 153 (Winter 2010): 113–31, 113.

43. Michael Neill, "'He That Thou Knowest Thine': Friendship and Service in *Hamlet*," in *A Companion to Shakespeare's Works: The Tragedies*, ed. Richard Dutton and Jean E. Howard, 319–38 (Oxford: Blackwell, 2003), 333.

44. Francis G. Schoff, in something of an overstatement, calls Horatio a "nobody." See Francis G. Schoff, "Horatio: A Shakespearean Confidant," *Shakespeare Quarterly* 7, no. 1 (1956): 53–57, 55.

45. Cicero, *De Amicitia*, 203.

46. Judith Butler, *Precarious Life: The Powers of Mourning and Violence* (New York: Verso, 2004), 20, 23.

CHAPTER 6

"Racked . . . to the Uttermost": The Verges of Love and Subjecthood in *The Merchant of Venice*

Lara Bovilsky

For some time now, criticism has taken *The Merchant of Venice*'s Antonio for an exemplary character: that is, his depiction has been argued to reveal representative early modern values associated with a wide variety of roles and phenomena. In these arguments, Antonio exemplifies the friend, the competition between homosociality and heteronormativity, the psychology and sociology of the emergence of venture capitalism, and, more recently, concepts as large as the differences between the individual and larger groups that generate ethical and political formations, and the content and operations of modern subjectivity itself. By contrast, in this essay I take as my starting point the inverse premise: Antonio has the most to offer early modern sexuality studies through analysis of the atypical and distinctive features of his sexual, affective, and economic depiction. I look briefly at his relationships with Bassanio and Shylock in order to offer an Antonio who does not exemplify trends in his culture (whether imagined as Venetian or Elizabethan) but rather one who enlarges our sense of the possibilities for agency and teleology within male friendship. I argue that Antonio's masochistic and other self-directed drives yield idiosyncratic forms of queer friendship, enmity, and subjectivity. These, in turn, are sufficiently unfettered by social and even humanistic conventions (such as expectations of self-care or obligations to the state) that they work to undermine the primary institutions represented in the play. I read Antonio, that is, as an anomaly but no less valuable for that in shedding light on the play's dynamics and concerns and in further clarifying the range within and tensions among early modern social and economic forms.

I therefore assert the value in identifying affective and queer idiosyncrasy as such and in noting the corrosive friction between Antonio's particular idiosyncrasy and the cultural, political, and economic institutions in which his character participates. Attending to both bonds and antagonisms linking the unusual and the representative, I take cues from analytics developed and modeled by Eve Kosofsky Sedgwick and Jonathan Goldberg. With Sedgwick, as beautifully described by Lauren Berlant, I affirm the value of parsing texts in order to locate "avowed and disavowed patterns of . . . desire, and then [to] understand[] those repetitions in terms of a story about sexuality that does not exist yet as a convention or an identity . . . the persistence of sexually anomalous attachment figures as the social potential of queerness, in which what counts is not one's 'object choice' as such but rather one's sustaining attachments, which are only sometimes also one's social relations."[1] I resist reading Antonio as instantiating the established cultural "convention[s] or . . . identit[ies]" brought to bear by recent criticism focused on the significance of his character. Likewise, as I will argue, reductive focus on the sex *tout court* of Antonio's object choice in the person of Bassanio, rather than on the representation of Antonio's desires for his treatment by Bassanio and his intimate relationships with other characters (Shylock in particular), has limited the usefulness and purchase of analyses of his sexuality. Investigation of the "anomalous" features of Antonio's attachments does not, however, reveal them as "sustaining" in any usual sense. Rather, Antonio repeatedly stresses the importance of total self-sacrifice in service to the desires of his beloved, wishing to be stretched to, or beyond, a limit he calls his "uttermost." Moreover, pursuit of his and his beloved's desires entails subordination of all other values and, therefore, can work to the harm of others. As we will see, Antonio's actions are in tension not just with institutions like marriage (as has been much remarked) but also with features of mercantilism and capitalism, the fortunes of Venice itself, and with conventional understandings of friendship and enmity. In entertaining fantasies of indifference or aggression to such institutions by representing Antonio's plot, the play registers and investigates resistance to them.

The role of male bonds in such resistance to central early modern English institutions and values is explored in Jonathan Goldberg's powerful chapter on "The Transvestite Stage" in *Sodometries*. In that chapter, Goldberg argues against the heterosexist frame within which most prior critics tended to read Elizabethan drama and the male-male relations therein. To offer another model, Goldberg analyzes the writings of Christopher Marlowe, writings that reveal both the general influence of authorized eroticized male-male bonds throughout the culture and the potential for political and social fracture found in male friendships. In this way, Marlowe's texts help delineate partly contradictory Elizabethan cultural logics according to which male bonds might be seen as at once integral and perilous to central institutions. As Goldberg shows, though, Marlowe's plays' male bonds do not themselves fully mirror those representative logics. Remarkable in a culture in which sodomy seems to have been "the word for everything illicit," Marlowe's work presents sodomy as a resource for the most valorized of Marlovian subjects: characters' agency and will.[2] As we will see, Marlowe is not alone in representing robust operations of agency and will in the service of male bonds and directed at culturally unsanctioned goals—if not in any predictably self-affirming or -stabilizing way.

Indeed, Goldberg argues that Marlovian sodomy does not catalyze something as coherent, stabilizing, or static as a character's "identity" in the modern sense; rather, "the identity that Marlowe gives to the sodomite is a fully negativized one against which there is no positivity to be measured."[3] Marlovian sodomy nonetheless enables "something like what Foucault calls sexuality" by delineating broad cultural spaces outside of regimes of marriage and inheritance for exertions of the will.[4] In his conclusion, Goldberg calls for future work that would use "what Marlowe makes available" in order to reassess what other period texts can tell us about the sex/gender system, renouncing all critical presumptions about that system.[5] The goal is to transform our understanding of sexuality and power relations in Elizabethan drama via new readings of friendship. "Even Shakespeare," Goldberg writes, "would be implicated" in this reassessment; he goes on to list numerous specific male friendships in Shakespearean plays whose analysis in these terms could enlarge our sense of the significances of male-male sexuality, existing both in culturally valorized forms and in those transgressing and disrupting cultural norms.[6]

The first example on Goldberg's list of potentially paradigm-shifting friendships is *The Merchant of Venice*'s Antonio and Bassanio. Goldberg offers a capsule reading of *Merchant*, focusing on Portia as the face of the play's conflicted handling of the friends and their intersections with systems governing sex and gender.[7] Portia "deform[s]" patriarchy by serving "in the father's place." However, ultimately she sustains "regimes of alliance close to those of heterosexual privilege"; her rescue of Antonio "police[s]" and "separate[s]" him from Bassanio. "At the end of the play," Goldberg concludes, "Portia is in the father's place and the wife's, but not the friend's."[8]

My own analysis turns to "the friend's place" as it is filled by Antonio, paired not just with Bassanio but also with Shylock. The two pairings are important because, as we will see, together they reveal surprising similarities and crossings between Antonio's relationships. Antonio transforms elements of conventional friendship until friendship resembles enmity in its effects—not just being willing, for instance, to sacrifice on behalf of Bassanio but encouraging Bassanio to make demands that would lead to painful sacrifice—and does the same with hatred, rooting it in mutual emotion and in thorough, intimate knowledge of the enemy. Both friend and enemy are recruited to further the other's relationship: Bassanio's monetary needs provide Shylock with a means to harm Antonio; Shylock's loan increases Bassanio's affective and financial debts to Antonio. The resultant asymmetries in intensity and suffering within the Bassanio-Antonio relationship make it an outlier friendship for the period, even as it continues to be classed as friendship and love by Antonio and other characters in the play.

The play offers a pointed framing of this friendship as at odds with cultural conventions of friendship in its accommodation of unlikeness and asymmetry. To underscore the discrepancy between cultural wisdom and *Merchant*'s example, typical discourses of friendship in the period are even incorporated into the play, cited by Portia herself as she determines to follow Bassanio to Venice. Portia takes it as axiomatic that friends are characterized by intense and multiform likeness and by a mutual, evenly weighed amity.[9] She therefore assumes that Antonio will embody "a like proportion" (i.e., symmetrical or harmonious likeness)[10] to Bassanio's "lineaments . . . manners and . . . spirit," that is, his physical features, characteristic demeanor, and nature:

> . . . in companions . . .
> Whose souls do bear an equal yoke of love,
> There must be needs a like proportion
> Of lineaments, of manners and of spirit;

Which makes me think that this Antonio
Being the bosom lover of my lord,
Must needs be like my lord. (3.4.11–18)[11]

Portia's list of the emphatically plural likenesses that the "equal . . . love" "must . . . needs" entail is typical of the period's assumptions about friends, and yet the play repeatedly distinguishes between Antonio and Bassanio along these very axes. For example, soon after Portia's musings, differences in the friends' manners and spirit appear to her (and the reader's or audience member's) very eyes when Bassanio makes a blunt offer of three thousand ducats to "Balthazar" (Portia in disguise) for services rendered at the close of the trial scene (4.1.407–8).[12] Seemingly startled by the starkness of Bassanio's strictly tangible, fee-for-service model, Antonio quickly makes a figurative and idealistic addition to the pecuniary thanks, insisting that Bassanio is wrong and that their debt may not be repaid: "And [we] stand indebted, over and above, / In love and service to you evermore" (4.1.409–10). Bassanio's quantification and monetization of emotion (gratitude as literal payment) and Antonio's insistence on a rhetorically infinite emotion presented alongside this (ongoing payment *in* gratitude), figured as a nondischargeable debt existing on another plane ("over and above") than the material, are each characteristic, as are the brashness and the earnest display of bonding with which the respective offers are made.

Bassanio and Antonio's relationship accommodates differences, then, in manners and spirit, as well as in degree and profession, and also in the proportionate weight pulled by each within the supposedly "equal yoke of love" itself: in lines that will be discussed at greater length below, Bassanio admits he "owe[s]" Antonio "the most . . . in love."[13] It should be less surprising, then, that while the presence of a male couple gives *Merchant* pride of place on Goldberg's Shakespearean list, whose rubric is "the relations between friends" in the plural, Antonio himself has disproportionately occupied the attention of critics tracking representations of queerness and friendship in the play.[14] My sense is that this fact testifies to some of Antonio's distinctive representational features without, however, these having often been taken up in recent criticism. This was not always the case. Over the last thirty years, predominantly historicist scholarship has generally centered its analysis on culturally illustrative examples, choosing to favor the representative case study over the contingent or exceptional one.[15] By contrast, early critical treatments of Antonio's portrayal and relationship to Bassanio—and these go further back than one might have expected—

tend to take advantage of their eras' premiums on descriptive particularity and analysis of character as desirable interpretive ends in emphasizing his specificity and representation as unusual.

For instance, E. K. Chambers's introduction to the play in 1904 echoes the play's own sore-thumb foregrounding of Antonio by likewise opening on the subject of his unresolved incongruity with the play's tone: "the melancholy of Antonio is a perpetual undertone . . . it claims your pondering in the first significant words of the play; nor is its meaning, there or elsewhere, clearly or explicitly set forth."[16] For Chambers, Antonio's portrayal is "out of harmony" with the rest of the play to the extent that he assumes it is ultimately intended not for the audience or play at all but instead as a kind of solace to Shakespeare, a "secret consolation of his private trouble" in the perhaps unlikely form of "an echo of those disturbed relations in his private life."[17] Though he therefore sees Antonio as "echo[ing]" a historical and psychological singularity rather than as an exemplar of a central early modern institution (eroticized friendship), Chambers does resemble a century's worth of subsequent critical accounts of Antonio in assimilating representations of Antonio's opening "sad[ness]" (1.1.1) and queerness, with the result that queerness is assumed to occasion a dysphoric frustration, isolation, and rejection.

If criticism sensitive to issues of queer sexuality in *Merchant* begins with Chambers at the turn of the twentieth century, it takes off starting in the 1960s by first timidly, then less timidly, reading Antonio's feelings for Bassanio as romantic, homosexual, gay, homosocial, erotic, or as hybrids of the above (e.g., "homoerotic amity").[18] But overwhelmingly, the point of access to what we might call Antonio's investment in Bassanio is not the context or nature of their friendship. Nor is the mere existence of a male friendship bond the cue: these critics generally do not read that other, less separable pair in the play, Salanio and Salarino, as romantically linked.[19] Instead, critics seize on Antonio's opening declarations that he is both sad and at pains to know the cause of his sadness.[20] Thus, in this work, Antonio's opening sadness has almost uniformly been reductively and, I would argue, punitively linked to his sexuality, itself also generally reductively imagined. This link casts sadness as the defining state of an anachronistically understood or thwarted homosexuality; Antonio is sad, read to mean "lovelorn," "disappointed," "frustrated," or even self-despising, such readings went (and still go), because he is experiencing a subconscious or inexpressible desire for Bassanio that is fundamentally out of place, even impossible, in a world dominated by a seemingly unquestionable heteronormativity.[21]

The assumption that same-sex desire is unavailable in Venice can be used to explain Antonio's putative confusion about his sadness, thereby resolving the nagging epistemological or motivational problems arising from Antonio's "ado to know [him]self" (1.1.6). Readings connecting Antonio's sexuality and confusion effectively argue or assume that Antonio's sadness results not only from failure and lack, from feeling unrequited or unrequitable passion, but also from proleptically embodying an identity whose time has not yet come. Surprisingly, such readings did not stop with the appearance of work by Alan Bray, Eve Kosofsky Sedgwick, Jonathan Goldberg, Jeffrey Masten, and many others, which showed just how timely male same-sex bonds, desires, and expressions were.[22] For instance, Steve Patterson's article on *Merchant* acts as though such work had never happened: "the present understandings of the ways that same- and cross-sex passions mattered in early modern England are still confused enough to allow for a convincing reading of Antonio as a prototype of the lovesick homosexual."[23] Note Patterson's "prototype," as if Antonio represents a quasi-evolutionary leap, a result of punctuated equilibrium in the evolution of sexuality. Invoking a "prototype" of what is referenced as a familiar modern category also spares the labor of engaging Antonio's specificity. In this reading, Antonio is simultaneously alone in his identity (a prototype) and what even Patterson refers to as a "modern cliché" (the "lovesick homosexual").[24] Moreover, he is awkwardly poised temporally—too soon to be homosexual but also "sadly outmoded" as "amorous friend," as "his society . . . re-evaluat[es] its definitions of love."[25] An even more recent version of such a reading is found in Arthur Little's essay on *Merchant* in Madhavi Menon's *Shakesqueer*; Little reads Antonio's speech as "mourning": "to be sure, he mourns the impending loss of Bassanio, but he mourns, too, a loss of an affirmative language and knowledge of his social and institutional place."[26]

When Antonio's sadness is equated most readily with his sexual identity itself, Bassanio implicitly serves as merely a male object of his affections in the abstract, significant structurally and not specifically. This Antonio, a frequent Antonio in the criticism, seeks a simple sort of satisfaction; he could be made happy if embraced or chosen by Bassanio, if Bassanio were not in pursuit of another, or if Bassanio were not in pursuit of a woman. These readings are not unuseful. But they flatten a specific characterization of sexuality, a question of the nature of attachment and desire, with all the meanings attachment and desire might be represented as possessing for the fictional subject and his real-world interpreting audience, into a minimalist matter equating sexuality with object choice indexed only by the sex of the object and the outcome of pursuit. Yet at the least they keep the relationship between Antonio and Bassanio in view, as more recent readings have not.

Likewise starting with the problem of Antonio's "sadness," recent influential work by Henry Turner and, most interestingly, Drew Daniel on Antonio has moved away from the particulars of Antonio's characterization and of his desires for Bassanio. Instead, in these two essays, the forces making Antonio sad are revealed as the selfsame structures (republican, capitalist, and/or Christian) interpellating Venetians into subjecthood and social contracts. In Turner's and Daniel's readings, there is effectively no qualitative difference between Antonio and any of the other members of his playworld (and, surprisingly, virtually no role for sexuality in that world). Turner has Antonio's actions show us in the abstract what friendship, enmity, and justice are for all ethical subjects; for him, political and philosophical logics mean that "otherness is never determinable or distributable to any one person," and thus Antonio cannot signify in his argument in his role as an individual. Turner's analysis has all the characters illustrating general ethical and political principles; all, including Antonio, are examined as exhibiting and governed by larger, uniform structures rather than distinct figurations: "Is Antonio Other to himself, as are all characters? The answer must be yes . . . We are led to the unexpected conclusion that early modern democracy is as antithetical to the friend as it is to the enemy, since one can never be friends with everyone, and the bond between two weakens as it generalizes to include the many."[27]

Similarly, in a dazzling argument working (for a start) to refine psychoanalytic approaches to the early modern and Shakespearean world, Daniel reduces what he calls Antonio's melancholy and masochism to psychic structures emptied of specific content, at once synecdochic and mimetic of his collective. In fact, Daniel's reading of Antonio's sadness is undertaken in part just to redress some of the former readings I have just criticized. For Daniel, Antonio's opening monologue does not depict a unique or pathologized homosexuality but a larger Venetian subjectivity: "Instead of an isolated, inconsolable figure at odds with the heteronormative comedy in which he suffers, we can see the symptomatic logic through which Antonio's showy declaration of his sadness and his frightening embrace of his own domination mirror the broader forms of subjection that drive the subjects of Belmont and Venice throughout the play."[28]

Daniel's subsequent reading of those forms of subjection is wonderful but, as Jacques Lezra writes in response, unusual for a psychoanalytic reading in that it does not offer an explanation of its central character's represented motives or emotions.[29] Instead, in Daniel as in Turner, Antonio serves a metonymic and allegorical function, standing in for a host of roles, metrics, dynamics, and values of the culture. The disappearance of an account of Antonio's particularity is especially striking in Daniel's essay, as it is the best—really, practically the only—treatment to date of the play's ample delineation of Antonio's masochism, which Daniel reads as the progressive transformation ("revision," "modulation," "*Aufhebung*," "transition") of Antonio's melancholy.[30] The particular masochism Daniel locates in Antonio is derived from Krafft-Ebing and possesses a decidedly nineteenth-century flavor, not least in its impersonal cast. In this spirit, explicitly ventriloquizing Antonio, Daniel writes: "exactly where I am simply and coldly treated as a bondsman by a master, it is there that I am most clearly enjoying masochistic pleasure."[31] Daniel's reading of the Antonio-Shylock relationship emphasizes the contract as a means of pleasurably detaching masochistic subjects from the human agents of their torment. The contract itself makes "a certain masochistic pleasure . . . available for Antonio to enjoy."[32] Thus, for Daniel, presumably Shylock partly displaces Bassanio in the engine of the masochism plot precisely because of the coldness of his affect for Antonio and his willingness to script their future obligations to one another in a bond rather than through the happenstance of encounter.[33] Or rather, in Daniel's view, the bond itself eventually displaces the human agents, beneficiaries, and victims it names as sources of pleasure or torment: "the bondsman stands in thrall to the literal text of the bond, rather than to the master who is its representative."[34] I will return to the question of whether this is the best characterization of Antonio's desires and of the relationship between Antonio and Shylock.

In fact, I think Daniel is exactly right to raise the question of something like masochism in order to understand how Antonio occupies what Goldberg calls "the friend's place" in the play.[35] Masochism seems a plausible explanation, for instance, of the depiction of Antonio's move to stake his body on the profitability of his profligate friend's pleasures. It can also be a potent ground for explanation of his insistence on clearing Bassanio's debt at the cost of his life and of what I have elsewhere referred to as his "increasingly hopeless bleats of submissiveness" during the trial, explicitly calling for Shylock's knife so long as Bassanio is there to see it fall.[36] Even after the contract with Shylock has been voided, masochism seems an apt description of Antonio's move to assume blame for Bassanio's fecklessness in giving away his wedding ring to the disguised Portia, when Bassanio had promised that he would sooner die (3.2.183–85). When Antonio laments or boasts that "I am th'unhappy subject of these quarrels" between spouses (5.1.238), the characteristic nature of his gambit, reviving both playwide tension between marriage and friendship and Antonio's particular positioning as liable for Bassanio's faults, prevents an audience from puzzling over his willingness to take the force of Portia's anger.

Antonio's masochism thus takes the form of substantial exertions of agency in the service of becoming a passive subject of harm or negative affect. This is most literally figured in his self-description at the start of the trial, when Antonio rhetorically pivots between the vocabulary and grammar that signal activity and passivity: " . . . I do oppose/My patience to his [Shylock's] fury, and am armed/To suffer with a quietness of spirit" (4.1.9–11). In making proximate opposition and patience, arming and suffering, the speech labors to condense the will to suffer into a single tense or voice.[37]

While Daniel offers a useful frame with which to interpret Antonio's figuration, I contest three parts of Daniel's argument, which seem to mistake the kind of masochism represented in the play: first, the claim that Antonio's masochism takes over from his melancholy in any sort of sequence, emerging only with the bond plot; next, the assumption that Antonio, in signing Shylock's bond, seeks an impersonal form of cruelty; last, the effort to make Antonio thereby figure the largest and similarly most impersonal subjectivizing structures of the Venetian republic. These three components of Daniel's argument seem to erase Antonio's particularity and thereby the complex queer exchanges in the play, which present men disappointing and depriving one another, even enraging and destroying one another, as among the most meaningful possibilities for queer affect and subjectivity. These forms of affect are distinctive and not readily assimilable to the culture that surrounds them. In fact, they exploit and often undermine Venice's economic, juridical, and social institutions in order that they might intensify and flourish.[38]

I therefore think that Antonio's place in the play evokes something more like Goldberg's vision of a "fully negativized," Marlovian sodomitical consciousness that—while it participates in and may pointedly resemble its culture's hierarchies and power relations—is not identifiable with the generalized structure of its culture.[39] In this way, Antonio's bond of friendship with Bassanio resembles the homosocial pairs and networks that undergirded early modern social and cultural institutions, while the bond of enmity he shares with Shylock may resemble the burgeoning ethnic and religious tensions that supported nascent national identities and changing ways of understanding individual identities. Antonio's plot, however, mobilizes both relationships in the service of a self-destructiveness at times competing directly with the state's political and economic needs and with the class and ethnic solidarity championed in the Portia-Bassanio plot.[40] Meanwhile, Antonio's represented desires and subjectivity, while not masochistic in the Krafft-Ebing sense glossed by Daniel, indeed center on his own disappointment and consumption by other men.

Is the failure to be chosen, openly adored, or favored by Bassanio a problem for Antonio? Or, to put it another way, is the sadness Antonio announces to his less intimate friends Salanio and Salarino at the play's start caused by his secondary status in relation to Portia or by an absolute sense of being secondary in Bassanio's eyes? Perhaps not. Indeed, based on his self-representation to Bassanio, his sadness might more plausibly result from not initially being rejected enough. From the first, Antonio's efforts to shape Bassanio's response to him position Bassanio as a key agent, or partner, in fantasies in which Antonio undergoes total destruction. Recall their initial encounter in the play: Bassanio meets with Antonio and, prompted by Antonio, who has evidently been told that details about Bassanio's courtship of a "lady" are forthcoming, parries Antonio's question about her by mentioning instead the possibility of a solution to his financial problems, solving which he calls his "chief care" (1.1.119, 127). Bassanio notes that he numbers Antonio among his creditors, owing him "the most in money and in love"—that is, he has received more than he has repaid in both currency and affection (1.1.131). Antonio must press for details a second time and cues tongue-tied Bassanio that to help him: "be assured/My purse, my person, my extremest means/Lie all unlocked to your occasions" (1.1.137–39). In response, Bassanio retreats into still-vague claims that supplying him with more money to fritter on what he earlier described as "showing a more swelling port/Than [his] faint means would grant continuance" (1.1.124–25)—clothing and gifts he cannot afford—would be justified as an investment that will bear fruit and return all of Antonio's vanished loans to Antonio.

Bassanio's vagueness, need to contextualize his request, and, most of all, insistence that he will not cost Antonio, that he will repay his debts "in money and in love," offend Antonio. Evidently, unpaid or even increasing debts in money—and, perhaps, in love—are more desirable than reprehensible to Antonio. There follows Antonio's most overt and bitter criticism of Bassanio in the entire play:

> You know me well, and herein spend but time
> To wind about my love with circumstance;

> And out of doubt you do me now more wrong
> In making question of my uttermost
> Than if you had made waste of all I have. (1.1.153–58)

When the actual request comes for money that, Antonio says, he does not have at the ready, Antonio jumps at the prospect of extending himself further and adopts a metaphor of agonized extension: "go forth," he tells Bassanio, "Try what my credit can in Venice do; / That shall be racked, even to the uttermost" (1.1.179–81).

"Extremest means"; "my uttermost"; "even to the uttermost." Antonio's diction in these quotations reveals the special hold on his fantasy of the superlative or verge, pointing to a vividly, repeatedly imagined and yet strategically vague finality. The "extremest" and "uttermost" evoke a limit combining temporal, economic, and personal elements, the last only expressible in metaphors that are themselves displaced onto Antonio's credit and possessions, which will be "racked" or "made waste." When reading Antonio's rebuke of his friend above, it is worth dwelling on Antonio's disappointment at what he views as Bassanio's mistake. This is Bassanio's "making question of [his] uttermost" even though Bassanio "know[s] [Antonio] well." Bassanio's question-making includes his misrecognition of the importance of the verge to Antonio and his mismeasurement of the extent—"uttermost"—to which Antonio would be willing to offer or suffer on Bassanio's behalf or, perhaps preferably, at his request, if not as a result of Bassanio's direct action (they must deputize Shylock for this).

The less offensive alternative Antonio offers, making waste of all he has, is a startling possibility at this point of the play, since Antonio has described himself to Salanio and Salarino as, if sad, still beyond financial risk.[41] Antonio's self-description to Bassanio as ready to supply his extremest means and his uttermost reveals him as desiring to augment whatever Bassanio might demand, desiring to be asked for that uttermost resource of self. Bassanio notably does not believe he is making any such demand, as his nervousness around Shylock's terms will indicate ("You shall not seal to such a bond for me" [1.3.150]). At that juncture, Antonio will go out of his way to convince Bassanio that he, Antonio, is in no danger, lest he be unable to achieve endangering himself. Yet in their first conversation, Bassanio's reluctance to believe that self-endangerment and a permanently unpaid debt are acceptable requests from Antonio is exactly what Antonio rebukes. According to Antonio's speech, laying waste to all Antonio has would be doing him "wrong," but to "mak[e] question of" his willing sacrifice of what is so elliptically described as his "uttermost," Antonio declares, does him "more wrong."

What wrong? Since questioning Antonio's willingness to sacrifice all does him no *material* wrong (in the way that laying waste to him would), Antonio presumably means that in questioning his will to sacrifice and exert his uttermost, Bassanio is mistaking who Antonio is, what he wants, and the nature of his relationship to Bassanio, the venture he would like them to make together. Bassanio is less intimate friend than misrecognizing stranger in that scenario. But Bassanio "know[s] [him] well." It is being made waste by a friend or other intimate that Antonio insists is to be his preferred superlative ruin. If in the rhetorics of friendship, a willingness to ruin oneself for one's friend is commonplace, Antonio's vivid prompting of the ruin and his developed vocabulary for it are more unusual.

Bassanio's slowness here to demand is frustrating to Antonio, yet it should be pointed out that if Antonio is *seeking* a person who would "owe [him] most . . . in love," offering less love than he receives, and who would most spectacularly default on that debt, Bassanio's very reluctance to confide and to demand (signaling deficits in his love and trust) fits with the desired package. It is thus not surprising that Antonio turns to Shylock effectively to delegate Bassanio's work, until now sluggishly performed, of laying waste to all he has. The circulations of affect, need, credit, and reprisal or payback among the three men generally serve to conceal the agency and origins of the circulated materials. For instance, a Jewish tradesman's money is repackaged as gentle and gentile for Bassanio's use, when laundered through Antonio's credit, so that any taint of Jewishness may be disavowed in Bassanio's Christian courtship.[42] Similarly, Shylock's increasing insistence on exploiting Antonio's vulnerability can diminish the audience's awareness of the fact that Bassanio's demands on Antonio—and Bassanio's willingness to drop his concerns about the terms of the bond in order to make use of the money—are the source of this vulnerability.[43] Harry Berger's rich account of Shakespearean redistributions of ethical complicities allows us to recognize this dynamic ultimately as Antonio's use of Shylock to produce the script in which Bassanio lays him waste and receives the tribute of Antonio's uttermost fantasized in the play's first scene.[44] Antonio appears to believe that in so doing he can most powerfully be revealed as Bassanio's "love," the role he claims during the trial scene when, at the point of the knife, he feels he has clearly outperformed the love of Bassanio's marriage: "Commend me to your honourable wife . . . bid her be judge / Whether Bassanio had not once a love" (4.1.270–74).

Yet pace Daniel, Antonio's bonds to Shylock are also not impersonal, and Shylock is not merely a pawn in Antonio's bid to be consumed by Bassanio. Shylock and Antonio have a long mutual intimacy rendered to us in far more detail than Antonio's with Bassanio, and seemingly reflecting a great deal more mutual understanding. Shylock and Antonio's story is composed of numerous acts of economic and personal abuse directed at Shylock by Antonio. The catalog of these is mostly a familiar one. Antonio has rated or harangued Shylock about his Jewishness and his profession on the Rialto in public, "there where merchants most do congregate," that is, depending on whether Shylock's or Antonio's own peer group is signified by the congregation of "merchants," where the shame for or danger to Shylock may be most heightened (1.3.44–45, 103). As is much noted, Antonio has also offered physical insult and injury to Shylock, spitting on Shylock's clothing and beard and kicking him (1.1.108, 113–14).

As is much remarked also, Shylock notes that Antonio makes loans without interest "in low simplicity" and apparently in sufficient volume to drive down the rate of interest current with usurers (1.3.39–41). Antonio's performance of lending behavior encouraged by the church (and lamented in England for its diminishment), has often been seen as characterizing him as an ethical participant in mercantile culture, contrasted with the usurer seeking profit only or with the Jew represented as villain.[45] But he further claims that he has "oft" been sought out by "many" of Shylock's debtors, supplying them with funds to liberate themselves from the need to pay Shylock penalties—claims that do not seem to have been taken up in criticism—going far beyond prosaic acts of anti-Semitism or rogue Christian economic activism (1.3.102–15, 3.3.2, 3.3.22).[46] And this is not the end of his activities undertaken to thwart Shylock. In order to "disgrace[] and hinder[] [Shylock], to laugh at [his] losses, mock at [his] gains, scorn [his] nation, thwart [his] bargains, cool [his] friends and heat [his] enemies," to quote Shylock's litany of complaints against Antonio (3.1.49–52), Antonio has kept close account of him, perusing his plans and assessing his values attentively in order to frustrate and demean them, respectively. Although the discourses of anti-Semitism saturate Antonio's actions, so far as we know, no other Jew in Venice has personal cause to resent him.[47] And although during the trial Antonio will tout his absolute passivity in relation to Shylock—"I do oppose / My patience to his fury" (4.1.9–10)—his prior history with Shylock reveals him as instead relentlessly active and interfering, conducting a strikingly personalized economic assault. No one cares about Shylock more than Antonio does.

The passion for Antonio thereby aroused in Shylock—"I will have the heart of him!" (3.1.114–15)—provides an alternate source of the destruction Antonio fantasized coming at Bassanio's hands.[48] Moreover, using Shylock successfully positions Bassanio as the formal cause of that destruction, so that the proof of Antonio's status as Bassanio's love may emerge in the sacrificial wake of Bassanio's very indifference and self-regard. Bassanio could never owe Antonio or anyone more than that result: "to you I owe the most in money and in love." Antonio acts toward Shylock as he wishes Bassanio would act toward him, racking him to the uttermost, and he acts toward Bassanio as Shylock acts toward others, steadily increasing the debt of love Bassanio owes him as if with usurious, uxorious interest.

Far from being identifiable with the forms of subjectivity of nascent capitalist or republican Venice, this merchant's actions are anticapitalist at every turn: lending without interest; undermining systems of credit; intervening in private contracts; inverting any rational principle of self-interest, etc.—even precipitating Shylock's loan of money without interest. These actions also subvert the republic, for Antonio risks the justice and reputation of the state in the service of producing a sublime moment of restorative personal destruction (3.3.26–31). His willingness to yield to Shylock's focused rage and to exact Bassanio's totalizing debt to himself aims to secure a lasting affective intensity for his own male bonds alone, meanwhile impoverishing the institutions of marriage and, perhaps, of conventional friendship and enmity alike.

The Antonio effect may be mapped, although it is not readily generalizable to other characters in this play. The dearest goal of this form of active passivity, this triumphantly negativized sexuality—that is, being consumed and ground to pieces against the hard hearts ("than which what's harder"? he asks [4.1.78]) of his accomplices, the careless youth and the persecuted Jew—seems *nearly* Marlovian. As in Marlowe, the near success of a willful and hyperbole-favoring agent in achieving his ends threatens to raze all competing antagonists and institutions but ultimately does not. Yet in the meantime, the almost single-minded pursuit of his desires sets Antonio apart from the rest of the Venetian polity; indeed, his desires limn a kind of subjecthood so different from and indifferent to the conventions of Venice as to be nearly absolutist in its unique forms of agency, meaning-making, and self-regard. This queer subjecthood may partly serve to reveal the more conventional institutions of the culture from which it is so sharply distinguished. But it is neither reflection nor inversion of those institutions. Tonally, affectively, and economically, as debtor and creditor, enabling and harrying, it has a hand in homosociality and marriage, capitalism and religion, love and enmity, even as it repeatedly subverts their central values, expressions, and goals. Nor do these institutions persist uncontested or unaltered by its resistant trace; they remain "much bound," if not "infinitely bound" (5.1.135–36), to the merchant of Venice.

NOTES

1. Lauren Berlant, *Cruel Optimism* (Durham, NC: Duke University Press, 2011), 123.

2. Jonathan Goldberg, *Sodometries: Renaissance Texts, Modern Sexualities* (Stanford, CA: Stanford University Press, 1991), 122. I am most interested in male characters in *Merchant*, but it is worth noting that Goldberg's readings show how Marlovian sodomy enables strong actions and a variety of postures in relation to will for both male and female characters.

3. Ibid., 124.

4. Ibid., 124, 122.

5. Ibid., 141, 108.

6. Ibid., 141.

7. Goldberg draws on Karen Newman's fine reading of Portia as a powerful and "unruly" woman. See Karen Newman, "Portia's Ring: Unruly Women and Structures of Exchange in *The Merchant of Venice*," *Shakespeare Quarterly* 38, no. 1 (1987): 18–33, revised as "Portia's Ring: Gender, Sexuality, and Theories of Exchange in *The Merchant of Venice*" in her collection of essays, *Essaying Shakespeare* (Minneapolis: University of Minnesota Press, 2009), 59–76.

8. Goldberg, *Sodometries*, 142.

9. Alan Bray, Jeffrey Masten, and Laurie Shannon provide exemplary treatment of these associations and the period's general pleasure in homonormativity. See Alan Bray, "Homosexuality and the Signs of Male Friendship in Elizabethan England," in *Queering the Renaissance*, ed. Jonathan Goldberg, 40–61 (Durham, NC: Duke University Press, 1993); Jeffrey Masten, *Textual Intercourse: Collaboration, Authorship, and Sexuality in Renaissance Drama* (Cambridge: Cambridge University Press, 1997); and Laurie Shannon, *Sovereign Amity: Figures of Friendship in Renaissance Contexts* (Chicago: University of Chicago Press, 2002).

10. *Oxford English Dictionary*, 3rd ed., s.v. "proportion."

11. William Shakespeare, *The Merchant of Venice*, ed. John Drakakis, Arden Third Series (London: Methuen Drama, 2010). Text references are to act, scene, line of this edition.

12. Abundant other differences will have suggested themselves to Portia and other readers of the trial scene, of course. I choose this as a less familiar

example, perhaps more telling for its occurrence at a seemingly unfraught and low-stakes narrative moment.

13. Lars Engle offers a strong (and rare) analysis of the implications of the differences in class between Antonio and Bassanio. See Lars Engle, "'Thrift Is Blessing': Exchange and Explanation in *The Merchant of Venice*," *Shakespeare Quarterly* 37, no. 1 (1986): 19–37. The nature of the friendship as rooted in difference is sufficiently palpable that individual productions often add to the differences I have just specified: for instance, regularly casting Antonio as older than Bassanio, as in the 2004 Michael Radford film production, which played a 56-year-old Jeremy Irons as Antonio opposite a 34-year-old Joseph Fiennes as Bassanio.

14. Goldberg, *Sodometries*, 142.

15. In the course of assessing boundaries between literature and history, Marshall Grossman notes that "each literary object is radically contingent with respect to the portion of the [cultural] system put into play within it" in "Limiting History," in *Rethinking Historicism from Shakespeare to Milton*, ed. Ann Baynes Coiro and Thomas Fulton, 65–84 (Cambridge: Cambridge University Press, 2012), 68. Unlike Grossman, I am not interested here in identifying an ethical or aesthetic residue possessed by literature outside of history. I am concerned with analytic losses and blindness to cultural diversity and conflict that occur when the standard form of critical argument correlates literary content with prevailing cultural logics and assumes that literary works do not routinely imagine alternatives to prevailing forms, institutions, and ideologies. Historicism's methodological dominance in literary studies is variously asserted and evaluated throughout the essays in Coiro and Fulton's volume in ways that implicitly bear on my essay's concerns; for instance, writing of religious subject matter, Andrew Hadfield suggests that "it might be worthwhile to redraw our current literary map and make it more representative." Andrew Hadfield, "Has Historicism Gone Too Far: Or, Should We Return to Form?," in *Rethinking Historicism*, 23–39, 24. For my part, emphasis on the "representative" is a problem; historicism might take stock of the cost of avoiding the exceptional.

16. E. K. Chambers, introduction to *The Merchant of Venice*, Red Letter Edition (London: Blackie and Sons, 1904), 86.

17. Chambers, introduction, 94. Compare E. M. W. Tillyard's description of Antonio as "strikingly different from all the sociable folk he has to do with, except Shylock." E. M. W. Tillyard, *Shakespeare's Early Comedies* (London: Chatto and Windus, 1965), 199.

18. See, for instance, an interesting range of such vocabulary in Engle, "Thrift Is Blessing," 19, 24, 26, 34. Steve Patterson, "The Bankruptcy of Homoerotic Amity in Shakespeare's *Merchant of Venice*," *Shakespeare Quarterly*

50, no. 1 (1999): 9–32. A longer developmental account of the role of male-male sexuality in *Merchant* criticism would include the various readings of Antonio's sexuality found in W. H. Auden's "Brothers and Others," in *The Dyer's Hand* (New York: Vintage Books, 1990 [1948]), 218–37; Graham Midgley, "*The Merchant of Venice*: A Reconsideration," *Essays in Criticism* 10 (1960): 119–33; John D. Hurrell, "Love and Friendship in *The Merchant of Venice*," *Texas Studies in Language and Literature* 3, no. 3 (1961): 328–41; Tillyard, *Shakespeare's Early Comedies*, 189, 199; Lawrence M. Hyman, "The Rival Lovers in *The Merchant of Venice*," *Shakespeare Quarterly* 21, no. 2 (1970): 109–16; and Leo Rockas, "'A Dish of Doves': *The Merchant of Venice*," *ELH* 40, no. 3 (1973): 339–51, 346.

19. John Drakakis's Arden Third Series edition of *Merchant* gives these spellings of the two characters' names and adds an additional character, Salerio, appearing in Belmont after Bassanio chooses the correct casket and in Venice at the trial. The first folio and first quarto texts offer five distinct full spellings and seven distinct speech prefixes evoking names of these speakers, so that the question of the separability of this duo is open. See Drakakis's explanation in Shakespeare, *Merchant*, 163–64 and 428–30.

20. For Keith Geary, for example, Antonio's "homosexual love" for Bassanio is the only possible explanation for dialogue that would otherwise be "fritter[ed] away." Keith Geary, "The Nature of Portia's Victory: Turning to Men in *The Merchant of Venice*," *Shakespeare Survey* 37 (1984): 55–68, 58, 59.

21. "Lovelorn" and "frustrated" are Patterson's words; "disappointed," Catherine Belsey's. See Patterson, "Homoerotic Amity," 9, 10; Catherine Belsey, "Love in Venice," *Shakespeare Survey* 44 (1992): 41–53, 49. Seymour Kleinberg argues that "Antonio is also in despair because he despises himself for his homosexuality." See Seymour Kleinberg, "*The Merchant of Venice*: The Homosexual as Anti-Semite in Nascent Capitalism," in *Essays on Gay Literature* (New York: Haworth Press, 1983), 113–26, volume also published as *Journal of Homosexuality* 8, no. 4 (1983): 113–26, 117.

22. See Goldberg, *Sodometries*; Bray, "Homosexuality and the Signs of Male Friendship"; Masten, *Textual Intercourse*; and Eve Kosofsky Sedgwick, *Between Men: English Literature and Male Homosocial Desire* (New York: Columbia University Press, 1985) and *Epistemology of the Closet* (Berkeley: University of California Press, 1990).

23. Patterson, "Homoerotic Amity," 9–10.

24. Patterson, "Homoerotic Amity," 9. Compare Kleinberg's argument that Antonio is characterized by "singularity" and as the instantiator of a transhistorical type: "a classic pattern . . . the earliest portrait of the homophobic homosexual." Kleinberg, "The Homosexual as Anti-Semite," 120.

25. Patterson, "Homoerotic Amity," 14.

26. Arthur Little, "The Rites of Queer Marriage in *The Merchant of Venice*," in *Shakesqueer*, ed. Madhavi Menon, 216–24 (Durham, NC: Duke University Press, 2011), 217. Belsey also describes Antonio as "mourning for friendship." Belsey, "Love in Venice," 52.

27. Henry S. Turner, "The Problem of the More-Than-One: Friendship, Calculation, and Political Association in *The Merchant of Venice*," *Shakespeare Quarterly* 57, no. 4 (2006): 413–42, 434. My brief treatment necessarily oversimplifies Turner's interesting argument. I do not mean to dismiss it, nor his considered Derridean critique of central myths of subjectivity, just to note that the cost of such analysis is differentiation of the characters.

28. Drew Daniel, "'Let Me Have Judgment, and the Jew His Will': Melancholy Epistemology and Masochistic Fantasy in *The Merchant of Venice*," *Shakespeare Quarterly* 61, no. 2 (2010): 207–34, 233, revised in Daniel's *The Melancholy Assemblage: Affect and Epistemology in the English Renaissance* (New York: Fordham University Press, 2013).

29. Jacques Lezra, "'Want-Wit' Discipline," *Shakespeare Quarterly* 61, no. 2 (2010): 240–45, 240.

30. Daniel, "'Let Me Have Judgment, and the Jew His Will,'" 216, 218. A partial treatment of Antonio's masochism emerges in Luke Wilson's engaging interpretation of *Merchant*'s poetics of risk. Wilson argues that Antonio vehemently opposes an insurantial mitigation of risk as incompatible with what Wilson finds his "narcissistic, and perversely self-destructive . . . insistence that the part must always entail the whole." For Wilson, "the ethic of risk [is] not only masochistic but antisocial too." Luke Wilson, "Monetary Compensation for Injuries to the Body, AD 602–1697," in *Money and the Age of Shakespeare: Essays in New Economic Criticism*, ed. Linda Woodbridge, 19–37 (New York: Palgrave Macmillan, 2003), 33.

31. Daniel, "'Let Me Have Judgment, and the Jew His Will,'" 222.

32. Ibid., 222, 221.

33. Presumably the bond merely facilitates different forms of interpersonal encounter (and of course the terms of the bond are exposed to juridical scrutiny, as they are litigated in this case), so it does not work even notionally as a contract in successfully limiting semantic or interpersonal ambiguity or in exhaustively scripting the nature of torment that can accompany encounter.

34. Daniel, "'Let Me Have Judgment, and the Jew His Will,'" 223.

35. Goldberg, *Sodometries*, 142.

36. Lara Bovilsky, *Barbarous Play: Race on the English Renaissance Stage* (Minneapolis: University of Minnesota Press, 2008), 69. Daniel offers a compelling reading of Antonio's desire to be seen under torture by Bassanio. Daniel, "'Let Me Have Judgment, and the Jew His Will,'" 220.

37. Antonio's language here recalls Harry Berger Jr.'s description of Shakespeare's frequent interest in representing complicity in victimization via such rhetorical gymnastics: "complicity and the site of agency are shuttled back and forth in the oscillation of discourses within one speaker's language." Berger notes that such speeches come as close as possible in English to more complex forms of agency expressible with a Greek middle voice. See Harry Berger Jr., *Making Trifles of Terrors: Redistributing Complicities in Shakespeare* (Stanford, CA: Stanford University Press, 1997), 322.

38. In a parallel argument, Melissa E. Sanchez turns to literary representations of female "excess and abjection," including masochism, as more likely to challenge cultural order and to disclose "the alterity and diversity of early modern sexualities." See Melissa E. Sanchez, "'Use Me but as Your Spaniel': Feminism, Queer Theory, and Early Modern Sexualities," *PMLA* 127, no. 3 (2012): 493–511, 494.

39. Goldberg, *Sodometries*, 124. Antonio decisively lacks the buoyancy and defiance of Marlowe's Gaveston, of course. A related (if perhaps inverse) possibility for thinking through Antonio's significance is found in Daniel Juan Gil's reading of *Troilus and Cressida*, which describes the eroticized hatred emerging in repudiation of the intuition of a humanity shared with another. In such a world, "the most fundamentally social desire is . . . the desire to kill." Daniel Juan Gil, *Before Intimacy: Asocial Sexuality in Early Modern England* (Minneapolis: University of Minnesota Press, 2006), 101.

40. Over and apart from his overt competition with Portia during the trial, the revelation in Belmont of Antonio's plight destroys Bassanio's imposture as a flush gentleman motivated by love.

41. Because of Antonio and Bassanio's intimacy—and perhaps the less-than-certain assumption that that Bassanio's "warranty/To unburden all [his] plots and purposes" to Antonio is symmetrical—Engle concludes that Antonio's claims that he is overextended are true and that his earlier self-representation to Salanio and Salarino as protected from risk with diversified capital enterprises is false. Engle writes that "we know from what Antonio says later to Bassanio that he is misleading his less intimate friends here," assuming that Bassanio hears only the truth (Engle, "Thrift Is Blessing," 22). But the opposite might also be true: Antonio might be misleading *Bassanio* in order to make manifest the form of his investment in him. Admittedly, a recurrent fantasy of total loss might be compatible with the pursuit of a poorly diversified investment portfolio.

42. See Lara Bovilsky, "'A Gentle and No Jew': Jessica, Portia, and Jewish Identity," *Renaissance Drama* 38 (2010): 47–76.

43. Turner also notes that Bassanio's willingness to suspend his concerns causes him to resemble "the enemy." Turner, "The Problem of the More-Than-One," 425.

44. Berger, *Making Trifles of Terrors*.

45. Some important readings of the play's depictions of changes in mercantile and proto-capitalist culture treating Antonio's and Shylock's actions in a largely realist vein may be found, for instance, in John Draper, "Usury in *The Merchant of Venice*," *Modern Philology* 33, no. 1 (1935): 37–47; Joan Ozark Holmer, "The Education of the Merchant of Venice," *SEL* 25 (1985): 307–35 and "The Merchant of Venice"*: Choice, Hazard, and Consequence* (New York: St. Martin's Press, 1995); and, more recently, Amanda Bailey, "Shylock and the Slaves: Owing and Owning in *The Merchant of Venice*," *Shakespeare Quarterly* 62, no. 1 (2011): 1–24. Walter Cohen's well-known treatment recounts relevant economic history (including the question of interest-free loans), emphasizing that the play engages but does not simply encode historical realities. See Walter Cohen, "*The Merchant of Venice* and the Possibilities of Historical Criticism," *ELH* 49, no. 4 (1982): 765–89. Theodore Leinwand weaves affect theory with economic history to read the play and is particularly interested in Antonio's interest-free loans. See *Theatre, Finance and Society in Early Modern England* (Cambridge: Cambridge University Press, 1999), esp. 2–19.

46. It is impossible to prove a negative. My search has not been exhaustive, but none of many consulted period economic histories, editions of the play, or literary critical works that investigate anti-Semitic contexts for the play or that tie Antonio's behavior to economic realities in England or Venice from Draper forward cite any historical precedent for Antonio's claim that he has "oft" delivered "many" from the "forfeitures" they owed Shylock (i.e., penalties or fines—for similar bonds?). It is surprising how little comment these extreme actions have received, as if anti-Semitism is an adequate explanation for the details of Antonio's extensive stalking and antagonizing of Shylock. Of the interest-free loans, however, Harry Berger Jr. anticipates my take, noting "[Antonio's] motive is not restrictively philanthropic. It has an antagonistic edge." Berger does not appear to differentiate the loans from Antonio's more targeted and unusual aid to Shylock's victims. See Harry Berger Jr., *A Fury in the Words: Love and Embarrassment in Shakespeare's Venice* (New York: Fordham University Press, 2013), 22.

47. In yet another characteristic muddying of the origins of circulated materials in the play, some or much of the loan is actually not Shylock's money but his coreligionist's, Tubal (1.3.53). Tubal clearly knows of Shylock's hatred for Antonio (3.1.70; 3.2.284) but is never explicitly represented as sharing it.

48. Only given Antonio's general malevolent foiling of Shylock's daily activities does it make sense for Shylock to revenge the loss of his daughter to Lorenzo on Antonio: Shylock's paranoia here has evidently been bitterly justified.

CHAPTER 7

Cities of the Stranger

Meredith Evans

> All these ways the world is a sea, but especially it is a sea in this respect: the sea is no place of habitation but a passage to our habitations. So the apostle expresses the world, *Here we have no continuing city* . . . .
>
> —JOHN DONNE, *LXXX Sermons*. [Ps. 61:20]

What's rotten in Denmark, so far as Claudius is concerned, is Hamlet. But Claudius is in luck, for the territory that Hamlet experiences as a claustrophobic "prison" is no such thing. It is, in fact, an island—or at least more of an island than not. Relative to Norway and Sweden, fourteenth-century Denmark was densely populated and relatively urbane; its sixty-odd towns (compared to Norway's mere dozen) were coastal and easily accessible by sea. However, this also made Denmark vulnerable to contagion: to the plague of Black Death, most immediately, but also to the mounting political pressures of its rivaling neighbors. Their issue, predictably enough, was title and land, but some things were still up for grabs. Now Danes once labeled "outlaws" for their opposition to the law of primogeniture—and for regicide too—were adopted by Sweden as a kind of cause célèbre while this rivalry played out not on Danish soil but on its waters.[1]

Hamlet was right, if literal-minded, to pronounce Denmark "a prison."[2] Like Pericles's Tyre, Denmark is "a wat'ry empire" (*Pericles*, 2.1.51) edged about by shorelines punctuated by multiple points of egress and (though Claudius does not care so much for *these*) ingress. What this means for Claudius, and for the destiny of *Hamlet*, is that the prince can easily be dispatched, especially given his unwitting collusion. Believing himself to be embarked on a diplomatic mission—a voyage not unlike Laertes's continental tour but more purposeful, as befits a prince of middle age—Hamlet will defer his scholarly pursuits in Wittenberg and instead set sail for England where, if all goes according to plan, he will promptly be executed.

Claudius's scheme is neither desperate nor delusive. Indeed, it demonstrates a sound, even canny understanding of international diplomacy that belies his long-standing literary reputation as an ineffectual, absentminded lush. England was conquered by Denmark in the eleventh century, but the chemistry between them was lacking; they were simply too geographically distant from one another to develop an antagonism of any lasting consequence or meaning. In *Hamlet*'s time, however, diplomatic relations between the two countries are still turbulent enough to be significant; that is, to be useful; manipulated for political advantage. Because England still owes Denmark remunerative fealty, Claudius quite reasonably wagers, it is likely to comply with his wishes, thus advancing his plot to murder his stepson and, finally, to secure his position as sovereign.

At the same time, Claudius recognizes that it would be ill advised for a novice king to personally apply or "put the strong law on" (4.3.3) the legal heir to the throne, especially if he hopes to sustain and strengthen the popular support he seems to be enjoying already. "*A flourish of trumpets and two pieces go off*" as soon as Claudius takes the stage (1.4.7). At least from Hamlet's privileged point of view—and much to his disgust—this expression of popular support, which has been neither inherited nor earned, is merely trumpeted by half-digested and gauche enactments of native customs (1.4.8–12). As only an insider "to the manner born" would know, these are customs "[more] honour'd in the breach than the observance" (1.4.15–16). Thus Claudius, with his reluctant recognition of his still tenuous hold on power and a strategy devised to secure it, also implicitly concedes that for all Denmark's geopolitical and military superiority, the King of England is *in fact* more powerful. Especially in contrast to his own untimely assumption of the throne, "England" represents a legitimate sovereign power. The one decides, while the other just schemes. England must kill Hamlet, because Denmark cannot.[3] At least, not yet.

So Claudius declares:

> . . . England, if my love thou hold'st at aught
> As my great power thereof may give thee sense,
> Since yet thy cicatrice looks raw and red
> After the Danish sword, and thy free awe

Pays homage to us, thou mayst not coldy set [i.e., ignore]
Our sovereign process, which imports at full
By letters congruing to that effect
The present death of Hamlet. Do it, England! (4.3.56–63)

But England does not. For Hamlet discovers the plot against his life and the rest, you might say, is history.

Still, why cannot Denmark just kill Hamlet? Put another way, why should Claudius be so politically circumspect now, when evidently he had no such compunction about killing Hamlet père? Here is one possible answer. The date of *Hamlet*'s composition and initial performance falls between the defeat of the Spanish Armada in 1588 and the expulsion of the Stuarts in 1688. While these dates might help to delimit a specific historical period, and thus also to locate *Hamlet* in its appropriate historical context, they are, arguably, too widely spaced, or perhaps simply too arbitrary, to contribute substantively to our understanding of either the text or its historical context.[4] For Carl Schmitt, however, they represent decisive moments for the emergence of the nation-state and, thus, for "political modernity" more broadly.[5] Seen in this way, these two events and the period they span are salient to our grasp of both the action of the play and its purported modernity. Defining or even locating political modernity as coincident with the rise of the nation-state is invariably contentious, but it is also familiar and, often, exigent; whatever its precise literary-historical purchase, its heuristic value is considerable.

According to Schmitt, early modern England lagged behind continental Europe in several respects. Lacking the advantage of a standing army or organized police force, it was—so it seemed—relatively incapable of transforming itself into a modern political body—that is to say, a sovereign state defined and consolidated by clear geographical boundaries and borders. For much the same reason, for Schmitt England represents an "exceptional" case, in the sense that it conspicuously lacked any marked geopolitical significance. In the decades preceding the 1648 Peace of Westphalia (or, say, between 1588 and 1688), Schmitt argues, incipient continental nation-states were staggering out of decades of war in order finally to erect "a public order of peace and security created and maintained by the legitimizing achievement of a new [political] entity." Meanwhile, Tudor England was just barely standing. In his blunt terms, it was, still, "barbaric."[6]

When Herman Melville asks us to consider, "once more, the universal cannibalism of the sea . . . whose creatures prey upon each other, carrying on eternal war since the world began"[7]—to consider, that is, the Leviathan—does he not sound oddly like Schmitt? Or else echo Schmitt's (by no means idiosyncratic) representation of barbarity as a "state" of monstrous undifferentiation, united neither by civil codes nor by the higher abstractions of juridical and political corporation but—as Ishmael puts it—composed simply of "Isolatoes" "federated along one keel" and driven thus by necessity? In Schmitt's view, which is itself heavily indebted to Hobbes, the "universal cannibalism of the sea," or the potentially infinite protraction of savage wars of predation, will only be mitigated, if not entirely arrested, with the establishment of sovereign nation-states erected on land.[8]

Is it that this hypothetical trajectory from *mare liberum* to "the *nomos* of the earth" is hardly pacific? Schmitt's relationship to Melville is even more direct than I have just suggested, and a fair bit stranger too. As Tracy Strong notes in his foreword to *Political Theology: Four Chapters on the Concept of Sovereignty*, Schmitt often "explained" his affiliation with National Socialism by referring to the titular character of Melville's *Benito Cereno*, in which the captain of a ship is temporarily overpowered by its "cargo" of African slaves who are eventually recaptured and executed—often signing his letters as "Benito Cereno."[9] If we follow Terry Eagleton's directives on how to read literature, we might recognize this as a peculiar form of (self-)address that "gives the fictional game away" by, in effect, "confessing" to its own artificial nature.[10] This seems right to me, as applied to Schmitt's pseudonymous correspondence, but less so of Melville's opening salvo (which is also Eagleton's main example here). "Call me Ishmael," *Moby-Dick* begins, and from this point on names, and other similarly arbitrary customs, just get stranger and give less and less away. For example, in this book there is a crippled beggar who for ten years displayed before him a painting of the "tragic scene" in which he lost his leg—even though, as Melville carefully notes, the stump itself was "as unquestionable a stump as any you will find in the western clearings." Obviously, this is not a man who can run for office ("Never a stump-speech does the poor whaleman make," is how Melville puts it), and yet, the world around him remained "incredulous."[11] In the face of such incredulity, or, say, illiteracy, the man pronounces himself an exile, "as much a savage as an Iroquois" and "owning no allegiance, but to the King of the Cannibals, and"—note—"ready at any moment to rebel against *him*."[12]

There is, of course, a great deal more to say, by which I mean, to think, about how such imagined affiliations and forms of identification as Schmitt's shape, or are shaped by, specific philosophical projects and political investments. Here, I simply note the indebtedness of Schmitt's thought to the "New World" conjured by nineteenth-century colonialism as a counterpoint to the so-called barbarism of sixteenth-century England and, by extension, to emphasize how wilder cards, like aesthetic judgment and literary taste, inform what may primarily be geopolitical, historical designations. Perhaps misidentifying Shakespeare with the "national poet" that he would only later become, Schmitt's argument about England's political belatedness recruits its ostensible cultural belatedness to the same purpose.[13] Thus, Schmitt opines, the classical theater of Racine and Corneille could only have arisen in the context of the modern sovereign state, adding that it is therefore quite "understandable that Voltaire would see in Shakespeare a 'drunken savage.'"[14]

I am inclined to dispute both the validity and truth of Schmitt's claim. However, Voltaire's remark is not so clearly or completely derogatory as its iteration might initially suggest.[15] Surely this "drunken savage" ("drunken sailor" might be the more appropriate idiomatic phrase) cannot be too far removed from Tudor England; too far removed, that is, from the same "barbaric" nation that, as Schmitt will also argue, made an enduring and exceptionally profound contribution to the form of civilization announced by the Industrial Revolution.[16]

Then consider once more the Leviathan. Despite or perhaps by virtue of its remarkable savagery and barbarity—the slow pace of its political evolution—in the span of a mere century "the island of England withdrew from the European continent and took the step from a terrestrial to a maritime existence."[17] More specifically, Schmitt argues that by "[carrying] out the appropriation of the world's oceans" this small island decided a "new global order of land and sea," adding that in so doing it was "following the lead of seafarers and pirates."[18]

So, our present-day geopolitical order was established by following the lead of pirates. This hypothesis bears repeating for several reasons, but, in the relatively narrow ambit of this essay, it helps substantiate my claim that the reason why Denmark cannot just murder Hamlet and be done with it already is because England is not a fully sovereign nation-state.[19] Moreover, it offers an account of British sovereignty, including its particular political and economic entailments, as an empire founded—essentially, specifically, historically—on piracy.[20]

This claim might sound provocative but it is not, in fact, eccentric. For example, in the *Leviathan* Hobbes documents that "till there were constituted the commonwealths, it was thought no dishonor to be a pirate . . . but rather a lawful trade."[21] While the notion of a lawful raider would not sharply be defined until the eighteenth century, by the end of the Middle Ages "the juridical condition of the hired sea bandit underwent a decisive change. Pirates who acted in the name and interests of the state . . . acquired . . . an accepted place in the field of public law."[22] This is not to suggest that Shakespeare's audience would necessarily have looked upon piracy with the equanimity of a detached spectator (shipwrecks being an altogether different matter). Marina, who, like Hamlet, has been rescued by pirates, thinks they are "not enough barbarous" (*Pericles*, 4.2.61). For Shylock, they are "water-rats, water-thieves," and no different from any other kind of thief (*Merchant of Venice*, 1.3.20).

In contrast, in *Hamlet* pirates are "thieves of mercy" who abort what would have been a smooth passage to England, although a deadly one for Hamlet. Admittedly, Hamlet's final take on the matter of his sudden reversal of fortune tells a rather different story than the one I am offering here: "There's a divinity that shapes our ends, / Rough hew them how we will" (5.2.10–11). This tidy platitude is not necessarily easy to dismiss either. Even Horatio, a steady scholar and generally reliable witness, proclaims the explanation "most certain" (5.2.12). Yet the plot says otherwise, and so, for that matter, does Hamlet—twice (4.6.13, 5.2.13). Hamlet's "thieves of mercy" are nothing if not expedient, both dramaturgically and (as Claudius only hoped England would be) politically.

If Denmark cannot murder Hamlet because it (or he) is not a fully sovereign power, it is also the case that *Hamlet*'s pirates are not merely serving to advance the plot but also acting in the name and interests of an inchoate state. More specifically, they are acting in the name and interests of an *amphibious* state, by which I mean, "having two lives; occupying two positions; connected with or combining two classes, ranks, offices, qualities, etc."[23] They afford the space of time in which Hamlet will be able to return to Denmark and, though he will not last long enough to see it, finally re-establish the legitimacy of the Danish throne.

With this off-stage, twice-narrated event that has at least been determined, if not exactly "decided," by piracy, power, which in *Hamlet* has been operating under a thick fog of corruption, becomes something a little more transparent, just as it reveals "providence" to be nothing more (or nothing less) than luck. We might therefore read *Hamlet* as a literary chronicle of intersecting orders and disorders in which it is not so much vengeance that is at stake, or the reach of subjective agency, or even still the constitution of a coherent self-identity[24] but, rather, the work of contingency. By this I mean: the *disruption* of sovereign models of power based on the occupation of territory (that is, of land) and the privilege thereby accorded to "originality," to the "origin" as a marker of social and political legitimacy; as well as the *interruption* of teleological and naturalized representations of history.

The contingency I am pointing to in *Hamlet* is what Ágnes Heller has called, with reference to Shakespearean dramaturgy, "swing."[25] Whether swings of mood or, say, fortune, for Heller they all essentially "point to the unexpected and sometimes also to the undeserved." Thus, she argues, "in Shakespeare, there are only real swings. There is no deus ex machina; no good fortune appears without a prehistory."[26] Heller's correlative investigation of the "pause" is also pertinent here. Whatever the precise duration of Hamlet's absence from Elsinore, it remains a gap, an interval that needs to be filled in. This duration is of no significance in itself; rather, it is what gets coded. The pause is both "the openness of interpretation" and the occasion of interpretation itself. What Hamlet's thieves of mercy steal for him, then, is not simply an escape but a space of time that is also the condition of representation itself. It is the event Hamlet will relate to Horatio and, equivalently, the event during which he does so.

The pause, the freeze-frame is a moment of suspense that is similar to but importantly distinct from "periods of time" regarded as "immovable, infixed, and frozen round" (*Paradise Lost* 2.602).[27] In place of such "periods," take the wonderfully impossible point of view of Milton's Satan, who "Looks down with wonder at the sudden view/Of all the world at once" (3.542–43). Satan is without doubt clever, but he is still very far from the wicked "Cartesian" dualist he is often accused of being.[28] He is both himself and not himself, but, scandalously, he is neither bothered nor embarrassed by this. I cite these lines from *Paradise Lost* in connection with the "pause" as a kind of gloss on Heller's conception of it.[29] As Jonathan Goldberg has proposed, such tension is generative insofar as it reveals "the other side"—or rather *an* other side—"of the absoluteness of identity."[30] Addressing the need to rethink (that is, to think again) about the structures, figures, and habits of thought that articulate and occasionally forge our identities, Goldberg asks which logical dispositions, which imaginative dispensations, might facilitate a way of thinking about sameness that does not presuppose identity: one that is hospitable to, but far from pious about, difference. The "pause," I think, is one such dispensation. It is a dilated liminal passage in which self-identity is not so much "in flux" as it is suspended. Lifted momentarily from the rigid sequence of cause and effect it into what Saint Augustine terms "distension," it affords a sort of time out of time.[31]

To "[look] down with wonder at the sudden view/Of all the world at once" describes, as I have said, an impossible perspective. Impossible: to grasp at once and all of a sudden the intermissive discontinuities we are. And yet it is precisely the impossibility of this position or pause, the unlikeliness of ever occupying it too comfortably, which makes it valuable. Interrupting ostensibly fixed narratives and perhaps indefinitely deferring their resolution, it invites us to see the relationship between self and other, or even, truth and error, differently. In the sudden view of a world seen all at once, there is "no continuing city,"[32] no city that could adequately or with any permanence claim us as its own. And vice versa. Unless a man can be an island—a state of exception if ever there was one—what city or what land can legitimately be claimed as one's "own"?[33] If to claim a piece of land is to occupy it, then, one might ask further, what exactly does "occupy" mean? What does the designation of territory as either "occupied" or "unoccupied" tell us about how bodies of land are regarded and, ipso facto, used? What exactly is at stake in Schmitt's political history, which singles out England for making the unprecedented transition from a terrestrial to a maritime existence?

Almost by definition (pace Donne), land is at stake. Among other things, a stake is what you drive into the earth to establish a boundary and mark it as yours, a pole.[34] Hence the genius of one Occupy protestor's sign circa 2013: "What do we want? Time travel! When do we want it? It's irrelevant!" Hence, too, the tragicomedy of historical progress, which *Hamlet* represents as the slow, dull march to which we are easily accustomed and as the literally absurd show of force with which we must become familiar over and over again. Whatever Hamlet does or does not do, there is Fortinbras still, going "to gain a little patch of ground" with

> no profit in it but the name.
> To pay five ducats—five—I would not farm it,
> Nor will it yield to Norway or the Pole
> A ranker state should it be sold in fee. (4.4.18–22)

Along with Hamlet and Schmitt, Doll Tearsheet might also be called as an authority on the matter of occupation. A prostitute and an unpartisan witness to England's nationalistic military campaign against France, she would especially be attuned to the presumptively gendered and irredeemably violent discourse of territorial occupation. For Doll Tearsheet, picturing the world, or land, or for that matter a woman's body as a thing that can be staked out or territorialized is also a clear sign of cultural and linguistic decline:

> He a captain? Hang him, rogue, he lives upon mouldy
> stewed prunes and dried cakes. A captain? God's
> light, these villains will make the word as odious
> as the word "occupy;" which was an excellent good
> word before it was ill sorted; therefore captains
> had need look to 't . . . . (*Henry IV, Part 2*, 2.4.136–41)[35]

Claudius's murderous scheme to assume the place of sovereign is neither reflective nor pacific, but even he appreciates the political significance of pausing: "This sudden sending [of Hamlet] away" must, he sees, at least "*seem*/Deliberate pause" (4.3.8–9, italics added). If anyone can take a cue from Claudius, it is Hamlet. At sea, Hamlet is for once suitably attired, having exchanged his "inky cloak" (1.2.77) for a "sea-gown," which—he tells his friends so they can picture it—he wore "scarf'd about [him]" (5.2.13). Yet upon discovering Denmark's letter to England the first thing he does is remark how poorly his death sentence is written. He then rewrites the letter in his own hand, which, as it happens, is also a convincing imitation of the language of diplomacy (captains had need look to 't). Lauding the "peace" that should "stand a comma 'tween their amities" (5.2.42), he requests the "sudden death" of Rosencrantz and Guildenstern, "[no] shriving-time allowed" (5.2.47), and for a patch of time fortune swings.

Before Shakespeare's Merchant of Venice lost almost everything on the high seas, while England was repulsing the Spanish Armada, Giovanni Botero very well remarked that "one of the main reasons for the peaceful condition of Venice is the canals which so intersect the city that its inhabitants can only meet together with difficulty and after much delay, during which their grievance is remedied."[36] Whether conceived in spatial or temporal terms, the pause is a practical way of negotiating differences. Such canny city planning was of little use to Shylock, though it may well have helped his daughter, Jessica, to improvise a novel identity for herself. In any event, the *in*deliberate pause—a momentary suspension of the laws that normally inform agency, define identity, and direct our plots—proves pivotal in *Hamlet*, though supposedly anathema to Hamlet.

In broader terms, the indeliberate pause represents a significant theoretical interruption of static, familiar narratives of identity, whether national, cultural, or subjective. (To be, and not to be.) There are numerous examples one could cite in this connection but I think *Hamlet* is a particularly good one, in part because it maps speculative or imaginative freedom onto a political freedom of sorts. To flesh out the kind of freedom I have in mind, I would look, further, to those two other chronicles of intersecting orders and disorders: *Pericles* and *The Merchant of Venice*. I take my cue here from an unlikely source. John Ruskin's treatise on Venetian art and architecture, published between 1851 and 1853 as *The Stones of Venice*, opens on a characteristically high note of aesthetic nostalgia and moral edification:

> Since the first dominion of men was asserted over the ocean, three thrones, of mark beyond all others, have been set upon its sands: the thrones of Tyre, Venice, and England. Of the First of these great powers only the memory remains; of the Second, the ruin; the Third, which inherits their greatness, if it forget their example, may be led through prouder eminence to less pitied destruction. The exaltation, the sin, and the punishment of Tyre have been recorded for us, in perhaps the most touching words ever uttered by the Prophets of Israel against the cities of the stranger. [But we forget] . . . that they were once as in Eden, [a paradise]. [Tyre's] successor [i.e., Venice] is still left for our beholding in the final period of her decline: a ghost upon the sands of the sea, so weak . . . that we might well doubt . . . which was the City, and which the Shadow.[37]

"I would endeavor to trace the lines of this image," Ruskin continues, "before it be for ever lost, and to record, as far as I may, [its] warning."[38]

That Ruskin's narrative of the rise and fall of empire originates with the "domination of men over the ocean" is consistent with Schmitt's emphasis on the importance of maritime dominance for England's belated but undisputed emergence as a sovereign nation-state.[39] This is true even though Schmitt's landmark of decisive geopolitical transformation—his "origin"—is planted firmly between 1588 and 1688, while Ruskin's port of departure is the ancient city, and ancient history, of Tyre: a lost Eden, an island fortress-city, or, depending on which authority is consulted, an abandoned fishing village. The specific authority to which Ruskin alludes is Ezekiel 26–27:1–36, in which God in his vengeance promises that Tyre "shall become a spoil to the nations" and that the "renowned city, which was strong in the sea," will be engulfed by the sea and "to be built no more." But on Ruskin's shelf the King James Bible was probably never very far from *The Collected Works*, and in Shakespeare, Pericles is still Prince of Tyre. At some point in the course of the series of shipwrecks, contingencies, and generic distortions called *Pericles*, the Prince washes up on the shore and overhears three fishermen debating (obviously) the natural law of predation and how the man-made laws of countries—civil law, that is—might stand up beside it.[40]

In an apostrophe to the heavens, Pericles begs some mercy of respite. While the gods listen, or more likely remain silent, Fisherman 1 expresses pity for the castaways he looked on powerlessly. Fisherman 3 similarly recalls marveling at the pitiful spectacle of a "porpas" thrashed by the rough sea, adding only that if porpoises are "half fish, half flesh," how much more marvelous, then, that "fishes live in the sea," that they survive. But the fantastic scene of Shakespearean romance leaves few illusions intact. Mere fish live in rough seas exactly "as men do a-land": "the great ones eat up the little ones," just as the rich, like a great whale that consumes small fry and a "whole parish" too, prey upon the poor (5.66–68). Passing through the figure of an amphibious Leviathan, Fisherman 1 exchanges sea for land as the more appropriate vehicle for the political tenor of his speech. Were he to occupy the place of "good King Simonides," he states, "We would purge the land of these drones that rob the bee of her honey" (83–84). One possible implication of this otherwise imperious statement is that the king may not in fact be "good." Despite his royal lineage, it is an implication that Pericles seems to approve. Like the small fry devoured by a Leviathan, he too has been swallowed and spat out (and swallowed and spat out again). In terms that recall both Schmitt's and Ruskin's narratives of the uncertain, amphibian origins of British sovereignty, Pericles remarks (aside):

> How from the finny subject of the sea
> These fishers tell the infirmities of men,
> And from their wat'ry empire recollect
> All that men may prove or men detect! (5.85–88)

As I have proposed, Hamlet's offshore, unstaged, and unanticipated run-in with a band of pirates—in short, *Hamlet*'s pause—disrupts familiar models of sovereign power based on land, and, by extension, the privilege accorded to the "origin" as a marker of social and political legitimacy. Hamlet claims this privilege for himself as someone "to the manner born," but he stands even more to gain from its unanticipated interruption. If Elsinore is a "city of the stranger" no less than Tyre or Venice, and no more so for Claudius than for Hamlet, *Twelfth Night*'s Illyria—a country once known for piracy[41]—could also qualify. It too is an amphibious state: "barbaric," in Carl Schmitt's particular sense of that term, or as Sir Toby Belch might put it, a state temporarily fixed "in standing water, between boy and man" (*Twelfth Night*, 1.5.141–42). Additionally, many of Illyria's inhabitants are also "amphibious" in the sense (given above) of "occupying two positions; connected with or combining two classes, ranks, offices, qualities, etc."[42] The *Oxford English Dictionary*'s entry for the adjectival use of the word offers a fair gloss of Viola's suspended identity, citing Thomas Browne's *Religio Medici* ("We are onely that amphibious piece between a corporall and spirituall essence"), and Joseph Addison's scandalized remark in *The Spectator* (no. 435) of "an Amphibious Dress" not merely suited but "belonging to both sexes." In drag and the servant of two masters, Viola occupies two positions. ("I am not, what I am.") So too does her twin brother Sebastian, destined, as he is, for Olivia and beloved of Antonio. Antonio, however, somehow got himself involved in a "sea-fight 'gainst the Count his galleys" (3.3.26) and no sooner lands on the shores of Illyria than he is charged with being a pirate and a thief (5.1.72). While the nature of his crime is obscure, without much ado he is recast as an enemy of the state, thus leaving the several sets of lovers to contrive their own endings. In *Twelfth Night*, the narrative pause or hiatus marked by Antonio's absence (and by his eventual return) serves to advance the play's heteronormative telos and to facilitate comedic closure. In Illyria, the same space of time that was afforded to Hamlet works against Antonio, consolidating rather than disrupting the plot against him. As a place of stasis and arrest, Illyria cannot be interrupted as Denmark is interrupted. It is a continuing city where the rain, when it comes, just rains (5.1.381–400).

What are "cities of the stranger," then? These cities of kites and craws, or brave new worlds, or else a world elsewhere; a wilderness of tigers: Elsinore, say, or Tyre. What can be said of them more generally? For whom or to what do these watery shadows of empire present a threat, and how do you get there from here, anyway? However variously they are imagined in Shakespeare, the surest way to get there is by sea. Or else to follow the shoreline, insofar as that is possible. Unlike the sea, earth or land has "fixed and visible lines of geographical demarcation" and therefore helps "ensure that territory may be stably portioned among those who occupy it."[43] Indeed, good fences make good neighbors. But the apparently clear demarcation of land and sea—the shoreline—is amorphous. According to the *Institutes* of Justinian, "The shore of the sea extends to the point attained by the highest tide in winter,"[44] but as Fishermen 1 and 3 would know, this point cannot easily be fixed;[45] consequently, civil laws that take it as their foundation will be precariously balanced.

In the *Laws of England* Henry de Bracton recites the principle that "De balena vero sufficit, si rex habeat caput, et regina caudam"[46]: if a whale is captured on England's coast, its head must be apportioned to the king and its tail offered to the queen. (The Latin tag also serves as an epigraph to chapter ninety of *Moby-Dick*, "Heads or Tails.") For Bracton, this principle should be followed not according to any law or rights of water (which had yet to be established), but simply out of respect for the king. But this purely formal, arbitrary gesture of deference might attest less to sovereign power—as it is intended to to—than to its fundamental impotence, especially when confronted with the "watery empire" of the sea. Against the backdrop of land-based claims to state sovereignty that, for all their promise of stability, have more often proved fiercely divisive, what I am calling "cities of the stranger" suggest an alternate way of defining—or rather conceiving—political communities: both those we inhabit and those we may only wish to inhabit.[47]

> PERICLES. What countrywoman [are you]? Here of the shores?
> MARINA. No, nor of any shores . . .
> PERICLES. Where do you live?
> MARINA. Where I am but a stranger. (5.1.126)

"Call me Ishmael," she might as well have said. Or maybe, "As the indifferent children of the earth," which is Rosencrantz's somewhat astonishing reply to Hamlet's familiar greeting of "Hey, how's it going?"[48]

Like the privilege customarily accorded to origins, "original" is a familiar honorific normally bestowed with faith in its self-evident value, which is also to say, here, its *virtù*. Embedded in the term's etymology ("to rise," "to stand")[49] is the peculiar faith sometimes invested in self-made men, manmade things, and other such fictions: each and all of them erected on a hylomorphic conception of how things come to be, "in the beginning . . . ." By contrast, the significance of the pause, as I have tried to describe it here, has more in common with the generative stupidity of Spenser's Knight of Holiness or, again, Saint Augustine's interminable confessions, both of which—like Milton's poem too, in its way—are driven by an effort to elude the sternly linear, sequential temporality entailed by the very notion of a "beginning" or an "origin."[50] The indefinite shoreline, like the suspended pause, is an occasion to revisit impoverished critical vocabularies that stymie efforts—heroic, romantic, quotidian, ordinary, visible, invisible, scholarly, spontaneous efforts—to conceive of a world, including the murmuring swarm of its constitutive relations, in nondualistic terms. At least not terms always given in advance. Such efforts attest to a trans- or pre- or perhaps peri-personal ethical "sense of connection"—that is, to "an integrity always yet to be"[51] that allows us to engage the viscerally hypothetical nature of our individual, particulate identities at any given time and to interrupt the ostensive necessity of a world pivoting on familiar axes of identity and difference, past and present, figure and ground.

In the passage I have taken as my epigraph, the apostle to whom Donne refers is Paul, in his Epistle to the Hebrews, chapter 13. An exhortation to persist in the face of prosecution and political geographical displacement, the letter opens with the directive to "be not forgetful to entertain strangers" and urges its audience to venture "without the gate." Given a context in which the positions of stranger and host are highly unstable, the letter, as I read it through Donne, presents something other than a council of abstract universalism, "brotherly love," or the certitude of a world presumed to be "Immovable, infixed, and frozen round." This is very far from Ezekiel's cataphatic fury to undo the carefully assembled and beautifully adorned city of Tyre, whose "borders are in the midst of the seas": its daughters slaughtered, its princes stripped and dethroned, the unreal city will be swallowed by the sea leaving only "a place to spread nets upon" (Ezek. 26–27). But the sea, Donne continues, extrapolating, is "bottomless to any line which we can sound it with, and endless to any discovery that we can make of it." Here, then, is a topos of worldmaking, or else, if "eloquence is not our net," a trope of adventure, the pirated edition.[52]

NOTES

1. Goran Dahlbach, "The Towns," in *Scandinavia*, vol. 1, *Prehistory to 1520*, ed. Knut Helle, 611–34 (Cambridge: Cambridge University Press, 2003).

2. One of Hamlet's two best friends contradicts him on this point, first arguing that if Denmark is a prison, why then, the whole world is one, and then just flatly denying it: "We think not so, my lord" (2.2.249). But Hamlet's reply—"there is nothing either good or bad but thinking makes it so" (l.250–51)—is not a sign of particular insight or an index of speculative genius. He's just being sarcastic. In other words, I think we often mistake Hamlet for Rosencrantz.

Here as throughout, I cite the Arden *Hamlet*, ed. Ann Thompson and Neil Taylor (London: Arden Shakespeare and Cengage Learning, 2006). All other plays cited are from *The Arden Shakespeare: Complete Works*, rev. ed., ed. Ann Thompson, David Scott Kastan, and Richard Proudfoot (London: Arden Shakespeare and Cengage Learning, 2002).

3. See also *Hamlet*, 5.2.19–24.

4. For a general discussion of reading Shakespeare historically, see, for instance, Lisa Jardine, *Reading Shakespeare Historically* (New York: Routledge, 1996).

5. Carl Schmitt, *Hamlet or Hecuba: The Intrusion of the Time into the Play*, trans. David Pan and Jennifer R. Rust (New York: Telos, 2009), 60–61.

6. Schmitt, *Hamlet or Hecuba*, 63.

7. Herman Melville, *Moby-Dick*, Norton Critical Editions, 2nd ed., ed. Hershal Parker and Harrison Hayford (New York: W. W. Norton, 2002), 107.

8. Carl Schmitt, *The Nomos of the Earth in the International Law of Jus Publicum Europaeum*, trans. G. L. Ulmen (New York: Telos, 2003). This text was first published in 1950.

9. As Tracy B. Strong notes in the foreword to *Political Theology: Four Chapters on the Concept of Sovereignty*, trans. George Schwab (Cambridge, MA: MIT Press, 1985), xii–xxxvi, viii–ix.

10. Terry Eagleton, *How to Read Literature* (New Haven, CT: Yale University Press 2013), 24.

11. Compare Wordsworth: "smitten / Abruptly, with the view (a sight not rare) / Of a blind beggar" who carries a sign describing "whence he came, and who he was," as if admonishing the young poet "from another world." William Wordsworth, *The Prelude: 1799, 1805, 1850*, Norton Critical Editions, ed. M. H. Abrams, Stephen Gill, and Jonathan Wordsworth. New York: W. W. Norton, 1979), 7.637–47.

12. Melville, Moby-Dick, 221–22. Emphasis added.

13. Or, by Schmitt's own lights, the national poet he could only later become. My suggestion that Schmitt mistakes Shakespeare for his subsequent incarnation as England's "national poet" is hardly damning but this inconsistency may be worth noting. Schmitt's salutary and undeniably influential account of emergent political modernity implicitly draws on the very thing his analysis discredits; namely, the establishment of British sovereignty and consolidation of national identity *avant la lettre*.

14. Schmitt, *Hamlet or Hecuba*, 64.

15. The relevant passage can be found in Voltaire's *Dix-huiteme lettre sur la tragégie*: "Il semble que les Anglais n'aient été faits jusqu'ici que pour produire des beautés irrégulières. Les monstres brillants de Shakespeare plaisent mille fois plus que la sagesse moderne. Le génie poétique des Anglais ressemble jusqu'à présent à un arbre touffu planté par la nature, jetant au hasard mille rameaux, et croissant inégalement et avec force ; il meurt, si vous voulez forcer sa nature et le tailler en arbre des jardins de Marly." Voltaire, *Lettres Philisophiques Par M. de V*. . . (Amsterdam, Chez M. Lucas, au Livre d'or, 1734), 224, http://gallica.bnf.fr/ark:/12148/bpt6k72251b.4=+voltaire+lettres+philosophiques.langEN.

16. Schmitt, *Political Theology*, 15.

17. Schmitt, *Hamlet or Hecuba*, 64.

18. Ibid., 65.

19. If the sovereign is he who decides the exception and holds power over life and death, one might also say that King Claudius is sovereign *de jure* but not *de facto*. See, Schmitt, *Political Theology*. See also Giorgio Agamben's *State of Exception*, and particularly his claim that it is "possible to see the *iustitium* (in the sense of public morning [sic]) as nothing other than the sovereign's attempt to appropriate the state of exception by transforming it into a family affair." Giorgio Agamben, *State of Exception*, trans. Kevin Attell (Chicago: University of Chicago Press, 2005), 68.

20. See Barbara Fuchs's recent *The Poetics of Piracy: Emulating Spain in English Literature* (Philadelphia: University of Pennsylvania Press, 2013), which examines the disruptive agency of piracy in early modern Europe.

21. Thomas Hobbes, *Leviathan or the Matter, Forme, & Power of a Common-Wealth Ecclesiasticall and Civill*, ed. Ian Shapiro (New Haven, CT: Yale University Press, 2010), 54.

22. Daniel Heller-Roazen, *The Enemy of All: Piracy and the Law of Nations* (Cambridge, MA: MIT Press, 2009), 83.

23. I shall return to this point below, but compare with the *Oxford English Dictionary*'s entry for "amphibious," especially entries 2.a ("Of, pertaining to, suited for, or connected with both land and water") and 3 ("Having two lives; occupying two positions; connected with or combining two classes, ranks, offices, qualities, etc."). *Oxford English Dictionary Online*, s.v. "amphibious," http://owww.oed.com.mercury.concordia.ca/view/Entry/6627?redirectedFrom=amphibious&.

24. Instances of these familiar readings can be found in, for example, John E. Curran Jr., *Hamlet, Protestantism and the Mourning of Contingency: Not to Be* (Aldershot, England: Ashgate Publishing Company, 2006); Heather Hirschfeld, "Hamlet's 'First Corse': Repetition, Trauma, and the Displacement of Redemptive Typology," *Shakespeare Quarterly* 54, no. 4 (Winter 2003): 424–48; and Leroy F. Searle, "The Conscience of the King: Oedipus, Hamlet, and the Problem of Reading," *Comparative Literature* 49, no. 4 (Autumn 1997): 316–43.

25. Ágnes Heller, *The Time Is Out of Joint: Shakespeare as Philosopher of History* (Cambridge: Blackwell Publishers, 2000).

26. Ibid., 122.

27. John Milton, *Paradise Lost*, ed. Alastair Fowler (London: Longman, 1998).

28. See, for example, Stephen M. Fallon, *Milton among the Philosophers* (Ithaca, NY: Cornell University Press, 1991).

29. This is also as an illustration of what Foucault would describe as a generative tension extended between "the self as reason and the self as point."

Michel Foucault, *The History of Sexuality*, vol. 3, *The Care of the Self*, trans. Robert Hurley (New York: Random House, 1986), 279.

30. Jonathan Goldberg, *The Seeds of Things: Materializing Sexuality and Materiality in Renaissance Representations* (New York: Fordham University Press, 2009), 55.

31. Saint Augustine, *Confessions*, trans. Henry Chadwick (Oxford: Oxford University Press, 1992), book 11, 240.

32. John Donne, "Sermon LXXII," 1640 Folio, in *Seventeenth-Century Prose and Poetry*, 2nd ed., ed. Alexander M. Witherspoon and Frank J. Warnke, 86–97 (San Diego, CA: Harcourt Brace Jovanovich, 1963).

33. John Donne, *Devotions upon Emergent Occasions*, 1624, Meditation 17.

34. Another relevant definition of "stake" is, that to which someone whose loyalty is doubted is tied and then burned. *Oxford English Dictionary Online*, s.v. "stake," http://0-www.oed.com.mercury.concordia.ca/view/Entry/188759.

35. *Oxford English Dictionary Online*, s.v. "occupy": 8.a *trans.*: "To have sexual intercourse or relations with." In this connection, *OED* (8.b) also quotes John Florio's 1598 *Worlde of Wordes*: "*Tentuno*: a punishment inflicted by ruffianly fellowes uppon raskalie whores in Italy, who . . . cause them to be occupide one and thirtie times by one and thirtie seuerall base raskalie companions."

36. Giovanni Botero, "Relations, of the Most Famous Kingdoms and Commonweals Through the World" (1597), in *The Broadview Anthology of British Literature* (Peterborough, Ontario, Canada: Broadview Press, 2015), 210–11.

37. John Ruskin, *The Stones of Venice*, ed. J. G. Links (New York: Da Capo, 2003), 13.

38. Ruskin finds a strange bedfellow in Foucault. In *The Order of Things*, Foucault represents the crisis or rupture in the history of "man" as the image of "a face drawn in sand at the edge of the sea." Michel Foucault, *The Order of Things: An Archaeology of the Human Sciences* (New York: Vintage Books, 1994), 387.

39. See also *"Society Must Be Defended": Lectures at the College de France, 1975–7*, ed. Mauro Bertani and Alessandro Fontana, trans. David Macey (New York: Picador, 2003). Chapter 2, "14 January 1976," is of particular relevance.

40. Close cousins of *King Lear*'s samphire gatherers, who practice their "deadly trade" on a cliff's edge, the fisherman are the only laborers to appear in Shakespeare's romances.

41. Jonathan Goldberg, *Shakespeare's Hand* (Minneapolis: University of Minnesota Press, 2003), 79–104.

42. *OED Online*, s.v. "amphibious."

43. Heller-Roazen, *The Enemy of All*, 163.

44. Heller-Roazen, *The Enemy of All*, 64. To underscore the tenacity of this definition, Heller-Roazen also notes that, in France, this "remained the accepted criterion for the delimitation of the public domain along the Mediterranean until 1973." Ibid., 64.

45. The Bay of Fundy, for instance, has an extremely high tidal range, with a mean of 53.5 feet.

46. Henry de Bracton, *Bracton on the Laws and Customs of England*, Bracton Online, Harvard Law School Library, 13.3, http://bracton.law.harvard.edu/.

47. Jacques Derrida, *On Cosmopolitanism and Forgiveness*, trans. Mark Dooley and Michael Hughes (New York: Routledge, 2004), 21–22.

48. "How do ye both?" are Hamlet's exact words (2.2.241).

49. See *Oxford English Dictionary Online*, s.v. "origin," n. and adj.: classical Latin *orīgin-*, *orīgō* ancestry, coming into being, beginning, that from which something is derived, source *orīrī* to ris.

50. See Saint Augustine, *Confessions*, trans. Henry Chadwick (Oxford: Oxford University Press, 1992), 227.

51. See Goldberg, *The Seeds of Things*.

52. John Donne, *The Sermons of John Donne*, vol. 10, ed. George Reuben Potter (Berkeley: University of California Press, 1955), 307.

PART III

Universality

CHAPTER 8

What It Feels Like to Be a Body: Humoralism, Cognitivism, and the Sociological Horizon of Early Modern Religion

Daniel Juan Gil

Over the past ten years scholars have attempted to reconstruct how early modern subjects understood their own bodily and emotional life primarily through the early modern discourse of Galenic humoralism, itself inherited from classical antiquity.[1] The central conviction of Galenic/humoral discourse is that the body is a porous container for fluids that mechanically determine the health and emotional state of the person. Pioneering scholars like Michael C. Schoenfeldt, Mary Floyd-Wilson, Gail Kern Paster, and Bruce R. Smith have touched off a tidal wave of subsequent studies that impute to early modern culture a basically mechanistic picture of the human person.[2] This approach has produced what I see as an equal but opposite reaction, in the form of cognitivist accounts of emotional experience as the result of judgments by the self about its situation in the world. I see humoral and cognitivist approaches as mirror images of each other in that each assumes a basic distinction between mind and body, with the humoralists focused on the side of the body and the cognitivists on the side of the mind.

I argue that focusing on early modern religious discourse opens a different path to reconstructing early modern somatic and emotional life, not least because this discourse is, somewhat surprisingly, capable of escaping from the mind/body distinction. In particular I focus on the early modern discourse of resurrection, and here I focus on what I take to be the deepest (and certainly most ancient) version of this belief within Christianity—the notion that the person is the body and the body is the person so that if the person is to live again the body must live again, too. I argue that this belief deeply conditions how early modern subjects experienced, interpreted, and theorized their own bodily and emotional life in the here and now in ways that are quite different from either humoralism or cognitivism. Insofar as early modern subjects interpreted themselves in light of a theory of resurrection they declined to see their emotional and somatic life as the result of fluid hydraulics or purely mental judgments about things and people in the world. Instead, they understood their emotional and somatic experience as the fruits of deep, unconscious habituation into a historical world, as signs of how the embodied self is captured by a contingent social and historical world. From a resurrectionist standpoint, this way of treating somatic and emotional life is inseparable from the project of gaining awareness of another dimension of bodily life, a pulsating vital core that is at one and the same time the very thing that is socialized and also deeply resistant to socialization and that can be understood as the seed or sign of a future resurrection.

Thus, as against both humoralist approaches and cognitivist approaches, the discourse of resurrection I examine here bypasses mind-body dualism by positing in its stead a distinction between two forms of embodied experience: on the one hand, a historically conditioned and deeply habituated dimension of bodily life and, on the other hand, an experience of the body as the very thing that transcends a particular historical moment. From this standpoint, emotional life is valued precisely because it is a sign of the degree and quality of a person's habituation into a social world. Indeed, one of the major arguments I make here is that insofar as this religious perspective highlights how much of bodily life including emotional experience is the fruit of deep, unaware habituation into a contingent social world, this perspective delivers what we, in retrospect, can understand as a sociological framework on the self and the world, one that strongly anticipates Pierre Bourdieu's cultural sociology and his important concept of "habitus." Thus I claim that early modern resurrection beliefs represent—quite unexpectedly—one root of what ultimately becomes a theoretically articulated sociological awareness.

My argument moves in two waves. First, I critique humoral and cognitive approaches to emotional life and sketch out a theoretical alternative that draws heavily on Bourdieusian cultural sociology. Second, I argue that the place where early moderns themselves did this kind of proto-sociological "theorizing" of embodiment and emotional life was in the discourse of resurrection. To illustrate this intellectual history argument I analyze Henry Vaughan's translation of a German medical treatise by a Paracelsian thinker named Heinrich Nolle. Since we know something of Vaughan's background beliefs about resurrection from his poetry and religious writings, we will be in a position to see how those background beliefs condition the explicitly corporeal and implicitly sociological account of the body and emotional life that emerges in his translation of the Nolle text.

I

Before turning to the kind of alternative thinking about the embodied (and emotion-experiencing) self that I see in early modern resurrection discourse, I want to examine the current scholarship on humoralism and cognitivism in greater detail and to propose a theoretical alternative to both. At the heart of much of the scholarship on humoralism lie two questions that are logically separate but that are, in practice, often conflated:

1. How did early modern theorists of the emotions conceptualize and describe the emotions?
2. How did early modern people engaged in the practice of everyday life actually experience and interpret their emotional life?

Many early modern theorists did, in fact, turn to the classical discourse of the humors to conceptualize somatic and emotional life and to propose therapies for sickness or emotional dysfunction. The modern scholarly program devoted to answering the first question is ironic in that it does not ask if the humoral theories espoused by early modern writers actually corresponded to the real experiences of real people in early modern England. Rather, the scholarly program organized around the first question simply describes how early modern writers working in the humoral tradition imagined emotional life.

The second question is quite different from the first: it does not seek to describe how early modern theorists theorized the emotions; rather, it inquires what the actual emotional experience of early modern subjects was like: Why did early modern people experience the emotions they did? How did those emotions feel? How did early modern subjects interpret or understand their emotional life? To address this second set of concerns we need more than an ironic theory of the emotions. Rather, we need a theory of early modern emotional life that is true as an account of actual emotional experience. Such a theory may well require us to set aside some or even much of early modern humoral theory as a red herring.

In the practice of scholarship, answers to the first question (How did early modern theorists theorize the emotions?) are often made to seem like answers to the second question (What did early modern emotions feel like?). It is, of course, true that early modern humoral discourse must have captured some of the ways people experienced their own emotions in early modern England; to be persuasive as a theory, early modern Galenic humoralism would have to match everyday experience, at least for the elite readers of treatises on the passions. But at the same time, treating answers to the first question as answers to the second question often ends up creating a picture of early modern emotional life that is almost unimaginably strange to us. This strangeness is typically explained by the hypothesis that people's experience of themselves as embodied and as emotion-producing has changed dramatically from the early modern period to today, and that work that recovers the strangeness of the early modern experience is worthwhile precisely because it expands our imaginative understanding of human life and human experience. While this is doubtless at least partly true, it also covers up the methodological conflation of the two very different questions I posed above.

To evaluate whether (or to what extent) early modern humoral discourse gives us an account of how early modern people experienced their somatic and emotional lives, we have to assess whether humoral theory is a logically or empirically plausible account of anybody's somatic and emotional life. The cognitivist approach that has been dominant in psychology and that has started to play an increasingly important role in scholarship on early modern emotions sees the humoral model as radically underplaying the role of subjective judgment in producing emotion. From the cognitivist standpoint, the self cares about many things in many different ways, and it is judgments by the self about what matters to it that account for emotions, both positive, when the self's concerns are advanced, and negative, when the self's concerns are blocked. By contrast, the humoral approach is radically anticognitivist insofar as it sees felt emotions as the mechanical result of the fluid makeup of the body, and it sees changes to the makeup of the body as the path to changing emotional life. From the cognitivist standpoint, what is wrong with the humoral model is that it is too mechanistic or hydraulic, blunting the role that subjective judgments about the world play in producing an emotional life that is (and, therefore, *feels*) saturated with subjective thought.

Of course, a major reason that today's scholars have been so drawn to the humoral model is precisely that it challenges the Cartesian vision of the autonomous, thinking self that is assumed by cognitivist accounts of emotional life. Indeed, for many contemporary scholars, the cognitivist model is wrong precisely because it overvalues the conscious, judging mind, when at least some of emotional life seems very bodily and to have a certain autopilot quality to it. But endorsing the humoral vision of an essentially mechanical emotional life is not a critique of the Cartesian account of mind but an equal and opposite reaction to it. Indeed, Descartes himself endorses a completely mechanical account of emotional experience as the necessary counterpart to his purely cognitivist account of mental life.[3] Whereas the humors provide a purely mechanistic, almost robotic account of the emotional life (making no appeal to mind at all), the cognitive approach posits a disembodied mind as the ultimate explanation for emotional life. What both approaches share is a commitment to the fundamental separateness of mind and body. Pure humoralism and pure cognitivism are mirror images of each other, both fundamentally committed to mind-body dualism.

One model that allows us to move beyond the sterile debate between these mirror-image dualisms is Pierre Bourdieu's cultural sociology.[4] On the face of it, Bourdieusian sociology does not project a theory of emotions at all. In fact, however, a theory of emotions is implicit in Bourdieu's account.[5] Implicitly, Bourdieu's sociology provides a powerful perspective on emotions by evading any differentiation of the mind and the body, pointing instead to a primordial state in which people are socially imbricated and habituated within a particular social world. For Bourdieu, most of life is unconscious and habitual, the product of unaware socialization. From this perspective, it is wrong to imagine that human beings fundamentally operate by making conscious judgments about what matters to them in the world and what they wish for (as the cognitivists assume). When this kind of abstract, reflective consciousness appears at all, it appears in a secondary way, upon the foundation of the vast, silent sea of an unconscious, habituated form of life. As Bourdieu writes in *The Logic of Practice*,

> The conditionings associated with a particular class of conditions of existence produce *habitus*, systems of durable, transposable dispositions, structured structures predisposed to function as structuring structures, that is, as principles which generate and organize practices and representations that can be objectively adapted to their outcomes without presupposing a conscious aiming at ends or an express mastery of the operations necessary in order to attain them. Objectively "regulated"

> and "regular" without being in any way the product of obedience to rules, they can be collectively orchestrated without being the product of the organizing action of a conductor.[6]

For Bourdieu, people are born into a particular quadrant of the social world and they are socialized into skillfully dealing with it. It is only when things go awry, or when people move from one area of the social world to another—only, in other words, when people find themselves not at home anymore—that people bring their practice to reflective consciousness and try to articulate explicit rules and criteria for defining their own goals and possibilities. As Bourdieu sees people, they are habit machines who are born into particular social worlds; their habits reflect their social world and glue them into it.

On Bourdieu's account, people always habitually (and therefore unconsciously) care about many things, wishing for or holding onto some things and disavowing or spurning others. These attitudes do not require conscious judgments; they are implicit judgments, they are inscribed in the body in an almost automated way, and one of the main ways one's habituated situatedness appears in the world is through emotional responses. Bourdieu uses the term "habitus" for this constitutive habituated way of caring about the world that manifests itself as a textured emotional life. From this standpoint, we can say that emotional responses are not triggered by conscious or even unconscious judgments about the world (as the cognitivist theory would have it), nor are they the product of purely physical forces in the body (as the humoralists would have it); rather, emotional responses simply are the ways in which the subject is habituated into a social world. From a Bourdieusian perspective, emotional experiences do not require a mentalistic judgment about a world that is separate from the self; rather, emotional responses follow from the unconscious, skillful ways of dealing with a social world that one has in virtue of being social. People are born and socialized into a particular corner of a particular social world and because of the situation they are in, things matter to them implicitly or habitually, and these implicit or habitual connections between selves and other people and things in their world define emotional states that "work," as if on autopilot. This "autopilot" quality is what the scholarship on humoralism imagines that it captures when it buys into an early modern discourse that describes merely physical substances as generating emotional experience. But to describe the emotions as the result of ("dumb," as it were) humoral imbalances is to deprive them of the significant (if implicit) meaningfulness that they always have for people whose lives are habitual patterns within particular social worlds, a meaningfulness, in other words, that comes from the fact that people always are in a situation in which things matter and in which emotional life is one measure of who and what matters and how.

The scholarship on humoralism blunts this implicit, habituated meaningfulness of emotional experience, and this blunting falsifies the phenomenology of emotional experience, the way it must have been felt and experienced in early modern England just as it is experienced now, because of the basic ontological reality of humans as socially embedded and socially habituated.

In essence, my complaint about the scholarship on humoralism is that it is too ironic, refusing to take a philosophical stand on the ontological question of emotional life (where it comes from, how it relates body and mind, how it relates the individual and his or her social horizon). Absent a non-ironic theory of emotional life, scholarship adopts a bad faith, ironic sensibility, describing early modern culture as though it were free to define the experience of emotions on the basis of a false belief, namely, that the humors mechanically determine emotional experience. While such scholarship is often right in its reconstruction of early modern humoral discourse, it is surely wrong in its (explicit or implicit) claim that this discourse provides a window into how emotions were experienced and understood in day-to-day life. What humoral scholarship lacks is attention to the fact that people's real emotional experience always takes place within a horizon of intelligibility provided by a social world that is defined by concrete, practical, habituated life. That is as true today as it would have been in the early modern period, so that understanding the spectrum of emotional experiences and how people related to them in early modern England would require more than raiding literary texts for snippets of humoral (or, for that matter, cognitive) thinking. Rather, it would require reconstructing (or "objectifying," as Bourdieu would put it) the entire (conflicted) social universe that early modern people were habituated into and that provided the horizon of intelligibility for their emotional experience just as much as the social world we are habituated into provides the horizon of intelligibility for our emotional experience.

II

Obviously, people do not need an explicit sociological theory to, in fact, experience emotions in light of a sociological horizon. Even absent any explicit sociological theory of the emotions in the early modern period, it should nonetheless be possible to reconstruct some of the features of the sociological horizon in light of which people experienced and interpreted their emotions. To do so we would have to look at various early modern discourses (including the literary) in a way that is informed by the sociological theory I have sketched above. A related but separate question is whether early moderns had any discourses in which they could in fact articulate a *theory* of a sociological horizon for emotions. As an explicit scientific discourse, Bourdieusian cultural sociology is obviously not present in early modern England, but I suggest that early modern culture does nonetheless contain some discursive antecedents to the kind of Bourdieusian theoretical approach I sketched above. The early modern discourse that comes closest to theorizing emotions in the way Bourdieu would is the discourse of the resurrection of the flesh. I see early modern resurrection beliefs as the site of a primary, spontaneous theory-work that parallels the theorizing I have attributed to Bourdieu. This is because belief in the resurrection of the body forces people to theorize how (and to what extent) the embodied self is embedded in a contingent social world that affects and conditions all corporeal experiences (even seemingly spontaneous or "natural" experience) and how (and to what extent) the embodied self can be imagined as separable from the contingent social world that it inhabits.

Seeing the discourse of resurrection as the site of a proto-sociological theory of the emotions that rejects mind-body dualism may seem surprising to scholars who assume that early modern resurrection beliefs primarily see death as a liberation of a transhistorically pure soul from the body. But ideas about resurrection are quite conflicted in the early modern period. The body-soul dualism that emerged in the scholastic Middle Ages, and that does play an important part in Calvinist and Puritan writings, is nevertheless always in tension with resurrection theories that are monist in insisting that the person is the body and the body is the person so that if the person is to live again, the body must live again. From this point of view, death is not liberation of the separable soul; it is the true and total death of the person (a position sometimes called mortalism) until the apocalyptic future in which the body is reconstructed and the person lives again. Moreover, while much resurrection thought is apocalyptic, there is a powerful countercurrent that insists that resurrection is somehow immanent in the creation we have now—in the sense of already unfolding in the here and now so that it is possible to catch sight of the "seed" of a future resurrection in the here and now. I focus on this immanent and monist strand of resurrection thought and the way it affects how somatic and emotional life are experienced and interpreted. Looking at the self in the light of such a theory of resurrection has the effect of forcing attention quite insistently to the body and yet seeing the body itself as split between a sociologically conditioned set of experiences that must, per force, be left behind at resurrection and a fleshly life that is other than the life of the socialized person and that is nevertheless his or her very essence insofar as it is precisely what shall be resurrected. This basic point of view is well illustrated in the poetry and religious writings of Henry Vaughan.

Vaughan is noteworthy for holding an explicitly monist and immanent understanding of resurrection. He denies that the soul can live on separately from its body, so that any post-death life is utterly dependent on the apocalyptic reconstruction of the body. Vaughan therefore rejects any comforting fantasies of souls continuing to live after the death of the body, as it were, by ascending directly to heaven. For him, death is total and complete until the end of time when bodies will be remade, a position he shares with Milton. But at the same time, Vaughan believes that it is possible, based on careful reflection on the experience of the body as it exists here and now, to catch sight of what a resurrected body will be like.[7] Though my focus here is on his religious and medical writings, Vaughan is best known for his powerful religious verse, much of which is devoted to searching himself in order to discover the material reality of a resurrection body that is already within himself and that displaces him from his conventional sociological coordinates.[8] Vaughan's goal in his poetry, in other words, is to uncover within himself the "Traces, and sounds of a strange kind," as he puts it in "Vanity of Spirit,"[9] that point forward to resurrection. Bypassing any soul/body distinction, Vaughan's searching analysis of himself splits his bodily life into two: on the one hand, a socialized and historicized life and, on the other hand, a life that, in its material strangeness, is alien to his time and place and therefore the substrate of resurrection.

Vaughan's search for the physical signs of a future resurrected life is heavily indebted to the important language of "seeds" that derives from Paul's great statement on resurrection in 1 Corinthians 15 (which I give here in the authorized translation that Vaughan used):

> But someone will ask, "How are the dead raised? With what kind of body do they come?" Fool! What you sow does not come to life unless it dies. And as for what you sow, you do not sow the body that is to be, but a bare seed, perhaps of wheat or of some other grain. But God gives it a body as he has chosen, and to each kind of seed its own body. (1 Cor. 15:36–39)[10]

The seed metaphor that he derives from Paul leads Vaughan to see resurrection as beginning in the here and now, with a part of the physical body already now containing the potential for resurrection. This perspective can be termed "immanent eschatology of the body" because it sees the resurrection of the body as immanent in the sense of *within the creation as it exists now*, following the resurrection of Christ as the "first fruits" (as Paul puts it in 1 Corinthians 15:23) of a more general process.[11] As Vaughan puts it in his 1652 collection of prayers and meditations entitled *The Mount of Olives*, death is total death and yet it is possible even now to see the corporeal trace of a future resurrection:

> Grant I beseech thee that this Celestial seed may take root in me, and be effectual to my salvation; Watch over my heart, O Lord, and hedge it in with thy grace, that the fowles which descend in the shadows of the Evening may not pick it out.[12]

For Vaughan, therefore, there is a natural body that will die, but within that body there is already now a seed that can "take root" within the self and thereby anticipate (now, in this life) what the resurrection of the whole body will be like in the future.

The notion of a seed or essential core that is present within the body—that is, indeed, the animating principle of all bodily life—and that anticipates a post-resurrection body is a recurring principle in Vaughan's writing. The transformative potential inherent in the language of seeds is one that we are only beginning to be aware of. In addition to its prominence in Christian discourse, the language of seeds also appears in classical discourses of generation and change, as well as proto-biological discourses of reproduction and embryology. Indeed, the language of seeds is a powerful entry point into early modern culture precisely because it fuses these different discourses into a sometimes unstable whole. Jonathan Goldberg's magisterial *The Seeds of Things: Theorizing Sexuality and Materiality in Renaissance Representations* traces some of these discursive connections and uses them to generate a brilliantly unsettling entry point into early modern culture.

My concern here is to describe how the "seed" language functions within a Pauline frame of reference to bring to consciousness a sociological sensibility about the embodied self and its experience of emotions. In Vaughan's poetry as well as in his religious and medical writing, the assumption that the seed of the resurrection body is already now within the socialized self affects how emotions are understood and experienced. Since one of the privileged ways people gain awareness of their bodies is through emotional experience, from the perspective of seeking the "celestial seed" within the self, emotions are interpreted as signs of the degree and quality of attachment to the social and historical world. From the perspective of the immanent eschatology of the body, when the self undergoes emotional experience, that experience must be queried as to the information it gives about, first, the part of the bodily self that is a habitually and conventionally social self and, second, about the part of the bodily self that is not a conventionally, habitually social self but that is, instead, pointing forward through time to an apocalyptic future. From this perspective, emotional experience is not understood mechanically but informationally; it gives information about two separate things.

First: somatic and emotional experience gives information about the part of the embodied self that is socially habituated. Rather than seeing the body as mechanical, the immanent resurrection perspective understands emotional experiences to testify to the degree and quality of situatedness in the world. From this perspective, the believer is born and socialized into a corner of a social world and because of the situation he or she is in, things matter to him or her implicitly or habitually and it is these implicit connections that come to light in emotional experience. Emotions are driven by a habitual way of being in the world—a habitus—and if properly attended to, emotions allow for this habitus to be brought into consciousness. In contrast to the humoral view, the resurrection perspective does not imagine everyday emotions to be mechanical or automated (nor, in contrast to a cognitivist account, are they understood to be voluntaristic, the result of "mere" judgments); rather, they are understood as driven by, and therefore also encoding information about, the way the self is caught by the social world. As Vaughan puts it in the dedication to Sir Charles Egerton in one of his religious self-help books, *Flores Solitudines* (1654), emotions testify to implicatedness of the self in the world, for "Man himselfe in his outward part, which was taken out of the world, feeles the like passions with the world."[13]

This perspective on the embodied self strongly anticipates the Bourdieusian notion of habitus. But from the standpoint of monist immanent resurrection theory, seeing the body as socially habituated is only the necessary condition for touching the vital principle within that is never fully subordinated to a historically and socially conditioned form of life.

Therefore, second: somatic and emotional experience can be understood to give information about the part of the embodied self that is *not* socially habituated, the part of the self that remains *other* to a socially defined identity, the part of the self that is the "celestial seed" of a future resurrection of the flesh. From the standpoint of immanent resurrection, persons become aware of the socialized, habituated world in them, and in becoming aware of it they are detached from it. But this newly conscious perspective on the self and its emotional life is experienced as a new set of emotional possibilities that point to the positive presence of something within the self that is moving away from being socially conditioned by the world. The quasi-sociological detachment from the social world produced by the search for a resurrection body within produces its own distinctive emotional life. For instance, Vaughan ends *The Mount of Olives* with a partial translation of Saint Jerome's "Life of Paulus" in which he emphasizes that the desert fathers had "here upon earth already begun the heavenly life; and regenerate Prophets who were indued not onely with holy habits, but had received therewith the Spirit of promise: for I have known many of them that were so free from malice, perverse thoughtfulnesse and suspition, as if they had never known that there were such evill wayes to be followed in the world. Such a great tranquillity of mind, and such a powerful love or longing after goodnesse had wholly possessed them."[14] The possibility of becoming "regenerate" amounts to cultivating the "celestial seed" that Vaughan here terms the "Spirit of promise," so that the body is itself infused with the spirit in a way that anticipates resurrection. Cultivating the resurrection body in the here and now aims for a transformation in which the self is detached from the conventional world, and this detachment is experienced as a radical transformation of emotional life in which some new emotional experiences become dominant and other emotional experiences wither away.

It should be obvious how far we are from the mechanistic humoral account of emotional life in which emotions represent physical substances sloshing around in the body and in which a cure to somatic or emotional discomfort is to change the makeup of these fluids. It should be equally clear how far we are from any cognitivist account in which emotions represent judgments by an autonomous self about what is conducive or antithetical to its wishes. If we approach early modern emotional life through the framework of resurrection, we begin to see a theoretical account in which the emotions are not mechanical fluids but are instead understood and *felt* to testify to the degree and quality of embeddedness in the historical social world and the degree and quality of displacement from the historical social world, and in which changing the emotions means effecting a change in the basic way a person is habituated into the world as reflected in his or her emotions—that is, a change in what Vaughan calls the "habits" and what Bourdieu calls "habitus."

III

Vaughan functioned as a community physician for much of his life and he published several therapeutic texts. One of them is a translation of a medical treatise by the German hermetic writer Heinrich Nolle entitled *Hermetical Physick: Or, The Right Way to Preserve, and to Restore Health*. This text is interesting because it vectors Vaughan's immanent, monist resurrection theory into a seemingly secular medical therapeutic discourse and by doing so draws out some of the implications of that resurrectionist theory as applied to the life of the body and the emotions. Like much Paracelsian medical theory, *Hermetical Physick* is animated by an explicit (and amusing) hostility to the "Dogmatical" or "vulgar Philosophy" of Galenic humoralism.[15] But rather than dismissing humoralism outright, the text recontextualizes humoral discourse as one pole of a two-pole theory of life that is heavily indebted to the notion of corporeal resurrection and the vision of a seed of resurrection that lies within the historical and socialized body.[16] The effect of this recontextualization is precisely to endow humoralism with a sociological horizon. What appears in explicitly religious discourse as a conflict between the body caught by a historically contingent social world and the seed that is already pointing forward to resurrection appears in Vaughan's medical writing as a conflict between an essential core that seeks eternal life and an envelope of humoral life that is understood as the product of unaware socialization.

The Nolle/Vaughan text is striking for its explicit attack on humoralism on the grounds that it is a "bare received Theorie" disconnected from empirical observation. In contrast to this theory, the Nolle/Vaughan text advocates careful empirical observation that

> layes open the most private and abstruse closets of nature, it doth most exquisitely search and find out the natures of health and sickness, it provides most elaborate and effectuall Medicines, teacheth the just Dose of them, and surpasseth by many degrees the vulgar Philosophy, and that faculty which is grounded upon the principles of the common, supposititious knowledge, that is to say, it doth much exceed and out do the Galenical Physick. . . . Now all the knowledge of the Hermetists, proceeds from a laborious manual disquisition and search into nature, but the Galenists insist wholly upon a bare received Theorie and

> prescribed Receits, giving all at adventure and will not be perswaded to inquire further then the mouth of their leader. (3–4)

Vaughan criticizes the Galenists for believing in their dogma as against what can be learned from careful empirical observation of the body that "layes open the most private and abstruse closets of nature." And what looking into the most private and abstruse closets of nature reveals is not the fluid dynamics of four humors entering in varying states of equilibrium or disequilibrium but a single, homogeneous principle of life that he calls the "radical seed" or the "radical balsam" or, sometimes, the "radical humor."

> The Radical seed, is the innate balsame of the body, which if it be advantaged with perfect digestion, will yeeld effusion, and a balsame of the same nature as it selfe. In this balsame the body lives as in his proper seed. (28)

This is the central conviction of Vaughan's medicine: that all human bodies have within themselves an identical core, a substance that is the essence of life and that attempts to maintain itself through time. It is a perspective that maps readily (and at times, as I will show, explicitly) onto the Pauline vocabulary of the seed of resurrection.[17] From this perspective, sickness always has the same structure: it is always a weakening of the one underlying substance of life, the radical seed. Vaughan does not understand the body as a mechanism that can get out of whack in many different ways (as the Galenists do), nor does he imagine that there are many varieties of bodies each requiring its own kind of medicine (its own "prescribed Receits"). In place of the Galenic/humoral approach of applying many different medicines to adjust many different kinds of bodies back into a static balance, for Vaughan the goal of medicine is to strengthen the dynamic, inner principle of the "radical seed" or the "radical balsam."

According to Vaughan, when it is strong, this radical seed has the quasi-alchemical ability to digest the stuff a person eats and the stuff a person's body produces into more of itself.[18] He understands sickness not as bodily humors getting out of balance but as this inner principle losing its vigor and therefore its ability to digest what is alien into more of itself. He writes, "Therefore, because health depends upon the strength and vigour of the radical balsame, sicknesse must needs proceed from the weaknesse and indisposition of it" (32). And because of his singular conception of human life, Vaughan believes that there is a universal medicine that would cure any disease by strengthening this one principle:

> This universall Cure is performed by a naturall medicinall Balsame, consentaneous to the nature of man, which resolves, discusseth and consumes the Seminary tinctures of all impurities and diseases: but corroborates, confirms, and conserves the innate humane Balsame; for (as Paracelsus teacheth) so long as the radicall humour keepes in its due quantity and proportion, no Disease or indisposition can be perceived. And in this way of Cure, the pluralities, particularities, and orderly Rules of Symptoms and Prognosticks, have no place for all Diseases (what ever they be) are universally & perfectly cured by this one universall medicine. (85–87)

This rather strange idea of a universal medicine is logically necessary given Vaughan's picture of human life as basically always the same: an inner principle—the balsam or radical seed or, in this passage, "radical humor"—attempting to maintain its vigor. The universal medicine is understood as being of the same substance as the radical seed (it is "consentaneous to the nature of man") so that giving it to a patient would amount to feeding the radical seed with itself.

But after noting the theoretical possibility of a universal medicine that would strengthen the radical seed directly, though he admits that he has not found it, Vaughan turns his attention to treating the symptoms that occur when the radical core weakens. "Next to the universall, is the particular cure, by which the roots of diseases, and the Seminal tinctures themselves, are not always taken away; but the bitter fruits of them, the Symptoms" (49). For Vaughan, symptoms are caused when the core is no longer strong enough to transform a hostile environment into more itself—"when," as Vaughan puts it, "our internal natural Alchymist is insufficient of himselfe to separate the pure from the impure" (99). For Vaughan, as for early modern Galenists, impurities in the environment enter into the body through food but also through more occult mechanisms. When the radical seed is not strong enough to digest them into more of itself, these impurities accumulate on the periphery of the radical seed and produce essentially humoral symptoms, which Vaughan thinks are indeed correctly theorized by the Galenic thought. Vaughan/Nolle write that their goal is to merge the best of Galenic medicine with their own theory of the radical seed. Having shown the errors of Galenism ("their Errours being first laid aside") they will now salvage those Galenic ideas they find useful: "I unite it with the Physick of the more sober Galenists, that theirs by consoclation with ours, may become perfect and irreprehensible" (7). But more than a merger of equals, what the treatise accomplishes is a massive recontextualization of Galenic symptomology as one pole of a two-pole theory in which the essentially non-humoral core of life gives rise to an envelope of humoral life that can then sicken the whole organism. After all, for Vaughan/Nolle, it is not the balance of humors but the strength of the radical seed that defines the essential health of the person: "the radical Balsame [is] the vital seed, and the very root or fundamentall of humane nature" (73). But this radical seed is, at the same time, surrounded by a second life that functions humorally.

Thus, the picture that Vaughan offers is one in which a radical core of life energizes a secondary form of life, a humoral envelope that can turn back on the core and suffocate it when the core becomes weakened. In place of the Galenic/humoral vision of the human being as *essentially* a container of humors that need to be mechanically balanced against each other to arrive at a more or less neutral state (mere dogmatism or even a scholarly "hallucination" [49], as Vaughan would have it), Vaughan sees the human body as internally divided between the *essential* core of the radical seed that aims for perpetuation and that transforms what the body ingests and the fluids the body produces into more of itself and a veneer of humoral life that creates symptoms only when the inner core weakens. The job of the physician is to assist the in-dwelling process of perfection by applying the one universal drug that will strengthen the radical seed by feeding it more of itself. And when the universal cure is not available, the physician can treat the symptoms of humoral imbalance that arise on the periphery, as it were, of the self's essential core.

It should be obvious how readily the Vaughan/Nolle physiological model maps onto Vaughan's understanding of resurrection in which there is a bifurcation between the historically contextualized person as he or she exists now and the "seed" of a future resurrection that is already present inside the body as its animating principle. In place of the resurrection body, we have in *Hermetical Physick* the radical seed or radical balsam, and around that we have the humoral veneer that envelops and sickens the radical balsam. Indeed, in *Hermetical Physick* Vaughan notes that when a physician strengthens the radical balsam, he is doing the work of resurrection before the actual day of resurrection when the "Almighty Physician himselfe will be pleased to heal us" (89). In fact, Vaughan's model of strengthening the radical balsam by applying the universal medicine (if only a physician could find the universal medicine!) blurs the line between medicine and resurrection so much so that he worries that a physician equipped with the universal drug might accidentally produce eternal life before death, so that he is forced to affirm that in such a case God would intervene arbitrarily to ensure that medical interventions do not "carry us alive beyond those bounds, which the very Father of life will not have us to transpasse" (106).

But none of this would seem to point to a sociological sensibility on the self and its corporeal life that I have claimed resides within resurrection theory. In fact, however, Vaughan connects the humoral body that grows out of the radical seed to a historically contingent social life. For Vaughan, the humoral envelope that surrounds and sickens the radical seed is, in fact, the place where the social world digs into the self and rewires it, where the social world becomes flesh. Thus, instead of a simple model of a radical seed enveloped by hostile humoral life, Vaughan actually gives us a model of a transhistorical radical seed that aims for eternal self-perpetuation enveloped by a socialized and historicized fleshly life that derives from a particular social and historical world. In essence, weakness in the radical seed makes the person vulnerable to being penetrated and rewired by the social world. This social perspective is suggested by the fact that Vaughan begins his discussion with a whole series of what I would term "lifestyle cures." Some of these cures are very much in line with standard Galenic practice that is concerned with managing what is brought into the body through eating and drinking and with managing the effects of exercise and sleep habits. Thus Vaughan offers such narrow lifestyle cures as "Eat not greedily, and drink not immoderately" (20). But Vaughan goes on to offer lifestyle cures that indict a whole European way of life and its supposed superiority over the "Salvages, Barbarians, and Canibals" (17). In fact, the treatise suggests that curing the diseases of the humoral envelope requires a cultural reform program and a vast change in lifestyle that is designed to effect at least a limited detachment of the self from the historical and social world it inhabits.

Vaughan's focus on a broad reorientation of self and world is, in fact, suggested by the fact that his discussion of therapies begins with the admonition to "Lead a pious and an holy life" (11), "For Piety (as the Apostle teacheth) is profitable for all things, having the promise of this present life, and of that which is to come" (12). But for Vaughan/Nolle, piety is not a narrowly religious matter, for it amounts to a wholesale rewiring of the self and its relation to a historical world. "Wonder not therefore, that so many in this age perish so suddainly and so soon. Impiety now bears the sway: true and unfeigned charity hath no place to abide in; Perjury, Treachery, Tyranny, Usury and Avarice, or (where these are not,) a vicious, lascivious, and loose life, are every where in request" (12). What Vaughan accomplishes through his attacks on the European form of life is to socialize the humoral envelope that grows when the radical seed weakens and loses its quasi-alchemical capacity to digest everything alien it encounters into more of itself. Lifestyle causes trouble by ensconcing itself in the humoral part of the body that is at odds with the radical seed, the part of the body that is aiming for perfect and everlasting bodily life. The life of the humors is a life embedded in a social universe, and the goal of the physician is to effect a limited detachment of the body from its habitual, mindless imbrication in social life, which strengthens the flesh at the expense of that within the body that aims for historical transcendence.

IV

From Vaughan's perspective, therapeutic interventions are not designed to restore mechanical balance (the goal of Galenic medicine) but to effect a wholesale rewiring of the self so that the life of the body will not be directed by the socialized flesh but by the radical seed or radical balsam, the principle within that seeks eternal life. And from this perspective, somatic experience (including emotion) is informational. It gives information about the relationship of the self to a contingent historical world. This information is important for Vaughan's medicine because he understands health to be a medically assisted displacement from this contingent historical world.

I want to end my discussion by looking more specifically at the implications of this model for reconstructing early modern emotional life. It is striking that one of the only extensive additions Vaughan makes to his translation of the Nolle treatise has to do with how to interpret emotion, namely the felt emotion of joy in the context of sexual experience.[19] Vaughan adds a long, marginal note to a section entitled "Use not too frequently, the permissions of Marriage." In the original Latin treatise written by Nolle, the thinking about the health effects of sex (for men) is quite mechanical: the expenditure of procreative "seed" is understood as an expenditure of essential life force and, if done immoderately, it can cause death. It might be tempting to see this seed as precisely the radical seed that Vaughan's resurrection somatics posit as the core of life, but this is where Vaughan himself adds a corrective supplement to the original text. Vaughan's supplemental comment tells the story of a man who, after a long courtship, gains the love of an especially "handsome" woman and is then found dead the morning after his wedding. The mechanical account of sex that the original Nolle text proposes would cast this as an instance in which too much emission of semen has led to death. But Vaughan steps back from the simple mechanical-hydraulic account in which emission of semen leads to death and in its place he posits the crucial mediating role of emotions, and especially what he terms "excessive joy:"

> It was not long before the publishing of this peece, that I was told by a very noble Gentleman, that in his late travailes in France, he was acquainted with a young French Physician, who for a long time had beene suiter to a very handsome Lady, and having at length gained her consent, was married to her, but his Nuptial bed proved his Grave, for on the next morning he was found dead. It was the Gentlemans opinion, that this sad accident might be caused by an excessive joy, and for my part I subscribe to it; for a violent joy hath oftentimes done the worke of death: this comes to passe by an extreame attenuation, and diffusion of the animal spirits, which passing all into the exterior parts, leave the heart destitute, whence followes suffocation and death. Scaliger Exercit. 310. gives the reason of this violent effusion and dissipation of the Spirits: Quia similia maxime cuprint inter se uniri, ideo spiritus, veluti exire conantur ad objectum illud externum atum ac jucundum, ut videlicet cum eo vniantur, Illud{que} sibi maxime simile reddant. If any will suspect, that together with this excessive joy, there was a concurrency of the other excess mentioned by my Author, I permit him his liberty, but certainly I thinke he will be deceived. (29)

The "other excess mentioned by my Author" is the purely mechanical expenditure of semen. But bypassing any simple expenditure-of-semen-equals-death theory as too mechanistic, Vaughan adds another, to us strange, cause of death—namely "excessive joy . . . for a violent joy hath oftentimes done the worke of death."[20] Vaughan cites Scaliger for an explanation of the killing power of joy; the Scaliger citation reads, in my translation: "Because similar things principally desire to be united among themselves, on that account spirits, for example, try to go out to that external object which is agreeable and pleasing, so that, of course, they may be united with it, and may give back that thing that is especially similar to them."[21] The quotation suggests that Vaughan (following Scaliger) understands joy to give information about how the self inhabits the world. More specifically, joy is a movement of a part of the self out into the world with an enervating immediacy. For Vaughan, joy is the *feeling* of the self investing itself into the world, and that feeling is pleasant but also painful insofar as it takes the self away from the transhistorical body within, the radical seed, the seed of resurrection. It may be that what we are glimpsing here is a basic fact about the early modern phenomenology of joy, namely that no matter how pleasurable the feeling of possessing the thing that causes joy might have been, early modern joy also contains a pain built upon the recognition that it ties the person to a contingent and passing world that is itself destined to die. Vaughan takes it for granted that too much joy has the power to kill (separate from the mechanical emission of seed as a cause of death) because of the excessive growth into the world, the over-attachment to the world that it vehiculates and betokens.

From this perspective, excessive joy does not admit of a simple humoral-hydraulic response. The solution to the Frenchman's problem is not to refrain from emitting more fluid semen. That is too simple, for the underlying problem is that the body is fundamentally caught by a social world that implants itself into the self and that leads the self to implant itself into the world. And that is precisely the information that the emotion conveys. As it was experienced (Vaughan imagines) by the Frenchman before his untimely death, his joy contained a threat, the threat of a death that results from being thrown out into the world. And that threat is essential to the phenomenological experience of the emotion. "Curing" the Frenchman would mean not forbidding mechanical sexual emission but attending to the emotion itself, becoming aware of the relation to the world that the emotion registers so emphatically, and then effecting a slow and gradual retraining of the basic habits by which the self inhabits the world.

One way of understanding Vaughan's marginal comment about "killing joy" is that it opens up a field a sexuality not governed by Nolle's mechanical imagery of sex as physical emission of the radical seed.[22] Instead, it suggests an experience of sexuality mediated by emotions that are the terrain on which the relation of the self and the world are registered and brought home. Leo Bersani has taught us to see sexuality as a beneficent crisis of selfhood, and killing joy would seem to qualify for such a crisis.[23] But Vaughan does not see killing joy as a beneficent at all. For Vaughan, killing joy is all bad because it represents a kind of explosive screwing of the self into the world; by contrast, the kind of transcendence of the self that Vaughan aims for (his account of "health") is a transcendence in the other direction, as it were, not out into the social world where the self is dissipated but back into the body, into the core of the body in all its pulsating, living strangeness, something that excess joy takes you away from by admitting the siren call of the world. The field of a sexuality mediated by emotions that Vaughan opens up here contains a vision of the body as socialized and yet as potentially unhinged from that social world. This form of sexuality treats somatic experience, including the emotions, as the terrain on which persons become aware of, and therefore become capable of transforming, the nexus between self and world.

I have argued that the immanent, monist resurrection belief that animates Vaughan's poetry also provides an important framework for understanding how early modern people experienced and interpreted their somatic and emotional life as socially habituated. To some extent, the "official" discourse of humoralism is a red herring—at least if our scholarly interest is in recovering the phenomenological experience of early modern emotional life. To the extent that contemporary scholars are interested in recovering the felt reality of early modern bodily and emotional life, they should bypass humoral discourse in favor of reconstructing a Bourdieusian vision of the social world that people are unconsciously habituated into in ways that "show up" as quasi-automatic emotional responses. Moreover, I have argued that although Bourdieusian sociology is not present as a discourse in early modern England, an analogous kind of theory-work is done in a surprising register, namely the discourse of the resurrection of the flesh, especially when that discourse is informed by the most immanent and monist commitments. Vaughan's translation of the Nolle treatise is a site where the proto-sociological vision granted by a monist, immanent resurrectionism is "secularized," so to speak, into an alternative kind of "scientific" theory that might be deserving of scholarly attention as a sociologically savvy rival to humoralist theory.

NOTES

1. For their help with this essay I want to thank Cora Fox, who organized a Shakespeare Association of America panel on the subject of emotions that allowed me to get going on this subject, and Curtis Perry, who offered a wonderfully thoughtful response to the version of this argument that I presented there. I would also like to thank Aaron Kunin and Ariane Balizet for their generosity in responding to earlier versions of this paper.

2. The major works that defined the paradigm include Michael C. Schoenfeldt, *Bodies and Selves in Early Modern England: Physiology and Inwardness in Spenser, Shakespeare, Herbert, and Milton* (Cambridge: Cambridge University Press, 1999), Mary Floyd-Wilson, *English Ethnicity and Race in Early Modern Drama* (Cambridge: Cambridge University Press, 2003), Gail Kern Paster, *Humoring the Body: Emotions and the Shakespearean Stage* (Chicago: University of Chicago Press, 2004), and Bruce R. Smith, *The Key of Green: Passion and Perception in Renaissance Culture* (Chicago: University of Chicago Press, 2008). These groundbreaking accounts of humoral thought in early modern England were often quite nuanced (especially in the case of Schoen-

feldt who tracked the persistence of stoical self-fashioning in the midst of humoral thought). By contrast, second generation scholarship on humoralism is characterized by increasing simplification of the basic model—something we might term "vulgar humoralism" on an analogy to vulgar Marxism. One example, of the many one could cite, is Sandra Clark, "Macbeth and the Language of the Passions," *Shakespeare* 8, no. 3 (September 2012): 300–11. My polemic about the absence of a sociological perspective in modern scholarship on the humors notwithstanding, it is important to note that attention to the sociological significance of the theory of the humors does play a role in the best humoral criticism, but it often appears secondarily, in terms of how humoral thinking is applied to social registers of identity. For instance both Paster and Floyd-Wilson implicitly pose the question: Given early modern beliefs about somatic and emotional life as fundamentally mechanical, how did early moderns coassemble humoral beliefs with social commitments they already had—for example, that women and the lower classes are undisciplined?

3. For an account of the extent to which Descartes imagines corporeal passions that operate independently of whether they are consciously sensed by the mind see Gary Hatfield, "Mechanizing the Sensitive Soul," in *Matter and Form in Early Modern Science and Philosophy*, ed. Gideon Manning, 151–86 (Leiden, Netherlands: Brill, 2012).

4. See Pierre Bourdieu's *Distinction: A Social Critique of the Judgment of Taste*, trans. Richard Nice (Cambridge, MA: Harvard University Press, 1984). I tend to inflect Bourdieu's model in a Heideggerian direction because I find useful the notion that emotions (especially background emotions) are the way a world comes to light to a person. For the connection between Heidegger and Bourdieu see Hubert L. Dreyfus, *Being-in-the-World: A Commentary on Heidegger's* Being and Time, *Division I* (Cambridge, MA: MIT Press, 1991). For a set of useful articles on the Heideggerian framework for analyzing emotional life see the Summer 2012 special volume of *New Literary History* edited by Rita Felski and Susan Fraiman, with several essays focused on mood as something that discloses a world, an idea I assume throughout this discussion. In some ways, I would describe my own methodology in this essay as an attempt at historical phenomenology, an effort to attend to the knowledge encoded in the felt experience of emotions and other bodily phenomena.

5. A scholarly program of applying Bourdieusian cultural sociology to the problem of emotional life in early modern England could also take the discourse of early modern humoralism as an object of sociological analysis and explore the ways this discourse is a symptom of the dynamics of early modern culture. This would certainly be an interesting research program but it would not reveal an answer to the second question I posed above, the

question of how real people in early modern England really experienced their emotional life.

6. Pierre Bourdieu, *The Logic of Practice*, trans. Richard Nice (Stanford, CA: Stanford University Press, 1992), 53.

7. While the general belief that at some point after death the body will be physically reconstituted was almost universally held in early modern England, the specific terms of that belief could vary quite a bit. As Carol Walker Bynum sketches it in *The Resurrection of the Body in Western Christianity, 200–1336* (New York: Columbia University Press, 1995), the early church was almost defined by its commitment to bodily resurrection (as opposed to mere persistence of the soul), despite continuing attacks on this view by proponents of the basic philosophical/metaphysical assumptions of the Hellenistic world, which was comfortable with body-soul dualism but was unable to accept the notion of a dead body being reanimated. As she describes it, the tension between Hellenistic philosophy and corporeal resurrection in the first three centuries of the Christian movement gave rise to several attempts to defend the idea of corporeal resurrection by working out its metaphysics. In early modern England, mainstream puritans (following Calvin) tended to favor a dualist understanding of resurrection in which the soul of the elect goes to heaven immediately after the death of the body and waits there to be reunited with its body at the end of time. Vaughan (together with Milton) articulates a resolutely corporealist account that includes the mortalist assumption that death is truly death until the body is reconstructed at the end of time. For an account of Vaughan's effort to distinguish himself from Puritan critics by means of a distinctive theory of resurrection, see Jonathan F. S. Post, *Henry Vaughan: The Unfolding Vision* (Princeton, NJ: Princeton University Press, 1982), 122–26. Despite the doctrinal atypicality of Vaughan's understanding of resurrection, it is nonetheless true that even mainstream puritan dualism is shadowed by a persistent emphasis on the centrality of the body as both caught by the social world and able to transcend it. This is evident, for example, in Richard Baxter's *The Saints' Everlasting Rest*, an influential effort to describe the way the joys of the elect in this world prefigure the joys of the elect in the hereafter. It is the corporealist strain in even dualist resurrection theory that I draw attention to as the basis for recovering the sociological backdrop to somatic and emotional life. For a sophisticated account of resurrection beliefs and the rise of modern psychology see Fernando Vidal, "Brains, Bodies, Selves, and Science: Anthropologies of Identity and the Resurrection of the Body," *Critical Inquiry* 28 (2002): 930–74.

8. My discussion here is a theoretical accompaniment to a study of the role Vaughan's resurrection beliefs play in his poetry, particularly as an explanation for his formal experimentation. See my "The Resurrection of

the Body and the Life of the Flesh in Henry Vaughan's Religious Verse," *ELH* 82, no. 1 (2015): 59–86.

9. Quoted from Alan Rudrum, ed., *Henry Vaughan: The Complete Poems* (New Haven, CT: Yale University Press, 1976). For a philosophical account of what I here term "immanent resurrection," including some discussion of the implications of this theory for an understanding of poetic language, see Karmen MacKendrick, "Eternal Flesh: The Resurrection of the Body," *Discourse* 27, no. 1 (2005): 67–83.

10. The intellectual origins of early Christian understandings of resurrection is a complex topic, beyond the scope of this essay. In addition to Bynum, see Raymond Martin and John Barresi, *The Rise and Fall of Soul and Self* (New York: Columbia University Press, 2006). I have also consulted two classic studies that are undertaken from within a theistic mindset: N. T. Wright, *The Resurrection of the Son of God* (Minneapolis, MN: Augsburg Fortress Press, 2003), and Dale B. Martin, *The Corinthian Body* (New Haven, CT: Yale University Press, 1995). For a useful sketch of how early modern philosophers tried to produce an exclusively corporeal account of resurrection see Lloyd Strickland, "The Doctrine of 'the Resurrection of the Same Body' in Early Modern Thought," *Religious Studies* 46 (2010): 163–83. Strickland examines the early modern interest in the question of what defines the identity of the person in a reassembled body, drawing special attention to Leibniz's notion of a vital "flower of substance" that has no physical extension but nevertheless defines a person's identity. What Vaughan's distinctive theory of resurrection adds is attention to the immanence of resurrection, to the ways in which a future of bodily reassembly can be pre-experienced in the here and now.

11. Though what I term "the immanent eschatology of the body" is easy to locate in Paul's letters, I certainly do not mean for my claims here to address the voluminous body of work on Paul's own understanding of the body. It is noteworthy, however, that the new life Paul describes in his letters is not understood as a positive place to stand but only as a characteristic displacement from Jewish and Greco-Roman ways of life. It is a non-foundational foundation, as it is powerfully theorized by Alain Badiou's *Saint Paul: The Foundation of Universalism*, trans. Ray Brassier (Stanford, CA: Stanford University Press, 2003). The implications of Badiou's account for early modern English culture are powerfully examined by Jonathan Goldberg, *The Seeds of Things: Theorizing Sexuality and Materiality in Renaissance Representations* (New York: Fordham University Press, 2009), 20–25. My interest in reasoning with and through early modern religious discourse rather than subjecting it to a kind of sociological debunking is indebted to the brilliant work on political theology by both Julia Reinhard Lupton and Graham Hammill. See Lupton's *Citizen-Saints: Shakespeare and Political Theology* (Chicago: University of Chi-

cago Press, 2005) and Hammill's *The Mosaic Constitution: Political Theology and Imagination from Machiavelli to Milton* (Chicago: University of Chicago Press, 2012).

12. Henry Vaughan, *The Mount of Olives: Or, Solitary Devotions.* (London: n.p., 1652), 21, Early English Books Online, http://gateway.proquest.com/openurl?ctx_ver=Z39.88-2003&res_id=xri:eebo&rft_id=xri:eebo:citation:99863671.

13. Henry Vaughan, *Flores Solitudinis Certaine Rare and Elegant Pieces* (London: n.p., 1654), 4, Early English Books Online, http://gateway.proquest.com/openurl?ctx_ver=Z39.88-2003&res_id=xri:eebo&rft_id=xri:eebo:citation:15076156.

14. Vaughan, *The Mount of Olives*, 108.

15. Heinrich Nolle, *Hermetical Physick: Or, The Right Way to Preserve, and to Restore Health. By That Famous and Faithfull Chymist, Henry Nollius. Englished by Henry Uaughan, Gent* (London: n.p., 1655), 49, Early English Books Online, http://gateway.proquest.com/openurl?ctx_ver=Z39.88-2003&res_id=xri:eebo&rft_id=xri:eebo:citation:99868485. Florian Eberling argues that early modern European hermetical thought is split between an occult tradition and a proto-chemical tradition often associated with Paracelsus. Especially in the realm of medicine, the latter played an important role in critiquing the Galenic tradition by emphasizing empirical observation, especially of the impact of chemical medicines on the body. See *The Secret History of Hermes Trismegistus: Hermeticism From Ancient to Modern Times*, trans. David Lorton (Ithaca, NY: Cornell University Press, 2007).

16. The Nolle text is a Paracelsian account and many of its distinctive ideas derive from Paracelsus. I argue that Vaughan's primary commitment is to a distinctively Christian understanding of immanent, monist resurrection—as is evidenced by his religious and poetic writings—but that in this translation he vectors these interests through a Paracelsian framework in ways that reveal the implications (in terms of an embedded sociological framework) of both Paracelsian medicine and a widely shared, intuitive Christian resurrectionism. Noting the overlap between the hermetic tradition and Christian thought, Michael Thomson Walton argues that "the shared illuminative epistemology of chemical philosophers . . . is closely related to the Christian notion of personal enlightenment by the Holy Spirit at Pentecost." See Michael Thomson Walton, *Genesis and the Chemical Philosophy: True Christian Science in the Sixteenth and Seventeenth Centuries* (Brooklyn, NY: AMS Press, 2011). For accounts that track the influence of hermeticism on Vaughan's thought and work see A. W. Rudrum, "'The Night': Some Hermetic Notes," *Modern Language Review* 64, no. 1 (1969): 11–19, as well as E. C. Pettet, *Of Paradise and Light: A Study of Vaughan's Silex Scintillans*

(Cambridge: Cambridge University Press, 2011), 70–75. For a broader contextualization of Vaughan's ideas in early modern hermetic and vitalist thought see Diane Kelsey McColley, *Poetry and Ecology in the Age of Milton and Marvell* (New York: Ashgate, 2007).

17. Beyond its commitment to empiricism (on the grounds that reality is sowed with secret knowledge that can be gleaned through careful observation), the tradition of "chemical medicine" (as Sujata Iyengar refers to it in *Shakespeare's Medical Language: A Dictionary* [London: Continuum, 2011)]) also contains a set of metaphysical assumptions that often include the kind of bipartite model that I describe here in my discussion of the Vaughan/Nolle text. In their discussion of Paracelsus, Martin and Barresi write, "Paracelsus ascribed to humans a corporeal constitution consisting of two sorts of flesh. One of these, the elemental body, has its 'origin in Adam' and is 'course.' . . . The other flesh, the astral body, is not from Adam. It is 'subtle' and not capable of being 'bound or grasped, for it is not made of earth.' It is what makes humans capable of spiritual activities. . . . Humans, Paracelsus wrote, are the divine in a state of becoming." Martin and Barresi, *The Rise and Fall of Soul and Self*, 117. I argue that the Vaughan/Nolle text shows how a Christian framework centered on an immanent understanding of resurrection can be inflected into this bipartite, hermetical schema.

18. Justin E. H. Smith argues that Leibniz saw the "flower of substance" as a hard kernel with very little extension, inside of which is a mathematical point that contains the soul that survives all change, even fire. But Smith says that Leibniz eventually rejected this view in favor of the idea that what gives a body coherence and continuity is that it is constantly changing the environment into more of itself via nutrition (*Stoffwechsel* in German). Thus, nutrition creates a kind of quasi eternality (together with reproduction), an idea that also plays a role in the Nolle text. See Justin E. H. Smith, "'Spirit Is a Stomach': The Iatrochemical Roots of Leibniz's Theory of Corporeal Substance," in *Matter and Form in Early Modern Science and Philosophy*, ed. Gideon Manning, 203–24 (Leiden, Netherlands: Brill, 2012).

19. Vaughan's additions to the original are revealed when we compare the translation Vaughan published in 1655 with the original Latin published by Nolle in Hanover in 1617. This text is available in the microfiche series "History of Science Landmarks." My thanks to the library of the University of Oklahoma for making a copy of this microfiche available to me.

20. Strange but not altogether atypical in early modern literature. I see one possible analogue of this experience in *King Lear* when Edgar reports that his father died because "his flaw'd heart,/Alack, too weak the conflict to support!/'Twixt two extremes of passion, joy and grief,/Burst smilingly" (5.3.189–92). Quoted from Stephen Orgel and A. R. Braunmuller, eds., *William Shakespeare: The Complete Works* (New York: Penguin Books, 2002).

21. I thank Brian Warren for his help with this translation.

22. In making this suggestion I am drawing on Margaret R. Miles's wonderful discussion of Augustine's understanding of post-resurrection sexuality in which the resurrected transcend the use of genitals in order to engage instead in a sex of the whole body (as Milton's angels do, too). See "Sex and the City (of God): Is Sex Forfeited or Fulfilled in Augustine's Resurrection of Body?," *Journal of the American Academy of Religion* 73, no. 2 (June 2005): 307–27.

23. See Leo Bersani, "Is the Rectum a Grave?," *October* 43 (1987): 197–222. This article is reprinted in Jonathan Goldberg, ed., *Queering the Renaissance* (Durham, NC: Duke University Press, 1993); see also Leo Bersani's *The Freudian Body: Psychoanalysis and Art* (New York: Columbia University Press, 1986).

CHAPTER 9

Woman as World: The Female Microcosm / Macrocosm in Shakespeare and Donne

Lynn Maxwell

In John Donne's "Sappho to Philaenis," Sappho asks Philaenis, "for if we justly call each silly man / A little world, what shall we call you then?" (19–20).[1] As several critics have noted, she uses this question as part of her rejection of a poetics of comparison and metaphor.[2] Yet her query also has the effect of problematizing the concept of the microcosm / macrocosm and drawing attention to the way it intersects with gender. The microcosm / macrocosm relation, by which man is construed as analogous to the world, was understood as more than metaphor in the early modern period. As the sixteenth-century French poet Guillaume de Salluste Du Bartas put it:

> In Man's self is Fire, Aire, Earth, and Sea;
> Man's (in a word) the world's Epitomé
> Or little Map, which heer my Muse doth try
> By the grand pattern to exemplifie.[3]

By the seventeenth century, when Donne penned "Sappho to Philaenis," the concept had made the rounds from Plato and medieval theologians to early modern humanists and Neoplatonists. In the hands of early modern thinkers the schema of microcosm / macrocosm was used to justify the humanist focus on man and his relation to the universe and God's "grand pattern." Yet it was also under continuous development by early modern philosophers as new discoveries were made about the nature of the world and universe that challenged man's place in creation.[4] We can see the ubiquity of the model and its openness to challenge in Sappho's question, which simultaneously presumes that her readers will accept the hypothesis that every man is "a little world" while posing it as a conditional statement open to question.

Sappho invites us to ask what it means to understand a self as "a little world" and how gender enters into the equation. If women can be understood as little worlds, as participating in the microcosm/macrocosm analogy, how does that relate to thinking of them as land to be explored or territory to be conquered, as locations to be plowed and planted? Which is to ask, to what extent is there space for female agency and subjecthood in the possibility of woman as world? Finally, how does this trope relate to other tropes of female selfhood and questions of relationality? Taking up Shakespeare's *A Comedy of Errors* and his *Rape of Lucrece*, alongside several of John Donne's poems, but particularly his "A Valediction: of Weeping" and "Sappho to Philaenis," in this essay I argue that gender matters in the formulation of the microcosm/macrocosm relationship. When women are imagined as worlds the trope becomes more invested in bodies and bodily reproduction than when applied to men. Yet this shift is not absolute; even as the gendered microcosm/macrocosm trope fails to treat men and women equally, we can still find moments when the figure helps to expand the possibilities of the female self together with moments in which the expansive female body threatens to overrun the model.

Generally, the microcosm/macrocosm model heightens the importance of man by figuring passions on a grand scale and suggesting that knowledge of the self and regulation of the passions are important goals. Thus Hamlet promises the ghost of his father that he will remember him, "while memory holds a seat/In this distracted globe," transforming his mind and self into a world with an uncertain future, made more uncertain by its current state of distraction, or literally, of being "drawn asunder" (1.5.96–97).[5] Similarly, in *King Lear*, Lear's mental unrest is figured through the microcosm; he is described as "striv[ing] in his little world of man to outscorn/The to-and-fro-conflicting wind and rain" (3.1.10–11).[6] As Lear's inner storm begins to suggest, microcosm and macrocosm are not understood as closed systems. Instead, since the individual is enmeshed in the world, the macrocosm can affect the microcosm and tempestuous weather in *King Lear* may exacerbate the storm within the king. Indeed, poetically at least, the relationship might also work the other way. As Marjorie Hope Nicolson observes, "Lear is losing his reason, nature hers, and the one inevitably reacts upon the other. The microcosm reflects the macrocosm, the macrocosm the confusion in the little world, until neither we nor Lear can tell which is more responsible for the confusion."[7] Since microcosm and macrocosm have a synecdochal relationship, questions of influence and agency become impossible to sort out.

The idea that the individual is not simply like the macrocosm but embedded in it has a long history. The sixth-century Pope Gregory the Great, who was largely responsible for incorporating the Neoplatonic microcosm/macrocosm into Christian thought held that man is best understood "by the title of the universe . . . in that in him there is set forth a true likeness and a large participation in common with the universe."[8] For the Italian Neoplatonists, man's place both within the universe and as a model of it provides a fertile ground for working out problems of man's freedom and salvation, ethical concerns that help differentiate between man and animal.[9] In Shakespeare, the analogy not only figures man as a world unto himself, it also reflects the state. Hamlet's distraction aligns with the rottenness of Denmark, and Lear's internal civil war corresponds outwardly. The microcosm/macrocosm analogy extends to man/state/world.[10]

Like Shakespeare, Donne also makes extensive use of the microcosm/macrocosm trope. Yet as Toshihiko Kawasaki argues, Donne's use of the trope shows not only a commitment to Neoplatonic systems of correspondences but also a unique preference for the microcosm over the macrocosm: "What is singular with Donne . . . is that his microcosm and macrocosm not only correspond to each other as two entities and symbolically reflect each other, but also that they represent a definite system of relative values: the smaller world is more valuable than the larger."[11] We can see Donne's preference for microcosm over macrocosm in his *Devotions upon Emergent Occasions*, when he writes:

> It is too little to call man a little world; except God, man is diminutive to nothing. Man consists of more pieces, more parts, than the world; than the world doth, nay, than the world is. And if those pieces were extended and stretched out in man, as they are in the world, man would be the giant, and the world the dwarf, the world, but the map, and the man the world.[12]

Donne's reversals of the trope—man as giant/world as dwarf, man as world/world as map—give rhetorical strength to his celebration of man.

Even as he questions the trope, suggesting it is "too little," he takes advantage of its power to suggest that man, like the world, is paradoxically almost unknowable because of his complexity and intuitively known through experience.

Throughout his poetry, Donne explores the limits of the trope. Sometimes he adds levels to the trope, a "macro-macrocosm above and micro-microcosm below," as Kawasaki describes it.[13] For example, in "The Good Morrow," both Kawasaki and Don Parry Norford find a chain of correspondences that moves "from the outside world to the 'little room' the lovers occupy, then to the pair conjointly, then to each party of the pair" and finally to their eyes, which become worlds in themselves:[14]

> My face in thine eye, thine in mine appears,
> And true plain hearts do in the faces rest,
> Where can we find two better hemispheres
> Without sharp north, without declining west? (15–18)

Other times Donne uses the new science to challenge the stability of the trope or, alternatively, reinvigorate it. In a verse epistle to the Countess of Bedford, Donne uses heliocentrism to explain how the correct relationship between body and mind has failed:

> As new philosophy arrests the sun,
> And bids the passive earth about it run,
> So we have dulled our mind, it hath no ends;
> Only the body's busy, and pretends;
> As dead low earth eclipses and controls
> The quick high moon: so doth the body, souls. (37–42)[15]

Here, the sun represents the mind, which should move or have "ends" but instead is stationary and "dull[]." The body's activity and priority over the mind is "pretend[]" and does not reflect the right order of things. By contrast, in Holy Sonnet 15, Donne imagines that the geographic discoveries of the seventeenth century might enhance the microcosm, when the speaker prays:

> You which beyond that heaven which was most high
> Have found new spheres, and of new lands can write,
> Pour new seas in mine eyes, that so I might
> Drown my world with my weeping earnestly,
> Or wash it, if it must be drowned no more. (5–9)

Sappho's question about "silly" man is just one of Donne's many explorations of the trope. However, it is the only such moment that explicitly foregrounds questions of gender.

There is no easy answer in Shakespeare or Donne to Sappho's implicit question of what women's relationship to the macrocosm might be. Certainly, it does not seem identical to man's. While both Shakespeare and Donne attach women to worlds and other macrocosmic possibilities, those connections are most often bodily and do not usually invoke the microcosm/macrocosm trope in order to figure an expansive self or articulate the value of self-knowledge and self-regulation implicit in the more classic applications of those tropes to men. Instead, the comparison of women to the macrocosm gets caught up with women's bodies, their reproductive parts, and their relationships with men (rather than with God or the universe).

In Shakespeare's *A Comedy of Errors*, we find a comic articulation of woman as world. Syracuse's Dromio finds himself with the wife of his Ephesian double and describes her as "spherical, like a globe; I could find out countries in her" (3.2.113–14). Not content with a brief comparison, Antipholus and Dromio push the trope to its limits as they continue:

> ANTIPHOLUS OF SYRACUSE. In what part of her body stands Ireland?
> DROMIO OF SYRACUSE. Marry, sir, in her buttocks. I found it out by the bogs.
> ANTIPHOLUS OF SYRACUSE. Where Scotland?
> DROMIO OF SYRACUSE. I found it by the barrenness, hard in the palm of the hand.
> ANTIPHOLUS OF SYRACUSE. Where France?
> DROMIO OF SYRACUSE. In her forehead, armed and reverted, making war against her heir.
> ANTIPHOLUS OF SYRACUSE. Where England?
> DROMIO OF SYRACUSE. I looked for the chalky cliffs, but I could find no whiteness in them. But I guess it stood in her chin, by the salt rheum that ran between France and it.
> ANTIPHOLUS OF SYRACUSE. Where Spain?
> DROMIO OF SYRACUSE. Faith, I saw it not, but I felt it hot in her breath.
> ANTIPHOLUS OF SYRACUSE. Where America, the Indies?
> DROMIO OF SYRACUSE. Oh, sir, upon her nose all o'er embellished with rubies, carbuncles, sapphires, declining their rich aspect to the hot breath of Spain; who sent whole armadas of carracks to be ballast at her nose.

> ANTIPHOLUS OF SYRACUSE. Where stood Belgia? The Netherlands?
> DROMIO OF SYRACUSE. Oh, sir, I did not look so low. (3.2.115–37)

Nell's body represents the world because it is spherical and through other bodily abnormalities and specificities; the "bogs" of Ireland, the "barrenness" of Scotland, the militant nature of France, the "chalky cliffs" of England, the heat of Spain, the riches of America and the Indies, and the "lowness" of Belgium and the Netherlands are all present. The exchange emphasizes the grotesqueness of Nell's body and explains why Dromio understands her claim on him as a threat; she is hardly the wife he desires, especially as her greatest claim to beauty seems to be her nose, "all oe'er embellished with rubies, carbuncles, sapphires." Undeniably, Dromio's association of Nell with a globe foregrounds her body rather than her inner self. If Nell is the world's "epitome," here, it is because of the size of her body and its irregularity. Dromio does not use the trope of Nell as world to elevate her, or situate her in relation to the cosmos, nor is he interested in Nell's interiority. Indeed, since Nell arguably never sets foot on stage, this caricatured blazon of her body together with Dromio's response to their encounter are the predominate means with which she figures in the play.[16] She is hardly a character, let alone a person, and her body proves a territory that Dromio can master rhetorically to solidify his bonds with both Antipholus and the audience.

At the same time, however, Nell's claim on him has sufficient power to haunt him until the very end of the play when, having discovered his twin, Dromio realizes that he has escaped Nell. After describing her as a globe, Dromio continues:

> To conclude, this drudge, or diviner, laid claim to me, call'd me Dromio, swore I was assured to her, told me what privy marks I had about me—as the mark of my shoulder, the mole in my neck, the great wart on my left arm—that I, amazed, ran from her as a witch. And I think if my breast had not been made of faith, and my heart of steel, she had transformed me to a curtal dog, and made me turn i' th' wheel. (3.2.137–44)

Dromio is uncertain whether Nell is "drudge" or "diviner," kitchenmaid or witch, and worries about the extent of her power, just as he worries about the extent of her body. Like Nell, Dromio's body is marked by certain irregularities and her knowledge of his "privy marks" threatens to give her absolute power over him. As Du Bartas articulates this relation, there is "No better knowledge, then Our Self to Knowe./Ther is no Theam more plentifull to scan,/Then is the glorious goodly Frame of Man."[17] Similarly, knowledge of "ourselves" promises power here, first to Dromio and then to Nell. Yet it is the wrong kind of power. Witchcraft replaces humanist understanding and Dromio genuinely seems to fear that his would-be wife might be able to transform him "to a curtal dog." His fear here suggests that his mastery is ultimately only rhetorical. His caricatured blazon does little to contain Nell's body or the threat it represents.[18]

The description of Nell differs from most figurations of man as world in Shakespeare's works, as when Prince Henry accuses Falstaff of being a "globe of sinful continents" (*The Second Part of Henry IV*, 2.4.258–59). Here the critique is not simply about bodily girth; Falstaff's virtue is in question, and the association of man with world is ethically tinged. In both *The Comedy of Errors* and *The Rape of Lucrece*, the association of woman with world is used to explore the possibility of masculine domination rather than narrate interior possibilities of agency and will. Yet, as we have seen, Nell's vastness increases the threat of her claim on Dromio. Similarly, when Lucrece's body is described in terms of worlds, her body becomes a site of expansive possibilities.

Whereas Nell's body is comically large and marred by irregularities, Lucrece's embodies an idealized feminine beauty and virtue. Thus Tarquin, on first viewing Lucrece, sees in her face a battle between "beauty's red" and "virtue's white," and his lust is driven by her perfections (65).[19] Standing over her sleeping form, we survey with him Lucrece's body, starting with one "lily hand" (386), then the next (393), moving to her closed eyes (397), "her hair, like golden threads" (400), and finally:

> Her breasts like ivory globes circled with blue,
> A pair of maiden worlds unconquerèd,
> Save of their lord no bearing yoke they knew,
> And him by oath they truly honourèd. (407–13)

As Coppélia Kahn has noted, the association of Lucrece's breasts with land reduces her to an object to be fought over, the battleground of a power struggle primarily between men.[20] The narrator makes clear, that "save of their lord" her breasts knew no "bearing yoke," reminding us that land is transformed by plowing and that the female body can also be brought to bear; both land and women are valued for their reproductive capacities.

The equation of the female body with unconquered territory is returned to incessantly in early modern texts. Sir Walter Raleigh's *Discovery of Guiana*, Donne's "To His Mistress Going to Bed," and Andrew Marvell's "To His Coy Mistress" come immediately to mind, as well as early modern maps on which female forms are inscribed. Yet this description of Lucrece offers something different, at least temporarily, by equating Lucrece's breasts with worlds rather than land. Of course, the shape of breasts has something to do with the metaphor. Yet when her breasts are described as being "like ivory globes circled with blue, / A pair of maiden worlds unconquerèd," Lucrece is figured not simply as land, to be taken, but as composed of complex systems existing outside and beyond man. Of course, these body parts are no sooner named than threatened with destruction. They may be "a pair of maiden worlds unconquerèd," but that status of "unconquerèd" is clearly only temporary. The very word "unconquerèd" works to normalize the state of being "conquered." Gazing on these "ivory globes" spurs Tarquin to action, and they become the site that Tarquin first assaults, as his violation of her becomes physical:

> His hand, as proud of such a dignity,
> Smoking with pride marched on to make his stand
> On her bare breast, the heart of all her land,
> Whose ranks of blue veins as his hand did scale,
> Left their round turrets destitute and pale. (437–41)

Her breasts become "the heart of all her land" rather than worlds unto themselves. At the same time, her body becomes a kingdom to be guarded and protected, and those same breasts are almost immediately reimagined as watchtowers from which her blood flees both to warn her of Tarquin's incursion and to escape his assault. In shifting from breasts as worlds to breasts as watchtowers, Shakespeare continues to operate within a microcosm/macrocosm system, but the macrocosm contracts, and as it contracts so do Lucrece's possibilities.

Lucrece's body here is inextricably linked to her selfhood. She understands the rape as an act that soils her body and justifies her suicide: "Ay me! The bark peel'd from the lofty pine, / His leaves will whither and his sap decay; / So must my soul, her bark being peel'd away" (1167–69). While body does not equal soul here, the two are deeply intertwined: damage to the body justifies the freeing of the soul. The narrator makes the point even more explicit when he offers an apology for women, using the trope of signet/seal:

> For men have marble, women waxen minds,
> And therefore are they formed as marble will.
> The weak oppressed, th'impression of strange kinds
> Is formed in them by force, by fraud, or skill.

Then call them not the authors of their ill,
No more than wax shall be accounted evil
Wherein is stamped the semblance of a devil. (1240–46)

Here the narrator makes sexual difference material through a trope that recalls early modern theories of reproduction, where the womb works like wax.[21] By aligning mind and body as spaces that respond in the same way to masculine pressures, the passage collapses distinctions between the two. Tarquin's bodily impression is doubled in Lucrece's mind, excusing all her desires and actions. At the same time that this collapse seems disastrous for female agency, it shows again that the poem insists on an equivalency between the female body and mind, as was also the case in the narrator's association of Lucrece's body with the macrocosm.

When philosophers and theologians explicitly take up gender around the microcosm/macrocosm, they generally hold that women's role in reproduction provides the basis for their different relation to the trope. Thus, the medieval nun and theologian Saint Hildegard of Bingen held that both men and women could be understood as microcosms, "O human, look at the human being! For human beings hold together within themselves heaven and earth and other things created, and are one form; and within them everything is concealed."[22] Yet she holds that women's elemental qualities are different from men's, changing their relationship with the macrocosm: "Woman's temperament, which sensitize[s] her to any spiritual force that happened to be 'in the air' [because of greater moisture] also ma[kes] her body more sensitive to the physical environment."[23] Perhaps more important, women's roles in reproduction also affect their relationship to the macrocosm and to the religious truths that Hildegard represents in the schema. Thus, she argues that women should not be priests, since consecrating the Eucharist requires the same active energy as conception and is accomplished "through a man, as the ground [is] ploughed not by itself but by a farmer."[24] For Hildegard, woman is more aptly compared to the church than to Christ and thus should take the more passive role in religious matters.[25]

Similarly, in his *Volumen Paramirum*, the occult philosopher Paracelsus argues that neither man nor woman alone is a complete human being and that both contribute seed for reproduction. At the same time, he holds that "Man is the Little World, but woman . . . is the Littlest World, and hence she is different from man. She has a different anatomy, a different theory, different effects and causes, different divisions and cares . . . . For the world is and was the first creature, man the second, and woman the third."[26] For Paracelsus, microcosm/macrocosm is both a binary in which the microcosm can be understood as requiring a male and female union and also a ternary in which the terms become microcosm/macrocosm/littlest world. Again, the woman's role in reproduction is what sets her apart, and ultimately what defines her since she provides a matrix for creation. In a troubling move, Paracelsus collapses woman to womb, arguing, "woman is enclosed in her skin as in a house, and everything that is within it forms, as it were, a single womb" (24). This collapse of body into self both elevates the importance of the womb and threatens female agency by making women only reproductive vessels, a possibility explored to its limits with the medical and alchemical notion of the homunculus or "little man," which provides a possibility of reproduction in which women supply no essential part.[27]

In Donne, too, we find a similarly messy and at times contradictory vision of female selfhood negotiated around the microcosm/macrocosm. To a certain extent, the flexibility with which Donne applies the trope to women mirrors the way he applies it to men, except Donne seems more uncertain about what he is celebrating. For example, in his juvenile *Paradoxes and Problems*, Donne suggests that women might not have souls, since "we deny souls to others equal to them in all but in speech, for which they are beholding to their bodily instruments: for perchance an ox's heart, or a goat's, or a fox's, or a serpent's would speak just so, if it were in the breast, and could move tongue and jaws" (141).[28] While *Paradoxes and Problems* is hyperbolic and satirical, the question recurs elsewhere in Donne's verse epistle to the Countess of Huntington, where he opines "Man to God's image, Eve, to man's was made,/Nor find we that God breathed a soul in her" (1–2). By suggesting that women might not have souls and by placing them lower in the chain of being, Donne, like Paracelsus, insists on female difference.

Yet where Paracelsus is clear about how women relate to both microcosm and macrocosm, Donne plays with a wide range of possibilities. Often women's bodies, rather than their souls, become the basis of the microcosm/macrocosm trope. Thus in "Elegy 2: To His Mistress Going to Bed," Donne commands, "Off with that girdle, like heaven's zone glistering,/But a far fairer world encompassing" (5–6). Yet in other poems, the female soul is explored through the trope. In a verse epistle to the Countess of Bedford, Donne treats woman as microcosm. He tells the Countess, "in your commonwealth, or world in you,/Vice has no office, or good work to do" (87–88).[29] Here the Countess's self is both "commonwealth" and "world" and the trope speaks to her virtue. Even more provocatively, in both "A Fever" and "The First Anniversary" a woman's death is equated with the death of the world. In "A Fever," he writes:

> But when thou from this world wilt go,
> The whole world vapours with thy breath
>
> Or if, when thou, the world's soul, go'st,
> It stay, 'tis but thy carcase then. (7–10)

Here the beloved is "the world's soul" and if the world continued after her death it would be "but thy carcase then." The same language appears in the "The First Anniversary" where the death of Elizabeth Drury requires the poet to perform an anatomy of the world. In both of these poems specific women are figured not simply as "little world[s]" but as integral to the world itself, as the world's soul, or the representation of all that is good in the world. Their sicknesses and deaths are figured as catastrophic for the fate of the macrocosm, and they offer exceptions to the rule in Donne's poetry that women are less than men.

When Donne uses the trope to figure a couple together, perhaps suggesting that man and woman together form one human being, as Paracelsus also holds at times, we find a similar range of treatments of gender difference. In "The Sun Rising," the speaker declares, "She'is all states, and all princes, I" (21); the speaker and beloved together form a world determined by gender difference as the male speaker is mapped onto the active role of ruling, while the female beloved becomes land to be ruled. Yet other lyrics, such as "The Good Morrow," insist on mutuality throughout, "Let sea-discoverers to new worlds have gone, / Let maps to other, worlds on worlds have shown, / Let us possess one world, each hath one, and is one" (12–14). Here the lovers' union multiplies their claims to the macrocosm and amplifies them both, promising immortality as "thou and I / Love so alike, that none do slacken, none can die" (20–21).

The association of women with worlds in "A Valediction: Of Weeping," proves one of Donne's most complicated, revealing both an interest in gender difference and suggesting that gender difference might matter only superficially. A careful reading of the poem reveals what is at stake in understanding woman as world for Donne. As in many of Donne's lyrics, the gender of speaker and beloved is not explicitly assigned. Yet the conventional reading of male speaker and female beloved seems most probable given the poem's metaphorics, particularly the naming of the beloved as "more than moon." This world-like position provides the beloved with tremendous destructive power over the speaker. Further, since the speaker is also imagined as a world, that power belongs to both speaker and beloved. Thus even as the poem plays with gendered metaphors and gendered possibilities, it insists on a more fundamental sameness between the two positions, a sameness reinforced by the ambiguity around gender and by the way Donne imagines and reimagines the possibilities of gendered impressions in the first two stanzas of the poem. Yet ultimately the trope speaks to the destructive possibilities of love. The lovers' mutual power does not create one greater human being as it does in "The Sun Rising" and "The Good Morrow;" instead it threatens to destroy them both.

In the "Valediction," the speaker invests worldmaking and world-destroying power in tears. Employing an extended conceit, the speaker imagines first how each tear might be imprinted by his lover, "For thy face coins them, and thy stamp they bear, / And by this mintage they are something worth" (3–4). The act of impression infuses the tears with value, because "thus they be / Pregnant of thee" (5–6). Since both coining and reproducing work via possibilities of impression, the slip from one to the other is accomplished seamlessly. The printed tears shift from being currency to being copies of the imprinted self, such that "When a tear falls, that thou falls which it bore" (8). Here, pregnancy results in reproduction, specifically the reproduction of the self. Donne seems to recall models of reproduction we saw in Shakespeare's *Rape of Lucrece*, yet here the model is transformed. The beloved prints copies of herself onto the speaker's tears, while the speaker occupies a passive position and his bodily secretions become a space for female writing. The ability to coin tears or imprint selves is no longer attached to masculine force and instead affords new possibilities for female agency around reproduction.[30]

Both the coinage metaphor and the reproductive one, however, suggest that if tears are productive, they can only be so in a relational space. The tremendous power of the beloved to print new selves depends on the availability of the speaker's tears. Once separated, "on a divers shore" the speaker insists that he and his beloved become "nothing," presumably because they are incapable of generating new life, both reproductively and emotively barren. Even together, their tearful union threatens loss. As the speaker insists "when a tear falls, that thou fall'st which it bore," becoming "nothing."[31] Unlike procreation, which generates offspring who can in turn generate offspring, lacrimation is a reproductive dead end. Tears might be selves, but those selves end in "nothing," bringing the trope and stanza to a close.

Yet the poem does not stop there. The second stanza seems to start over. As the speaker shifts from describing his own tears to those of his beloved, the metaphor shifts from pregnancy and reproduction to the construction of model globes; yet it follows the same pattern. Donne imagines artisans crafting globes from "a round ball" and "copies" of the shapes of continents: "A workman, that hath copies by, can lay / An Europe, Afric, and an Asia / And quickly make that, which was nothing, all" (10, 11–13). Like the metaphors of impression that dominate the first stanza, the creation of a globe depends on copying: "So doth each tear, / Which thee doth wear, / A globe, yea world by that impression grow" (14–16). Again, the speaker slips quickly from copy to original. In the first stanza, "pregnant of thee" collapses into "that thou . . . which it bore," now "globe" is replaced by "world" and once again the tears promise to become "all." The speaker, like the beloved, becomes a creative impressing force and occupies a powerful position.

If we continue to assume that the speaker is gendered male and the beloved female, this stanza seems to reinstate the gendered binaries of active male and passive female. Since they take their print from the speaker, the beloved's tears become another space where female matter, in this case tears, can be imprinted by masculine force. Of course since this is a mirror image of the power relations in the first stanza, where the female beloved imprints the male speaker's tears, the binary has already been destabilized. Still, the scope of creation is magnified when the man occupies the position of imprinter. We shift from selves to worlds, from microcosm to macrocosm. While ascribing multiple worlds to the female body could yield an expansive portrait of the female self, as we saw in Shakespeare's *Rape of Lucrece*, these worlds do not seem to have that effect. While they have something to do with the beloved—they are formed from her tears and emanate from her body—unlike Lucrece's breasts, these excremental effusions are fully external to her, she "wear[s]" them.[32] Thus, like jewelry, they could be read as a symbol of ownership, even more since every tear is imprinted with the speaker's image.

Just as the first stanza ends in loss, however, so does the second, and the mode of loss ascribes even greater agency to the female beloved. The speaker suggests each tear will be a world: "Till thy tears mixed with mine do overflow / This world, by waters sent from thee, my heaven dissolved so" (17–18). The tears of both speakers mingle, and the resulting "overflow" causes destruction. The scope of the metaphor seems to shift away from the tears and back to the speaker's self with the phrase "my heaven."

The beloved's crying seems to threaten the speaker's microcosm. Within the ecosystem of this world of self, tears are again tremendously powerful. The second stanza mirrors the first but also magnifies it. Yet since it magnifies both the scope of creation and the violence of destruction, it ultimately refuses the gender binaries that it begins to narrate.

In the final stanza, the idea of the self as the world becomes the central metaphor when the speaker names his beloved as "more than moon." Here the speaker is clearly a world himself set in relation to the beloved's "more than moon." Critics have been quick to read this reference to the moon as a classic Petrarchan invocation of the female moon, a possibility that genders the beloved female and also suggests a retreat from the poetic experimentation of the first half of the poem.[33] Yet Donne pushes the trope further than such readings would suggest. First, "more" invites numerous ways in which the beloved might exceed the moon. In *Seven Types of Ambiguity*, William Empson details the range of possibilities that could attach to the phrase:

> She is *more than Moone* because she is more valuable to him than anything in the real world to which he is being recalled; because she has just been called either the earth or the heavens and they are larger than the moon; as controlling tides more important or more dangerous than the sea; as making the world more hushed and glamorous than does moonlight; as being more inconstant, or as being more constant than the moon; as being able to draw the tides right up to her own sphere; as shining by her own light; and as being more powerful because closer.[34]

The role of the moon in other writings by Donne helps illuminate even further possibilities. In several of his sermons, Donne invokes the moon to describe the nature of man and the right relationship among man, the universe, and God. In a sermon preached at Paul's Cross, Donne relies on the Ptolemaic notion that beyond the moon all celestial movements are perfect, while below they are prone to errors. He reflects, "the poets afford us but one man, that in his love flew so high as the moon; Endymion loved the moon. The sphere of our loves is sublunary, upon things naturally inferior to our selves."[35] Naming the beloved as "more than moon" might serve to elevate her beyond the "sublunary," making her greater rather than "inferior" to the speaker's self. Similarly, in another sermon, Donne suggests that the moon acts as a mirror for the sun, metaphorically reflecting the light of God into the darkness of night.[36] Both of these possibilities invest the beloved with considerable importance. Yet, given new cosmological developments, there is one more possibility worth considering for "more than moon." Donne might be suggesting that his beloved is herself another world. Galileo Galilei's *Sidereus Nuncius* and Johannes Kepler's *Somnium* both treat the moon as a planet, insisting on a lunar landscape that consists of peaks and valleys, just like the Earth and shattering the Ptolemaic conception of the perfection of the spheres.[37] Further Kepler's *Astronomia Nova* imagines the Earth and moon exerting force on each other. He explains tides by insisting, "the sphere of influence of the attractive power in the moon is extended all the way to the earth, and in the torrid zone calls the waters forth, particularly when it comes to be overhead in one or another of its passages."[38] The attractive power of the moon, combined with its rapid motion, causes the ebb and flow of tides as "the waters are unable to follow so swiftly."[39] Yet it is not only the moon that must have attractive power for Kepler, instead:

> it follows that if the moon's power of attraction extends to the earth, the earth's power of attraction will be much more likely to extend to the moon and far beyond, and accordingly, that nothing that consists to any extent whatever of terrestrial material, carried up on high ever escapes the grasp of this mighty power of attraction.[40]

Earth and moon mutually attract and exert influence on each other.

"A Valediction: Of Weeping" provides one of Donne's more complex associations of women with world. Ultimately, the poem sustains both an interest in gender difference—since "more than moon" approaches the more gender-neutral possibilities of "world" but also retains some of the moon's feminine associations—and a powerful vision of selfhood that seems to transcend gender difference. The poem also raises the problem that if every man and every woman truly is "a little world" then they must relate to each other in the same way that planets do: via "attractive virtue[s]" whose very strength threatens mutual destruction at the same time that it promises mutual attraction. The reproductive possibilities of coining and printing prove illusory and the union of the two lovers hurtling toward each other, destined to part, promises only mutual annihilation. At the moment that Kepler and Galileo were developing new ways of conceptualizing "the movement of the spheres" and the relation of Earth and moon, Donne embraces the poetic possibility of planetary relations to figure desire, love, and loss. The vision of woman he lays out in this poem seems markedly different from his dismissive attitude in *Paradoxes and Problems*. Ultimately for Donne, the woman as world is a trope to be played with and manipulated, pushed to its limits in various directions and made to speak not only about female agency or selfhood but also about male/female relationships.

Taken together, Donne's figurations of the female as world suggest that we might indeed call Philaenis a "little world." After all, several women in Donne's poems are figured as worlds or associated with worlds, even as that association does not always work in the same way as a classic microcosm/macrocosm trope. However, Sappho insists on negating that possibility in her poem. Rather than calling Philaenis a "little world" or anything else for that matter, she declares:

> Thou art not soft, and clear, and straight, and fair,
> As down, as stars, cedars, and lilies are,
> But thy right hand, and cheek, and eye, only
> Are like thy other hand, and cheek, and eye. (21–24)

Sappho's refusal to find a world in Philaenis, here, does not seem particularly gendered. After all, it is not only Philaenis who is "not soft, and clear, and straight, and fair,/As down, as stars, cedars, and lilies are;" no person is. We can find the same sentiment in Francis Bacon's critique of Paracelsus. In *The Advancement of Learning*, Bacon writes:

> The ancient opinion that man was *microcosmus*—an abstract or model of the world—hath been fantastically strained by Paracelsus and the alchemists, as if it were to be found in man's bodies certain correspondences and parallels, which should have respect to all varieties of things, as stars, planets, minerals, which are extant in the great world.[41]

Just as Sappho cannot find "stars," "cedars," and "lilies" in her beloved, Bacon refuses to locate "stars, planets, [and] minerals" within man. Yet while Sappho's refusal could apply to all bodies, the fact that it is based on external appearances makes it unusual. Man is a microcosm, if we again recall Du Bartas, because "In Man's self is Fire, Aire, Earth, and Sea." Sappho seems to miss the point of the trope, which is usually about the interiors of bodies and selves, when she focuses on Philaenis's appearance.[42]

Sappho's mistake in making the trope about her sensory experience of Philaenis's body might remind us of Shakespeare's Dromio, the narrator of *The Rape of Lucrece*, and the speaker in Donne's "Elegy 2: To His Mistress Going to Bed." For all of these speakers, feminine bodily surfaces insert themselves in the trope, which causes confusion between metaphors of reproduction that insist on conquering, taming, writing, or cultivating the female body and the trope of the microcosm/macrocosm. If Sappho employed the microcosm/macrocosm trope to speak about Philaenis's interiority, it could provide her with a language for conveying Philaenis's importance and ascribing her agency. Certainly both of these goals seem to be Sappho's later when she tells Philaenis she should not engage in cross-sex relations:

> Thy body is a natural paradise,
> In whose self, unmanured, all pleasure lies,
> Nor needs perfection; Why shouldst thou then
> Admit the tillage of a harsh rough man? (35–38)

Here Sappho rejects the possibility that women are incomplete without a man and require a union to find "perfection." This idea, which we also find in Paracelsus and is implicit in other Donne poems, proves anathema to Sappho, who insists instead Philaenis need not look outside of herself. Indeed, Sappho wants to reassert herself as Philaenis's lover on the basis that such love is not transformative. Instead she insists "of our dalliance no more signs there are,/Than fishes leave in streams, or birds in air" (41–42). Sappho insists on Philaenis's completeness. Why then does she insist that Philaenis cannot be understood as a world?

Sappho's rejection of Philaenis as world should be understood as a reminder of how strongly woman's role in reproduction invades the trope. As we have seen, her misapplication of it to talk about Philaenis's body echoes other moments in early modern literature and philosophy where woman becomes aligned with world precisely because she is generative. Indeed, Sappho herself talks about Philaenis in similar terms when she describes her as "a natural paradise." While Sappho insists that Philaenis does not need "tillage," she struggles to erase the reproductive implications from the trope. To be a world as a woman is to be a body in flux, changing and changeable.

Yet Sappho finds a macrocosmic possibility for the stable female body she desires in the figure of the galaxy. Sappho prays:

> O cure this loving madness and restore
> Me to me; thee, my half, may all, my more.
> So may thy cheek's red outwear scarlet dye,
> And their white, whiteness of the galaxy
> So may thy mighty, amazing beauty move
> Envy in all women, and in all men love;

And so be change and sickness far from thee,
As thou by coming near keep'st them from me. (57–64)

When Sappho compares the whiteness of Philaenis's cheeks to the galaxy after having eschewed comparisons earlier in the poem, she suggests that Philaenis might not be a "little world" because she is something greater. She is galactic, not terrestrial. By elevating the scope of the comparison, she offers more expansive possibilities for selfhood. Yet there is something too large about Philaenis at the end of the poem. She is less a person and more a force of nature that can be neither controlled nor comprehended. Sappho's jealousy of Philaenis's new love is replaced by a desire that Philaenis's "mighty, amazing beauty move" everyone to "envy" or "love." Similarly at the end of "A Fever," Donne's despair fades as he realizes:

These burning fits but meteors be,
Whose matter in thee soon is spent;
Thy beauty, and all parts, which are thee,
Are unchangeable firmament. (21–24)

While the possibility of death and destruction is undeniable in the poem, the speaker reimagines the beloved not as world but as "unchangeable firmament." In both "Sappho to Philaenis" and "A Fever," the trope of woman as world ultimately is replaced with one of even greater scope, suggesting that the trope is too small to contain all the possibilities of the female self.

NOTES

1. All references to Donne's poetry and prose are to *John Donne: The Major Works*, ed. John Carey (Oxford: Oxford University Press, 1990). References are to line numbers unless otherwise noted.

2. See in particular, James Holstun, "'Will You Rent Our Ancient Love Asunder?': Lesbian Elegy in Donne, Marvell, and Milton," *ELH* 54, no. 4 (1987): 835–67. See also, Paula Blank, "Comparing Sappho to Philaenis: John Donne's 'Homopoetics,'" *PMLA* 110, no. 3 (1995): 358–68, and Madhavi Menon, *Wanton Words: Rhetoric and Sexuality in English Renaissance Drama* (Toronto: University of Toronto Press, 2004), 35–38.

3. Guillaume de Salluste Du Bartas, *Du Bartas his deuine weekes and workes translated: and dedicated to the Kings most Excellent Majesty by Iosuah Syuester* (1611), 155. Early English Books Online, http://gateway.proquest.com/openurl?ctx_ver=Z39.88-2003&res_id=xri:eebo&rft_id=xri:eebo:image:11251:95.

4. For a survey of the idea of the microcosm/macrocosm in philosophy see Ernst Cassirer, *The Individual and the Cosmos in Renaissance Philosophy*, trans. Mario Domandi (Philadelphia: University of Pennsylvania Press, 1963), 73–123.

5. Unless otherwise noted all Shakespeare references are to *The Norton Shakespeare*, eds. Stephen Greenblatt, Walter Cohen, Jean E. Howard, and Katherine Eisaman Maus (New York: W. W. Norton, 1997). References are to act, scene, and line. *Oxford English Dictionary Online*, s.v. "distract." I am not the first to suggest that this line has macrocosmic implications. In the Arden edition of *Hamlet*, this line is glossed as: "(1) while [my] memory has any power over my shattered frame; (2) while memory [in general] is a force in this disordered world." William Shakespeare, *Hamlet*, ed. Ann Thompson and Neil Taylor (London: Arden, 2006), 219. Rhodri Lewis argues that this gloss is inappropriate, suggesting that globe merely refers to the mind. Rhodri Lewis, "Hamlet, Metaphor, and Memory," *Studies in Philology* 109, no. 2 (2012): 609–41. See especially n43.

6. *The Tragedy of King Lear: A Conflated Text. The Norton Shakespeare* provides the first quarto, first folio, and a conflated version of *King Lear*. Citation is to the conflated text. The lines quoted derive from the first quarto and are also printed in *The History of King Lear*, scene 8, lines 9–10. For a careful reading of the microcosm/macrocosm trope around the storm in *King Lear*, see George W. Williams, "The Poetry of the Storm in *King Lear*," *Shakespeare Quarterly* 2, no. 1 (1951): 57–71.

7. Marjorie Nicolson, *The Breaking of the Circle: Studies in the Effect of the "New Science" upon Seventeenth-century Poetry* (New York: Columbia University Press, 1960), 17.

8. Saint Gregory the Great, *Morals on the Book of Job*, trans. by members of the English Church (Oxford: John Henry Parker, 1844), 1:326.

9. See, for example, Giovanni Pico Della Mirandola, "Oration on the Dignity of Man," in *The Renaissance Philosophy of Man*, ed. Ernst Cassirer, Paul Oskar Kristeller, and John Herman Randall Jr. (Chicago: University of Chicago Press, 1948), 225. Pico imagines the creator telling Adam, "We have made thee neither of heaven nor of earth, neither mortal nor immortal, so that with freedom of choice and with honor, as though the maker and molder of thyself, thou mayest fashion thyself in whatever shape thou shalt prefer."

10. The trope of microcosm/macrocosm often extends to multiple levels. Nicolson introduces the term "geocosm" for the terrestrial globe in order to differentiate between universe and world which are both commonly mapped onto the macrocosm. Nicolson, *The Breaking of the Circle*, 28.

11. Toshihiko Kawasaki, "Donne's Microcosm," in *Seventeenth-Century Imagery: Essays on Uses of Figurative Language from Donne to Farquhar*, ed. Earl

Miner (Berkeley: University of California Press, 1971), 27. Nicolson provides a good overview of the prominence of the trope in seventeenth-century literature. She argues that "Donne and his later contemporaries . . . were much more concerned about the nature of the macrocosm than was Shakespeare, more concerned too with man's relation to his earth." Nicolson, *The Breaking of the Circle*, 18.

12. John Donne, *Devotions upon Emergent Occasions*, in *The Works of John Donne*, ed. Henry Alford (London: John W. Parker, 1839), 508.

13. Kawasaki, "Donne's Microcosm," 27. Kawasaki connects the concept of "a great chain" of relationships to Neoplatonic philosophy, as does Don Parry Norford, "Microcosm and Macrocosm in Seventeenth-Century Literature," *Journal of the History of Ideas* 38, no.3 (1977): 409–28.

14. Norford, "Microcosm and Macrocosm," 421. Norford is paraphrasing Kawasaki, "Donne's Microcosm," 27–28.

15. John Donne, "To the Countess of Bedford," in *John Donne: The Major Works*, ed. John Carey (Oxford: Oxford University Press, 1990), 187.

16. In the Norton edition she prevents the Dromio and Antipholus of Ephesus from entering Adrian's house (3.1.48–61). However, in the First Folio (1623), the maid who answers the door is Luce. The Arden also follows the First Folio in not collapsing the two characters together. See *The Comedy of Errors*, ed. R. A. Foakes (London: Arden Shakespeare, 1968), 3.1.48–60.

17. Du Bartas, *Du Bartas his deuine weekes and workes translated*, 155.

18. The primary difference between the two Dromios is their marital status. Nell thus represents the greatest threat to the Syracusan Dromio's sense of self. For more on the language of witchcraft and the importance of Dromio's fear, see Kent Cartwright, "Language, Magic, the Dromios, and 'The Comedy of Errors,'" *Studies in English Literature* 47, no. 2 (2007): 331–54, especially 347.

19. References to *The Rape of Lucrece* are given in line numbers.

20. Coppélia Kahn, "The Rape in Shakespeare's *Lucrece*," *Shakespeare Studies* 9 (1976): 45–72. Since Lucrece is a married woman, the narrator's claim that her breasts are "maiden worlds," is particularly intriguing. They may be maiden insofar as she has not yet had children, or they may preserve their status as "maiden;" she has given Collatine access "by oath," thus their relation is not one of conqueror and conquered.

21. Since many early modern medical texts held that conception required both a male and female orgasm, the trope excuses Lucrece of any complicity in the rape as well as for the choices she makes after she has been raped. See Barbara Baines, "Effacing Rape in Early Modern Representation," *ELH* 65, no. 1 (1998): 69–98, especially 88.

22. Saint Hildegard, "Cause et cure," in *On Natural Philosophy and Medicine: Selections from Cause et cure*, trans. and ed. Margaret Berger (Cambridge: D. S. Brewer, 2009), 24. For more discussion, see Timothy Reiss, *Mirages of the Selfe: Patterns of Personhood in Ancient and Early Modern Europe* (Stanford, CA: Stanford University Press, 2003), 280–81.

23. Ibid.

24. Saint Hildegard, *Scivias*, ed. Adelgundis Führkötter and Angela Carlevaris (Turnhout, Belgium: Brepols Publishers, 1979), 1:290. Translated and quoted in Reiss, *Mirages of the Selfe*, 279.

25. This despite her insistence elsewhere that both men and women contribute to reproductive outcomes and that on a deep level gender difference does not matter.

26. Paracelsus, *Paracelsus: Selected Writings*, ed. Jolandi Jacobi and trans. Norbert Guterman (Princeton, NJ: Princeton University Press 1988), 36.

27. There is a long tradition that sperm carried the form of the father and that the mother simply provided matter and a womb. See Margreta de Grazia, "Imprints: Shakespeare, Gutenberg, and Descartes," in *Printing and Parenting in Early Modern England*, ed. Douglas A. Brooks, 29–58 (Hampshire, England: Ashgate, 2005) 32–33. Early modern alchemists sought to create children outside of a maternal womb, and seventeenth-century scientists believed that they saw such fully formed men when examining sperm under a microscope. See for example, Allison Coudert, *Religion, Magic, and Science in Early Modern Europe and America* (Santa Barbara, CA: Praeger, 2011), 95–98.

28. Reference is to page number.

29. Donne, "To the Countess of Bedford," 187–88.

30. William Empson suggests that the idea of a female signet here might be appropriate because there is something "royal" about the beloved. William Empson, *Seven Types of Ambiguity* (New York: New Directions, 1947), 140. John Carey also attaches the metaphor to sovereignty in "Notes on Two of Donne's Songs and Sonnets," *Review of English Studies* 16, no. 4 (1965): 50–53, 51. For an overview of how coining and printing typically attach to gendered bodies see de Grazia, "Imprints," especially 32–33.

31. For more on tears in Renaissance science, including tears as excrement, see Marjory E. Lange, "'The Brain's Thinnest Excrement': Renaissance Medicine," in *Telling Tears in the English Renaissance* (Leiden, Netherlands: Brill, 1996), 18–51.

32. Alternatively, the tears might wear her, as William Empson suggests in *Seven Types of Ambiguity* (140). If we read the tears as the active subjects here it lessens the possibility that the trope suggests an expansive female subject.

33. See, for example, Barbara L. Estrin, *Laura: Uncovering Gender and Genre in Wyatt, Donne, and Marvell* (Durham, NC: Duke University Press, 1994) 173–76. See also Kawasaki, "Donne's Microcosm," 30.

34. Empson, *Seven Types of Ambiguity*, 143.

35. John Donne, "From a Sermon Preached at Paul's Cross (24 March 1617)," in *John Donne: The Major Works*, ed. John Carey (Oxford: Oxford University Press, 1990), 268.

36. John Donne, "From a Sermon of 5 November 1622, Commemorating Deliverance from the Gunpowder Plot," in *John Donne: The Major Works*, ed. John Carey (Oxford: Oxford University Press, 1990), 320.

37. Galileo Galilei, *Sidereus Nuncius or Sidereal Messenger*, trans. Albert Van Helden (Chicago: University of Chicago Press, 1989), 46–47. Johannes Kepler, *Kepler's Somnium*, trans. Edward Rosen (Madison: University of Wisconsin Press, 1967). Galileo's work was first published in 1609 and Marjorie Nicolson argues that Donne had access to Kepler's *Somnium* as early as 1610. If "A Valediction: Of Weeping" was written after these works, it is likely these ideas could have influenced Donne's "more than moon." See Marjorie Nicolson, "Kepler, the Somnium, and John Donne," in *Science and Imagination* (Ithaca, NY: Cornell University Press, 1956), 67–74. We have been unable to conclusively date any of Donne's *Songs and Sonnets*; for a discussion of this, see *John Donne: The Major Works* (Oxford: Oxford University Press, 1990), 88.

38. Johannes Kepler, *Selections from Kepler's Astronomia Nova*, trans. William H. Donahue (Santa Fe, NM: Green Lion Press, 2004), 13–14.

39. Ibid., 14.

40. Ibid., 15.

41. Francis Bacon, *The Advancement of Learning*, ed. William Aldis Wright (Oxford: Clarendon Press, 1869), 133–34.

42. Bacon does not make the same error. His critique appears in a discussion of medicinal practices and Bacon is contesting the idea that "in man's body" there are parallels to everything that is "extant in the great world."

CHAPTER 10

The Nether Lands of Chouboli's *Dastan*

Madhavi Menon

In *The Comedy of Errors*, William Shakespeare maps the globe onto a woman's body and speaks of traveling to her nether lands.[1] As this mapping suggests, the "Netherlands" serve as a bawdy pun on the genitalia, but perhaps more significant, it suggests that travel is inevitably tied up with desire. This is an idea in which Shakespeare trades in several plays. Think, for example, of Othello's fabulous tales of travel that make Desdemona fall in love with him, or Puck putting a "girdle around the world" as he searches for the all-important love potion. Roaming to the nether lands brings one, in the words of John Donne, all the delights of a new found land.[2] The trope of travel was widely available to Renaissance poets as they wrote of desire; as we shall see, a similar trope extended to poets and poetry in other parts of the world. The title of my essay picks up on the pun of the nether lands to highlight the desire of travels both dramatic and sexual. Shakespeare has for long been the vehicle for such a double-edged travel, because he continually makes bawdy puns and because he has been made to travel the world, often in support of the colonial enterprise, as an icon of aesthetic and intellectual brilliance. In turn, Shakespeare has provided a stage, even for those critical of his iconicity, on which to enact a desiring and anticolonial encounter with that world.

In this essay I will map such a Shakespearean world that involves both geographical and sexual travel. But I will not address directly or at any length a text attributed to Shakespeare; the adjective "Shakespearean" is meant purely as an insubstantial signifier, a signifier that refers to ideas shared across space, language, and time. Indeed, the dual engagement with travel and desire that saturates Shakespeare's plays is also the hallmark of work by Jonathan Goldberg that goes far beyond Shakespearean texts.[3] Despite his repeated discomfort with the bardolatry of the Shakespeare industry, Goldberg has written a brilliant book on the desiring and anticolonial afterlives of *The Tempest* in the Caribbean in which he works on authors like Michelle Cliff, Jamaica Kincaid, and Sylvia Wynter.[4] The book is prefaced by the following quote from Wynter's *The Hills of Hebron*: "Yes, Shakespeare, he used to write books. . . . He made the English language reach up to the heavens, touch the stars. . . . At a time when the rest of his countrymen waited like jackals to rob the Spaniards who returned with their blood-stained plunder from the New World, he created men of grandeur, big villains, towering heroes, new world men."[5] Despite a discomfort with Shakespeare's iconicity, the traveling Shakespeare allows Goldberg to theorize about things foreign: about colonialism and about sexuality. Goldberg keeps finding in Shakespeare a mobility of identity, a queerness of desire—whether in the anus of Coriolanus or in the arse and poperin pear of Romeo and Juliet—that allows him to theorize a Shakespeare freed from institutional constraints, one who can speak in many tongues. It is in keeping with this dissident and elusive relationship that I offer, in a volume on worldmaking in early modern literature, an essay that is not on Shakespeare but which nonetheless maps a world that may be termed Shakespearean.

In Delhi, October 2011, the dastan *(tale) of Chouboli is being performed by two* dastangos *(tellers of tales). It is a tale of a princess who has vowed to marry only the man who can make her speak four times in one night. Such a man does indeed turn up, but she is a woman in disguise as a man. This person tells the princess four stories and gets her to speak four times. The two women get married to each other. And then . . . .*

The *dastangos* are performing on a minimalist stage—a mattress covered with a white sheet, with two bolsters on it, is at the center of the space. Flanking this mattress are two silver goblets containing some liquid—

water? wine?—that the dastangos sip during their performance. The performance itself lasts over two hours, with a short break in the middle. The language of the dastan is interchangeably Hindi, Urdu, and Rajasthani, with a smattering of English. Members of the audience understand primarily one or two of the languages and fractions of the others. But neither the lack of physical action on stage, nor the lack of props, nor the possible barrier of language, detracts from the enjoyment of the audience, all of whom laugh appreciatively, shout out raucous comments, and focus intently through the story of Shahzadi (Princess) Chouboli. The *dastangoi* demands of its audience skills not unlike those demanded of Shakespeare's first audiences: a tolerance for long speeches, a fascination with philosophical conundrums, an ability to understand puns, a taste for sexual fluidity, a willingness to be diverted by stories within stories. How, in this day and age of instant gratification and elaborate cinematic and theatrical productions, is such an event even possible? What *is* this event that demands of the audience rapt attention while only giving them language in exchange?

Dastangoi is a Persian word describing the telling—*goi*—of a *dastan*, or story, with the *dastango* as the teller of the tale. It is a medieval Persian art of storytelling that made its way to India in the sixteenth century when the dastan of Amir Hamza, supposed to have been an uncle of the Prophet, was by far the most popular.[6] The Mughal Emperor Akbar (1542–1605) was so enamored of this *dastan* that he commissioned its conversion into manuscript form, which resulted in the 1200-folio-long *Hamzanama*. In the nineteenth century, the dastan of Hamza was commissioned to be written in Urdu as a compilation of all oral and written sources—a team of three scholars supervised work for twenty-five years to produce forty-six volumes of the dastan, each running to about a thousand pages. In Hindustan—an area roughly corresponding to what we now know as North India and Pakistan—the *Dastan-e-Amir Hamza* might have been the most popular, but it was only one of many dastans available for narration. Between the sixteenth and nineteenth centuries, other stories like the *Bagh-o-Bahar* joined the repertory from which dastangos could pick their tales.[7] At heart an oral tradition, dastangoi was never solely or even primarily reliant on manuscript—dastan, rather, was the name given to stories that shared a set of themes. These involved war, romance, trickery, and magic, to varying degrees, and a good dastango would throw all of them in a brew he would concoct for the telling. Dastan insists on verbal inventiveness in the sometimes thousands of names devised for people and places as well as in the literary allusions to, and use of set pieces from, other genres and literary traditions.

Indeed, dastangoi flourishes on narrating stories within stories—the *Arabian Nights* would be a classic example of a dastan that relishes the interwoven intricacies of narrative, where one story leads not to a teleological end but rather to another story that in turn leads to another. As the example of the *Arabian Nights* suggests, the unending narrative of a dastan is inevitably set in relation to a desire understood in some way as being unbounded, if only in the sense of being out of bounds. The intricate, open-ended narratives and meta-narratives of dastangoi provide a map of desire and its fugitive movements in which the object of desire is not a thing to be obtained but rather an idea endlessly to be chased. Indeed, one of the ways in which dastangoi was denigrated in Hindustan was by being termed *bazaaru*—belonging too much to the marketplace and, by implication, to the lower realms of desire and longing. I will return to this aspect later, but for now, it is interesting to note that in nineteenth-century Delhi, every Thursday was the day designated for dastangos to gather on the steps of the famous Jama Masjid—the largest mosque in India, built by Emperor Shahjahan in 1658—and narrate their dastans. As an art form, dastangoi was never divorced from religion either in its setting or in its audience; if anything, the lines between practicing religion and enjoying desire were never drawn with finality. After all, dastangoi flourished alongside a Sufi literary and musical tradition in which a male poet expressed intense desire toward a male beloved.[8] The male beloved was considered synonymous with God, and in order to press the analogy home, the poet would often have to embark on a mode of itinerancy—traveling out of his gender, for instance, in order to narrate himself as the bride of God.

This itinerant mode of Sufi poetry is echoed in the dastan as it moves between realms, genders, and ideas. Borrowing one *sher* (couplet) from here, and one episode from there, dastan claims neither ancestry nor progeny: it emerges out of a mish-mash of traditions and leads to more of the same. Neither linguistically pure nor generically identifiable, dastangoi presents stories from everywhere and nowhere at once.[9] This tradition of storytelling does not demand that its audience be silent and invisible: since dastans were narrated in marketplaces and public chowks, audience members could walk away if bored and shout suggestions if they fancied themselves as better storytellers. Such interaction was true also of productions of Renaissance plays despite the proscenium stage—audience members often commented on what was going on before them. Again like Shakespeare's drama, dastangoi does not require verisimilitude—statues can come to life, bears can appear as characters, and as we will see later on, necklaces can speak. If anything, in insisting on magic as one of the key ingredients of a dastan, dastangoi flourishes on suspending what we understand as reality and forcing us to take seriously possibilities that we might otherwise not comprehend. Complicated tales, complex tropes, allegedly cheap desires—this is the stuff of which the itinerant dastan is made.

Much of this itinerancy has to do with the language of Urdu itself. Born in Delhi during the Delhi Sultanate in the thirteenth and fourteenth centuries, "the tree of Urdu grew in the soil of Sanskrit and [Braj] Bhasha, [and] flourished in the breezes of Persian."[10] No one knows quite when Urdu first "started," but the Sufi poet Amir Khusrau is most often acknowledged as being its progenitor in the fourteenth century. Except the language in which Khusrau wrote was not called Urdu—that name was an invention of the nineteenth century when one of the outcomes of British rule was the growing divide between Hindus and Muslims. Until the end of the eighteenth century, Hindi and Urdu were both known as Hindustani, with precursor names like Hindavi, but after that date Urdu (from *Zaban-e-Urdū-ē-Muallā*, the language of the military camp, or the language of the residence of the elite; even in its etymology, Urdu traverses a wide range of possibilities) became the new language increasingly identified by its Persian provenance. Urdu drew inspiration from multiple sources and was promiscuous in its linguistic affiliations; it cut across lines of community, religion, class, region, and even nation, and this caused no small degree of consternation to scholars. As Frances Pritchett describes it:

> Consider, for example, the classic list of vices provided by the censorious Ram Babu Saksena in his *History of Urdu Literature* (1927). Saksena charges Urdu poetry with (among other sins) showing a "servile imitation" of Persian poetry that has led to its "debasement" and has made it, according to its own enumeration of the charges: (1) unreal; (2) rhetorical; (3) conventional; (4) mechanical, artificial, and sensual; and (5) unnatural, for Persian poetry was often "vitiated and perverse." And unnatural things are of course doomed, if not already dying—for Nature is busy creating their fresh and natural replacements. It is actually kinder (as well as more prudent) to put them out of their misery, and to turn one's attention from morbid death to healthy rebirth.[11]

Pritchett's wonderful study of Urdu poetry in undivided India remains unparalleled as a document about language and its relation to politics. Examining in detail the denigration of Urdu for being "unnatural" in comparison with what the English considered "natural" poetry—their own—Pritchett asks: "But why? Only because the semantic dice have been loaded so heavily that the game is over before it starts. Because anything not 'natural' is, by definition, in one or another inherently negative state: it is affected, distorted, artificial, inauthentic, derivative, decadent, perverted, false. Anything not natural is, ultimately, 'unnatural.'"[12]

Urdu poetry and, by extension, the language itself started to become suspect in the eyes of moral purists who thought of it as being decadent, as the charge of "unnaturalness" makes clear. This was not only because of its enormous investment in the "play of words"—the puns and intricate metaphors that are integral to Urdu poetry—but also because it played with words—or so it seemed—in order to excite sexual frivolity.[13] Take, for example, a poem by Nazir Akbarabadi, who was a master of languages—he was reputed to know Arabic, Persian, Urdu, Punjabi, Brij Bhasha, Marwari, Purbi, and Hindvi—as well as a male poet who was dressed throughout his childhood as a girl in order to ward off the evil eye. Dismissed often as a bazaaru poet (which is perhaps why his poetry has been included in the dastan of Chouboli that I listened to in Delhi), Nazir writes fairly explicitly about male-male desire. In the poem that follows here, he recreates a scenario involving a contest being held to decide who will be the best seducer. The narrator in the poem is caught unawares by the contest and appears in disheveled clothes. It turns out, however, that despite the unkempt appearance, he is carrying his trump card with him:

> Listen friends, one day a whim struck a chieftain
> To watch the skills of master seducers, to have some fun.
> He ordered, let all the masters be brought—
> Thus suddenly by his servants I was sought.
> I was unprepared, but I did have my baby squirrel.
> . . .
> And when he saw my state, when he saw my lost look,
> He wondered, "A boy how would he manage to hook?"
> I knew what he was thinking, I did not have to be told.
> Not in my pockets or in my waistband but in my turban's fold,
> After much searching, I found my baby squirrel.
> Sitting near and watching was his twelve-year-old boy,
> Fairy-faced, a piece of the moon, a fair, plump toy—
> Friends, the moment he saw my baby, on sight of it,
> He was enchanted and demanded: "I want it, I want it,
> Come on quick, I want it in my hands, that baby squirrel."
> Anxious, desire driving him into an eager mood,
> Friends, he came running, right to where I stood—
> A hundred pleas, he begged: "Give it to me, give it to me!"

> His father screamed: "Throw out the man immediately!"
> How extraordinary the magic of this, my baby squirrel.[14]

Describing the boy as a fresh-faced piece of the moon was widely accepted code for an object of adult male desire. The squirrel is sexually suggestive because of its shape and slipperiness, while the fact that it is a baby alludes more generally to the pederastic desire at play in the poem. The "fair . . . fairy" is immediately and urgently enamored of the baby squirrel and is seduced by the narrator despite the latter's disheveled look. Ironically, the poet manages to seduce the prepubescent son of the chieftain who had wanted to test the poet's skill in seducing young boys. And at the end of all this drama, the pose of the naïf is maintained: How can this little thing of mine, this smooth twitchy object, win a contest in seduction? How is it possible that boys should be so drawn to my, ahem, squirrel? The subject of the drama of seduction—the squirrel—is also the object with which the seduction is accomplished. And the means of that seduction is the language of the poem that invites and challenges us to read Urdu in all its multiplicities.

It is this ability to speak in a forked tongue, in a language at once sexual and ordinary, seductive and prosaic, Persian and Brij Bhasha, that is the hallmark of popular Urdu poetry. This ability also indicates an inability to pin down the language of Urdu and its politics. And once this instability was transmuted into "unnaturalness" and made applicable to Urdu culture in general, the suppression by the moral police was severe. Importantly, this condemnation of the unnaturalness of Urdu coincided with the increasingly heavy hand with which the British established their political and military hold over India: Urdu became the linguistic site of an imperial battle. Once India lost, it was introduced to notions of linguistic sparseness and morality. Independence from the British in 1947 did little to change this new Victorian mindset that Hindustan and its Urdu culture had inherited in the middle of the nineteenth century when language was valued for its instrumentality rather than its rhetoric. As Pritchett points out, the high point of Matthew Arnold's praise of William Wordsworth's poetry was that it had "no style,"[15] and this lack was precisely what the British colonials used to elevate themselves and downgrade Urdu. Indeed, as she goes on to note:

> If [after 1857] Wordsworthian poetry was the touchstone of naturalness, [then] the whole Indo-Muslim poetic tradition was bound to appear "unnatural" in comparison—not just literarily decadent, artificial, and false, but morally suspect as well. And if, as many English writers

> argued, poetry was inevitably a mirror of society, then the cultural rot must go much deeper. The result was a sweeping, internally generated indictment with which Urdu speakers have been struggling ever since.[16]

Urdu suddenly became "unnatural" and Muslim rulers both wordy and sexually decadent: a colonial mission became fused with both a sexual and a literary one. Poetry was denounced for its very Shakespearean ability to travel in style.

Having internalized this colonial censorship, Muhammad Sadiq is able to write of the *ghazal* form (composed of rhyming couplets and a refrain, not unlike that of a sonnet) in 1964 that it "envisions love as 'a torture, a disease,' a 'morbid and perverse passion'—a view that is 'a legacy from Persia' and is 'ultimately traceable to homosexual love which had taken deep root among the Persians and Persianized Arabs.'"[17] It is striking how similar this denigration of love in the ghazal is to that of love in Shakespeare's sonnets. For instance, in 1793, George Steevens refused to include the sonnets in his *Complete Works of Shakespeare*: he thought them unworthy of such an exalted place as a collection of literature. His disgust at sonnet 20 (in which Shakespeare addresses "the master-mistress of my passion") is quite startlingly like that of Sadiq: "It is impossible to read [sonnet 20] without an equal mixture of disgust and indignation," Steevens states.[18] This disgust, apparently caused by the remapping of gender and desire, seems to cause great pain to these critics and so they take great pains to disavow what their poets have written: "great" poetry cannot be about "that" because "that" by definition belongs elsewhere. These denigrations of the "unnatural" mapped poetry onto desire and denounced both as being decadent, fanciful, and immoral. As Sadiq goes on to add: "over time the ghazal has gone from bad to worse. It has developed 'wholly in the direction of fantasy and unreality': 'facts give way to fancies,' and the imagination explores 'curious byways' as the ghazal evolves 'in its downward career.'"[19]

Little wonder, then, that dastangoi started to crumble along with the rest of the Urdu edifice. Openly disseminating wondrous tales, dastans were not contained either literally within a written text, or physically within an acting space, or metaphysically within one worldview, or socially within one milieu, or linguistically within one language, or sexually within conventional bounds. While this very lack of codification allowed dastangoi to get off relatively easily in the pecking order of denigration, it nonetheless died out in the twentieth century. As Mahmood Farooqui, the leading revivalist of dastangoi in twenty-first century India, argues:

> Seeking to yoke literature to social reform and emphasizing purity of thought and simplicity of style, Urdu's leading critics privileged truthful experience rather than exaggerated inventions. Desirous of mirroring western, more particularly Victorian, literary values they praised moralistic and realistic fiction and long narrative poems. Dastans, by then, were already an object of religious censure, women particularly were advised against reading them because it would corrupt them. At the same time colonial officers found Dastans to be immoral and obscene. Added to this was the growing contempt of Urdu's own critics who found Dastans to be childish, inconsistent, implausible, and too repetitive. The only permissible fictional form for the reformers was the novel and the Dastan was a veritable anti-novel, not a precursor to it but quite a different form.[20]

The dastan offended in terms of content, and it was also literally in bad form. Neither the ancestor of the novel nor the descendant of the narrative poem, the dastan did not fit any formal device that could be conjured up for it. It had no fixed shape, which is perhaps why, as Farooqui goes on to argue, it merged seamlessly into the film industry that to this day remains such a craze in India and Pakistan. Incorporating Hindi, Urdu, regional and international languages, marked by fertile tropes and poetic language, using set-pieces, time-tested plot devices of intergenerational conflict, male-female relations, song and dance, and desires that do not conform to gender types, dastangoi is both the descendant of Shakespearean drama and the precursor of Bombay's film industry. If Shakespeare were alive today, he would be writing for Bollywood.

In its commitment to such an itinerant antiteleology, dastangoi never actually reaches the end point of a story without simultaneously beginning a new tale—in the story of *Chouboli*, this happens four times, and even the end of the dastan does not seem final. The dastan announces its verbal inventiveness in the title itself with the pun on *boli* ("she spoke") encoded also in the name of the protagonist, Chouboli. This titular name is performative as well—Chou boli, four speeches, is the name of the person who speaks four times; this quartet of speeches is the very condition on which the story rests. The dastango's working script of Chouboli is a translation into Hindi and Urdu of Christi Merrill's English translation of noted Rajasthani author and literary activist Vijaydan Detha's quotidian Rajasthani script based on an oral tale he had heard being performed, with the help of a Rajasthani-inflected Hindi translation by Kailash Kabir.[21] As this brief itinerary suggests, the dastan of *Chouboli* is exemplary of the itinerant history that is an integral part of dastangoi. Dastan travels not only between nations and regions but also and between languages and desires.

The opening lines of the performed version begin with an invocation in Urdu from the poetry of Intizar Hussain, after which the story proper starts:

> May Lord Ram continue to bless us so that Chouboli's story may be narrated over and over again in every generation in every age in every realm in every region in every nation. May there always be born people to tell this tale and people to listen to it.

This opening invokes sacred figures from Hindu mythology yet uses more Urdu words than Hindi. The endlessness of the tale, its cyclical return, and the necessity of the audience, are all emphasized at the very beginning as the stage is set for the start of the tale. And thus it begins: a *thakur* (landlord) with impressive land holdings has one very bad habit. Every morning he likes to shoot 108 arrows though his wife's nose ring. His wife wilts in fear at her daily ordeal and complains to the niece of the estate manager, who exclaims in shock that if her husband were ever to use her as target practice, she would show him what's what. The wife, unfortunately, does not dare to say this to her husband in her own behalf and instead narrates what the manager's niece has said. The thakur, incensed at this challenge to his authority, and that too from a woman, demands the niece's hand in marriage so he can make her a part of his archery routine and thus teach her a lesson. The manager's niece, astonishingly, agrees to the marriage. On the first morning after the wedding, the thakur prepares to shoot 108 arrows through his new wife's nose ring when she begins to taunt his masculinity by observing that shooting arrows through a nose ring is no big deal; indeed it is a feat she too can achieve with ease: "If you are able to win the hand of Princess Chouboli, then I will acknowledge your mastery, not otherwise," she adds (10). It turns out that Shahzadi Chouboli has refused to marry any man except the one who can make her speak four times during the course of one night. Hundreds of princes have tried their hand at achieving this feat but have failed to make Chouboli's tongue move. As punishment for their failure, they have been imprisoned in a dungeon and made to grind fodder for horses.

The thakur sets off to achieve this difficult task but, like all the men before him, fails and is imprisoned in the dungeon. Then the manager's niece sets off in male disguise to see if she can win the hand of Shahzadi Chouboli. She succeeds by narrating four gripping tales to each of which the

Princess feels compelled to respond, thus fulfilling the condition of speaking four times in one night. True to the terms of the agreement, Chouboli and the manager's niece get married and head back to the village, with the unsuspecting thakur in their entourage as a servant. Taking pity on him, the manager's niece decides to set him free and allow him to take possession once again of his lands but makes clear that she and Chouboli will be the ones living together—the thakur is to be kept on only to protect them from other men.

Even at first glance, it is easy—perhaps astonishing—to see how much *Chouboli* shares in common with myths and literatures from other parts of the world. The princess who sets a seemingly impossible task for her suitors only to eventually succumb to love (Atalanta), the woman dressed as a man who succeeds where no man has done before (Portia in the courtroom scene), the continual storytelling of fantastic tales meant to stave off doom (Scheherazade)—all these threads are spun into the fabric that is *Chouboli*. Added to these multinational strains are the multiple forms and languages in *Chouboli* itself, so what the audience hears and sees during the performance is a mode of narrative that only redraws boundaries and allows us to ask what goes into the making of a boundary in the first place. What is the difference between Greek myth and Indian folktale, between Urdu and Hindi, between women and men? Can a popular folktale end with two married women living together happily ever after? Are cross-dressing women lesbians? Is there an identity to hold on to in the swirls of all these ruptures?

Whether or not they can be identified with certainty as lesbians, Chouboli and the manager's niece are intensely attracted to one another: "Thakurayin . . . usko dekhte hee uspe fida ho gayi" [The thakur's wife was smitten as soon as she looked at Chouboli] (19). After Chouboli has spoken for the second time in the story, and is thus halfway toward losing her cause, the manager's niece once again asks for the *hunkara* (call-and-response that necessitates audience participation) to be given, and Chouboli's necklace volunteers to do so. (In this dastan, both people and inanimate objects have agency to speak and respond; thus the dastango's call for audience participation is answered once by the necklace, another time by a lamp, and a third time by the darkness.) Chouboli fixes her speaking necklace with a fierce look of disapproval, which prompts the *kissago* (teller of tales) to chide her:

> Tum se chup na raha gaya to ilzam doosron ko kyun deti ho. Kya patta mera sundar roop dekh kar tum mujh par mar mitti ho aur man hee

> man apni pratigya todni chahti ho. // Chouboli ne baat ka jawab na diya aur sar jhuka kar baith gayi. (51)
>
> If you were unable to keep silent, then why blame others? Who knows, but perhaps you are so enthralled by my beautiful frame that you are secretly trying to break your vow. // Chouboli refused to answer and sat with bowed head.

There is something about Chouboli's anger that the manager's niece, aka kissago, aka *thakurayin*, aka Chouboli's lascivious suitor, finds irresistible:

> Lekin thaurayin ko Chouboli ka gusse se tamtamata hua chehra aur gusse mein uski nazo-adaa bohut bhayi thi. Woh agar mard hoti to woh yakeenan usse shaadi kar leti. Khair woh shaadi rachaane ko hee to wahan aayi thi. (40)
>
> The *thakurayin* was very attracted to Chouboli's face glowing with anger and all her mannerisms drenched in rage. If she [the manager's daughter] were a man, she would have married Chouboli. Still it was, after all, to conduct a marriage that she had come there.

The manager's niece is intensely drawn to Chouboli, and the repeated implication is that Chouboli is similarly drawn to the kissago. This same-sex attraction is initially presented in the same manner as Olivia's love for Viola is in Shakespeare's *Twelfth Night*; in both texts the implication is that the older woman falls in love with the masculine femininity or feminine masculinity of the young boy she sees before her. Even though Olivia and Chouboli might be falling in love with a person presenting as a man, it is the inability to tell woman from man to which they seem drawn. Thus, Olivia, after disallowing all amorous advances by men, relents at her steward Malvolio's description of the latest emissary sent by her suitor Duke Orsino:

> Olivia. Of what personage and years is he?
> Malvolio. Not yet old enough for a man, nor young enough for a boy; as a squash is before 'tis a peascod, or a cooling when 'tis almost an apple: 'tis with him in standing water, between boy and man.
> . . .
> Olivia. Let him approach: call in my gentlewoman. (1.5.138–42, 145)

In a surprise turnaround, Olivia agrees to see Cesario and, indeed, falls in love with her in short order. There is something in the description of Viola as being "between boy and man" that seems to have clinched the deal for Olivia. And what lies between a boy and man seems to be a woman.

Similarly, people try to dissuade the thakurayin from attempting to win Chouboli's hand by pointing to her youthfulness: "Tere to abhi dudh ke daant bhi nahin toote hain. . . . " [Your milk teeth haven't even fallen out yet], or "Jiski abhi masein bhi nahin bheegi hain, woh rajkumari se shaadi karne aaya hai [he who is still wet behind the ears, whose facial hair has not yet sprouted, he has the temerity to try and marry the princess] (17).

This gendered indeterminacy seems attractive to women all over the literary world. In *Chouboli*, the formal insistence on breaking down borders of language and genre is echoed by a sharp questioning of the boundaries between the sexes and interrogating the laws as they have been laid down for desire:

> Woh to khud aurat thi par uspar Chouboli ke husn ka nasha chadh raha tha; jab uski sachai saamne aayegi to na jaane shahzadi ka kya radde amal ho. Aur agar koi ummeedvar sach mein uska var jeet leta to—nahin, nahin, koi mard iss kaabil nahin tha ki woh Chouboli ka haath jeet sakey, kissi mard se haarne par usski aukat kam ho jaayegi, mardon ki to zaat hi bemurrawat hai, unhe kya hak pohunchta hai ki woh uski barabri karein. Chouboli poori aurat zaat ki numayinda thi, use surkhru hona hi tha. (53)

> She herself was a woman but she found Chouboli's beauty intoxicating: who knows how Chouboli will react when the manager's niece is revealed to be a woman! And what if some hopeful man had indeed won Chouboli in marriage—no, no, no man was worthy enough to win Chouboli's hand; if she had lost to a man, then her status would have been lowered. The entire race of men is selfish: What right did they have to try and match themselves with Chouboli? The princess is the gem of the entire female race, so the manager's niece had no choice but to win in her endeavor—her very being, and that of womankind, depended on it.

There is here a curious mix of defiance—men are worthless—and conformity—how will Chouboli react to the knowledge that the thakurayin is a woman? This passage both keeps men and women apart and ignores the differences between them. The double movement is interesting because it does not come down on the side either of conformity or defiance: it both questions heterosexuality and adheres by its norms. But what is even more interesting—and this is borne out also at the end of Chouboli's dastan—is that despite the conservative view of seeing men and women as being completely different species from one another, the manager's niece's love for Chouboli exists in the text entirely without negative comment and even with a certain familiarity: homosexuality does not excite the invocation of difference. There is never any moral opprobrium attached to it nor does it necessitate any explanatory apparatus: Chouboli is beautiful, and the manager's niece is deeply attracted to her beauty. The but-I-am-a-woman comment that is wheeled out every now and then is done so by the manager's niece herself, never by the narrative or by any other character in the story. And even the manager's niece, as we see, wheels it out only to send it packing with great dispatch.

But how do the two women explain their relationship? At the end of the dastan, when Chouboli and the manager's niece have to decide what to do with themselves—they are, after all, husband and wife—they must take recourse to the stories that lie before them. At least three of the four tales that the manager's niece or kissago or storyteller narrates have at their heart the dilemma of desire. In a tale provocatively titled "Who Is the Husband?" a woman has to decide between the mismatched trunks and heads of her husband and his best friend. This last story is rather bizarre: "In a village a Rajput and a Jat (thus belonging to two different castes) were the best of friends, lived side-by-side, day and night, all twenty-four hours they were inseparable, joined together like a body and its shadow" (61). Incensed at the way in which his in-laws have treated his friend, the Rajput enters a temple dedicated to Shiva and sacrifices his life in protest for the god not having honored his devotee's desire that his friend be treated well. When the Jat enters the temple to inquire after his friend, he sees him lying dead with his neck slit: "Looking neither right nor left, the Jat picked up the same sword, cut off his neck, and fell dead by the side of his friend. When the two were alive, they would lie together, now that both were dead, their blood mingled together as it flowed. Each man dissolved in the other's blood" (64). By dissolving into one another the two men have achieved the union they seem to have fervently desired through life and death.

The Rajput's new bride enters the temple, and is granted a favor by Parvati, Shiva's wife: she can rejoin the severed heads and bodies of her husband and his friend. In her nervousness the new bride attaches the wrong head to the wrong trunk and now faces a dilemma: "The bride was now in an odd predicament: which of the two was her husband? The one with the Rajput's body and the Jat's head, or the one with the Jat's body and the Rajput's head?" (65). The tale remains open-ended on what the bride will do. In a sense, of course, *what* she does is not important, nor who she chooses (the text gives us justification for two different choices); what is important is that this tale complicates the relation between desires and bodies. And while it may seem like a classic case of a woman being placed in the middle of a homosocial/-sexual relation, it is also a tale of complicating the particular identities that we attach to desire. For dastangoi, these complications of desire are part of its generic fabric: one cannot know who is speaking as what and when, whose desires are being mouthed by whom, because that takes away from the suspense of the tale—and its capacity to express desire.

The theater of the dastan thus brings into focus an anti-ontology in which being never coincides with itself. The question it poses is whether or not the audience can retain its hold on a self when the spectacle it has paid to watch insists on the impossibility of that self. Can we go to the theater and continue to have a self that owns its desire? This is the question that animates *Chouboli*: Does particularity explain desire, or can women and men have desires not confined to bodily identities? Can we be certain who is and who is not a man or a woman, and do our desires follow suit? What difference does it make to the audience when a narrative thread presents two women in love rather than a recognizably heterosexual love story? Does the former have the power to fight homophobia, or can it be even more radical than that? Can *Chouboli*, for instance, open us up to questioning the fundamental categories of gender and sexuality within which we narrate ourselves instead of merely providing an anodyne "acceptance" of lesbian love? Can *Chouboli* teach us to be skeptical of (our) identity?

By not legislating among lesbianism, bisexuality, and heterosexuality, Chouboli allows the same character to be all three at once. Both women are all of the above, but what is most important in the dastan is that like the multiple languages in which the story is narrated, their desires too are mobile and travel at will without needing an explanatory apparatus to identify them. Far from trying to make lesbianism palatable to what might inevitably be an unthinking or even actively homophobic audience, *Chouboli* refuses to identify its characters' desires. Or rather, it refuses to correlate their desires to an identity. Whether the particular verdict about the tale is hetero or homo, what is more interesting to contemplate is that most audiences simply do not want to undertake the difficult task of unthinking one's particularity, and so sexual identity of any kind becomes, yet again, the default mode into which the tale gets slotted; *Chouboli* gets described mostly as a tale of hetero fantasy and sometimes as a narrative of lesbian love. Indeed, it is easier to think of the dastan in terms of identity than it is to think of it as undoing identity altogether. Yet, the dastan of Chouboli moves itself and us out of categories of particularity.

The ability to let go of the differences that define us and others, the ability to withhold a correspondence between self and identity, necessitates an embrace of desire and a refusal to cling to the differences within which we live. This refusal is not skepticism so much as the ability to think anti-ontologically. It refuses to base itself in identitarian categories, preferring instead to interrupt the line that all too easily connects bodies with identities, affiliations, and desires. This is the primary reason why dastangoi seems to offer the performative equivalent of a queer universalism: its form and content both propose multiplicities but refuse to resolve into any one. It echoes a Shakespearean insistence on punning desire and travel; it maps worlds without giving us boundaries for them.

NOTES

1. Act 3, scene 2 in *The Comedy of Errors*, in *The Norton Shakespeare*, ed. Stephen Greenblatt et al. (New York: Norton, 1997), especially 135.

2. John Donne, Elegy 8 "To His Mistress Going to Bed." Consider especially the following lines: "Licence my roving hands, and let them go / Before, behind, between, above, below. / O, my America, my Newfoundland, / My kingdom, safest when with one man mann'd, / How am I blest in discovering thee!"(25–30). *John Donne's Poetry*, ed. Donald R. Dickson, A Norton Critical Edition (New York: W. W. Norton, 2007).

3. It is disheartening to note that there are very few studies that allow colonialism and desire to overlap as modes of scholarly analysis. There are terrific books on Shakespeare and colonialism, and fascinating studies of Shakespeare and desire, but the two rarely intersect; equally, Shakespeare is not usually taken as limning a horizon of inquiry, a world that may be termed "Shakespearean." Goldberg's work is a notable exception to all these rules.

4. For Goldberg, Shakespeare scholars' adherence to the Bard ignores the punning vagaries of a worldly Shakespearean encounter with desire. "I never intended to write a book on Shakespeare," (vii) he claims in the introduction to *Shakespeare's Hand*, because "finding ways to denaturalize the most canonical figure in English literature has never been easy or likely to be very successful. (Students, however, are more receptive and inspiring coconspirators on these matters than many professional Shakespeareans are.)" (xiii). Goldberg continues the criticism of professional Shakespeareans while outlining the reception his paper on *Coriolanus* received at a meeting of the Shakespeare Association of America: "I try assiduously to avoid such events, if only because even the most determined efforts to rethink Shakespeare seem stymied by their immediate incorporation into an institution that enshrines his canonical name and fosters the professional deformation that

characterizes all single-author societies, especially this one" (xvi). Jonathan Goldberg, *Shakespeare's Hand* (Minneapolis: University of Minnesota Press, 2002).

5. Jonathan Goldberg, *Tempest in the Caribbean* (Minneapolis: University of Minnesota Press, 2003), v.

6. See Musharraf Ali Farooqi, trans., *The Adventures of Amir Hamza* (New York: Random House, 2008), for more details of this iconic dastan.

7. I am greatly indebted to Mahmood Farooqui for these details about the history of dastangoi. Mahmood Farooqui, "What Is Dastangoi?," *Dastangoi: The Lost Art of Storytelling*, http://dastangoi.blogspot.in/2010/02/what-is-dastangoi.html.

8. For the Sufis, if the poetry of the *ghazal* derived from Persian, then it was easy to maintain the indeterminate character of the beloved since Persian is a genderless language; if the poetry was in Urdu, then the beloved was gendered male because the love of women was not considered exalted enough to be the subject of mystical music. Either way, the Sufis performed male homoerotic desire despite or because of its metaphysical convolutions.

9. Dastan literature belongs to a long and rich line of texts that Mohamad Tavakoli-Targi in *Refashioning Iran: Orientalism, Occidentalism and Historigraphy* (New York: Palgrave, 2001) terms "homeless texts," by which he refers to the "large corpus of texts made homeless with the emergence of *history with borders*, a convention that confined historical writing to the borders of modern nation-states" (9).

10. Frances W. Pritchett, *Nets of Awareness: Urdu Poetry and Its Critics* (New Delhi: Katha, 2004), 140. This passage is a quotation from the *Water of Life* by Urdu poet and literary critic, Muhammad Husain Azad.

11. Ibid., 159–60.

12. Ibid., 159.

13. Pritchett elaborates on this double movement: First, the identification of Urdu poetry with a "play of words" and second, a Victorian disdain for that play when compared to the instrumentality of the English language: "plainness and directness, this disdain for literary niceties, this concern with the real world, is part of what Azad wants from English. . . . English shows us how to use language instrumentally, how to short-circuit the play of words, how to get from feelings in the poet's heart to feelings in the reader's heart with a minimum of fuss in between. Mere words may be suspect, the autonomous 'game of words' may have been discredited—but feelings are reassuringly real and irreproachably 'natural.'" Ibid., 143.

14. Ruth Vanita and Saleem Kidwai, eds., *Same-Sex Love in India: A Literary History* (New Delhi: Penguin, 2008), 250.

15. Pritchett, *Nets of Awareness*, 167.

16. Ibid., xvi.

17. This is Pritchett's rendition of Sadiq's argument; many of the phrases are hers, some are Sadiq's. Pritchett, *Nets of Awareness*, xiv.

18. Steevens quoted in Dympna Callaghan, *Shakespeare's Sonnets* (New York: Wiley-Blackwell, 2008), 20. For more details about the nineteenth century's critical response to Shakespeare's sonnets, see Margreta de Grazia, "The Scandal of Shakespeare's Sonnets," in *Shakespeare Survey*, vol. 46, *Shakespeare and Sexuality*, ed. Stanley Wells (Cambridge: Cambridge University Press, 1993), Cambridge Collections Online, doi:10.1017/CCOL0521450276.004.

19. Sadiq quoted in Pritchett, *Nets of Awareness*, xiv.

20. Farooqui, "What Is Dastangoi?"

21. The printed version of the Chouboli story can be found in the following: Vijaydan Detha, *Chobuoli and Other Stories*, trans. Christi A. Merrill with Kailash Kabir (New Delhi: Katha, 2010). References to the dastangoi are from the unpublished working script used by Mahmood Farooqui and Danish Husain.

ACKNOWLEDGMENTS

This book recalls the conference at Brown University that occasioned it, so we thank first the Departments of Comparative Literature and English, the Renaissance and Early Modern Studies Program, and the Woods Lectureship Fund at Brown for their support, and Jonathan Kramnick, who helped organize the event. The opportunity for two days of exchange over ideas and meals sparked the work gathered here. We are deeply appreciative for the occasion and grateful to all those who attended the conference and made it a memorable event, an audience of valued friends and colleagues among whom we would mention Sharon Cameron, Irene Tucker, Elizabeth Wilson, Ashley Shelden, Brent Dawson, Susan Bernstein, Michael Moon, Tom Brooks, and Kevin, Emma, and Violet Pask; we thank all those who delivered papers (Aaron Kunin, David Glimp, Jennifer Summit, Rick Rambuss, Madhavi Menon, Lara Bovilsky, Robert Matz, Lynn Maxwell, Laurie Shannon, Jeff Masten, Lee Edelman, and Joseph Litvak); those who spoke about Jonathan Goldberg's transformative teaching (James Kuzner, Mary Fuller, Daniel Juan Gil, and Zachary Samalin); those who commented on various of his books (David Baker, Meredith Evans, and Elizabeth Hanson). Closing the conference, Helen Tartar spoke beautifully about working with Jonathan to make books worthy of their thinking, giving eloquent testimony to her engagement with his work for more than twenty-five years, first as his editor at Stanford University Press and more recently at Fordham University Press. Helen welcomed the idea of a volume arising from the conference, and we thank Tom Lay and Richard Morrison for their continued support of this project and the two readers who recommended its publication. The shocking news of Helen's death came as we were revising these pages for submission to the Press. To mark that wrenching loss and in appreciation of her rare talent and longstanding contributions to humanities scholarship, we dedicate this volume to her memory.

CONTRIBUTORS

LARA BOVILSKY is associate professor of English at the University of Oregon. She is the author of *Barbarous Play: Race on the English Renaissance Stage* (University of Minnesota Press, 2008) and of essays that have appeared in *ELH* and *Renaissance Drama*. She is completing a book entitled *Almost Human: The Bounds of Personhood in Early Modern England.*

BRENT DAWSON is faculty fellow at the University of Oregon. He works on Renaissance literature and contemporary literary theory. Two of his articles, published in *New Literary History* and *Renaissance Drama*, form part of a book project on early modern notions of worldhood.

MEREDITH EVANS is associate professor of English at Concordia University. She has published on Enlightenment philosophy and literature, seventeenth-century natural philosophy, and Renaissance drama. Her work has appeared in *Shakespeare Quarterly* and *Shakespeare Studies* and she has an article forthcoming in *Shakespeare's World of Words*, edited by Paul Yachnin (Bloomsbury Arden Shakespeare, 2015). Her current book project on Shakespeare in political theory focuses on the equivocal value of action and agency.

MARCIE FRANK is professor of English at Concordia University in Montreal. She has published on topics in eighteenth-century British literature and American twentieth-century literature. "Frances Burney's Theatricality" (*ELH* 82, no. 2) and "Melodrama and the Politics of Literary Form" (*Eighteenth-Century Fiction* 27, no. 3–4) derive from a book manuscript, *The Novel and the Repertory, 1680–1814*.

DANIEL JUAN GIL is professor of English at Texas Christian University. He is the author of *Before Intimacy: Asocial Sexuality in Early Modern England* (University of Minnesota Press, 2005) and *Shakespeare's Anti-politics: Sovereign Power and the Life of the Flesh* (Palgrave Macmillan, 2013). He is currently working on a book about secularism, religious beliefs, and the body.

David Glimp is associate professor in the Department of English at the University of Colorado Boulder. He is the author of *Increase and Multiply: Governing Cultural Reproduction in Early Modern England* (University of Minnesota Press, 2003) and the coeditor of two volumes: with Michelle R. Warren, *Arts of Calculation: Quantifying Thought in Early Modern Europe* (Palgrave Macmillan, 2004), and with Russ Castronovo, *After Critique?*, a special issue of *English Language Notes* (Fall/Winter 2013).

Jonathan Goldberg is Arts and Sciences Distinguished Professor at Emory University. His recent publications include "What Dost Thou in This World?," an essay on *Paradise Regained* that appears in *Milton Now: Alternative Approaches and Contexts*, edited by Catharine Gray and Erin Murphy (Palgrave Macmillan, 2014), and *The Seeds of Things: Theorizing Sexuality and Materiality in Renaissance Representations* (Fordham University Press, 2009).

Aaron Kunin is associate professor of English at Pomona College. He specializes in Renaissance literature and has wide-ranging research interests in poetry and poetics. His most recent book is *Cold Genius* (Fence Books, 2014).

James Kuzner is Joukowsky Family Assistant Professor of English at Brown University. He is the author of *Open Subjects: English Renaissance Republicans, Modern Selfhoods, and the Virtue of Vulnerability* (Edinburgh University Press, 2011) and of *Shakespeare as a Way of Life: Skeptical Practice and the Politics of Weakness* (Fordham University Press, 2016).

Robert Matz is a professor of English and senior associate dean in the College of Humanities and Social Sciences at George Mason University. His book, *The World of Shakespeare's Sonnets: An Introduction* (McFarland, 2008) was selected as a 2008 *Choice* Outstanding Academic Title. He is currently editing two early modern English marriage sermons to be published in a volume forthcoming from Ashgate. He serves on the Executive Committee of the Association of Departments of English.

Lynn Maxwell is assistant professor at Spelman College, where she teaches Shakespeare and early modern literature. Her work has appeared in the *Journal for Early Modern Cultural Studies*, and she has an article forthcoming in *Criticism*. She is currently working on a book project, tentatively titled *Wax Works: Wax Impressions, Figures, and Forms in Early Modern Literature*.

Madhavi Menon is professor of English at Ashoka University. She is the author of *Wanton Words: Rhetoric and Sexuality in English Renaissance Drama* (University of Toronto Press, 2004), *Unhistorical Shakespeare: Queer Theory in Shakespearean Literature and Film* (Palgrave Macmillan, 2008), *Indifference to Difference: On Queer Universalism* (University of Minnesota Press, 2015), and the editor of *Shakesqueer: A Queer Companion to the Complete Works of Shakespeare* (Duke University Press, 2011).

Karen Newman is Owen Walker '33 Professor of Humanities and professor of Comparative Literature and English at Brown University. She has written widely on early modern English and continental letters and culture and on Shakespeare and Renaissance drama. She is the author of *Cultural Capitals: Early Modern London and Paris* (Princeton University Press, 2007) and *Essaying Shakespeare* (University of Minnesota Press, 2009). She is currently working on the reception of Shakespeare in Europe and on early modern translation.

INDEX